CW01460662

Thawra hatta'l nasr!
Revolution until Victory!

A Marxist Analysis of the
Arab Revolution

Alan Woods, Jordi Martin *and* others

Wellred Books
London

Thawra hatta'l nasr! Revolution until Victory!
— A Marxist Analysis of the Arab Revolution
Alan Woods, Jordi Martin and others

Wellred Books, May 2011
2024 printing

Copyright © Wellred Books
All rights reserved
wellred-books.com

UK distribution: Wellred Books Britain, wellredbooks.co.uk
152-160 Kemp House, City Road
London
EC1V 2NX
contact@wellredbooks.co.uk

USA distribution: Marxist Books, marxistbooks.com
WR Books
250 44th Street #208
Brooklyn
New York
NY 11232
sales@marxistbooks.com

DK distribution: Forlaget Marx, forlagetmarx.dk
Degnestavnen 19, st. tv.
2400 København NV
forlag@forlagetmarx.dk

Typeset by Ainhoa Murguiondo
Cover design by José Mármol

ISBN: 978 1 900007 40 5

CONTENTS

EGYPT

Preface by Alan Woods

The present volume is a selection of the main articles on the revolutions in Tunisia and Egypt published on In Defence of Marxism (www.marxist.com) from January to March 2011. A reading of these articles will provide a blow-by-blow account of these dramatic and historic events.

In preparing this book we at first considered the possibility of reworking the material contained in the articles as a history. But it soon became evident that this was impracticable. Whatever advantages may have been gained in stylistic terms would have been cancelled out by the loss of immediacy.

For much of the time, we were publishing daily articles, particularly on the developments in Egypt. They hang together as if they were the chapters of a book. Moreover, these articles are not merely a descriptive account of the events. They provide a scientific Marxist analysis and a political commentary of each stage of the Revolution.

In the Preface to *The History of the Russian Revolution*, Trotsky writes:

> The history of a revolution, like every other history, ought first of all to tell what happened and how. That, however, is little enough. From the very telling it ought to become clear why it happened thus and not otherwise. Events can neither be regarded as a series of adventures, nor strung on the thread of a preconceived moral. They must obey their own laws. The discovery of these laws is the author's task.

I believe that the present volume follows this advice to the letter. It is not a list of isolated facts, in the style of English empiricism, but a coherent whole that seeks to determine the deeper processes and class forces that lie beneath the surface. Each article not only describes the events as they unfold, but tries to lay bare the role of the different classes, parties and individuals who make up the dramatis personae of the Revolution.

From such an analysis, it should be possible not only to explain where we have come from and where we are, but also to arrive at a scientific hypothesis as to which direction the situation is tending towards. I think that in general, our analysis was correct and accurately predicted the course that the Revolution actually took. By following the articles as they were written, the reader can judge to what extent we were right or wrong.

Of course, the Revolution is not finished and must still run through a whole series of stages, the precise course of which it is impossible to predict. There are too many variable factors both nationally and internationally to perform such a task. All that is possible is to predict the general line of development and indicate the different possibilities inherent in the situation. Whoever asks for more must seek the services, not of the Marxists, but of a professional astrologer.

Marxism is a science, but it is not an exact science. It has more in common with medicine, metrology or geology than with physics. It is impossible to predict an earthquake, although we know precisely where the fault lines are. The recent tragedy in Japan bears eloquent witness to this fact. It is impossible to conduct a controlled experiment with earthquakes. But nobody thinks that geology is not a science because it failed to predict the earthquake in Japan.

Many people would regard meteorology as a science. In recent decades they have accumulated new and powerful tools for predicting the weather: computers with awesome memory capacity and satellites that can plot the tiniest movements of weather systems from space. Yet despite this vast array of data, modern meteorology is incapable of predicting the weather for more than three days with any accuracy.

This fact does not condemn the method of meteorology or forbid us from attempting to predict the weather. It is merely an expression of the fact that the weather is a chaotic system. It is difficult to predict with accuracy because small variations can cause sudden and unexpected changes in the weather. Society is also a chaotic system in which a series of infinitely small changes can produce dramatic transformations when they reach the critical point where quantity is transformed into quality.

The method of dialectics is a closed book to bourgeois economists and sociologists who like to think that they follow a scientific method because they allegedly confine themselves to "the facts". But in the first place, as Hegel points out, the facts do not select themselves. A political analyst approaches the facts with definite presuppositions. Certain facts are selected because they are considered to be important, while others are ignored. Whether this selection is conscious or unconscious is of no relevance. But the way the question is posed will usually determine the answer.

In the second place, it is the business of science, not merely to enumerate a list of isolated facts, but to show the processes and general tendencies that lie behind the facts and manifest themselves through them. Before Charles Darwin could arrive at his theory of natural selection, he carefully examined and listed a great many observations from the natural world, cataloguing the most minute differences in the shape of birds' beaks, their size, colour and other physical characteristics. But the theory of evolution through natural selection is not merely a catalogue of observed facts but a brilliant theoretical generalization. What interests us is not the catalogue but the theory, not the isolated facts but the law that alone can explain them.

Foresight and astonishment

It is no accident that not a single one of the bourgeois "experts" were able to predict the Revolution in Tunisia or Egypt. On the contrary, they denied it even when it had already begun. A slavish worship of the established fact is the hallmark of empiricism. The bourgeois analysts look at the surface and do not see the processes that are taking place in the depths of society.

But dialectics teaches us that things turn into their opposite. Now all the bourgeois strategists, economists, academics and "experts" make a public exhibition of their perplexity. It is a graphic illustration of Trotsky's definition of theory as the superiority of foresight over astonishment.

On September 28, 2009 I wrote about the Gaza war as follows:

> The Middle East shows the idiocy of Bush's policy. All they succeeded in doing was destabilizing the whole of the Middle East. All the pro-western regimes there are hanging by a thread. Saudi Arabia is hanging by a thread. Egypt is hanging by a thread. Lebanon is hanging by a thread. So is Jordan, so is Morocco. These ruling elites were terrified by the demonstrations that took place during the Gaza war.

This was by no means the first time I had made the same point. I specifically mentioned Egypt, Saudi Arabia, Jordan and Morocco as unstable regimes that could be overthrown at any time. This could have been brought about by the Israeli attack on Gaza, which is why the imperialists put pressure on the Israelis to withdraw. In fact, the Gaza war produced mass demonstrations in all these countries, which indicated the existence of a profound ferment in society.

I did not include Tunisia in the list because I had not been following events there. But exactly the same arguments would apply. Of special interest are the articles published in our Arab language website, Marxy.com, which have traced the movement in Tunisia from its first beginnings. They alerted us to the revolutionary implications of the situation following the self-immolation of Mohamed Bouazizi in December. These articles are all the more important because they are written by active participants in the revolutionary movement in North Africa.

By paying careful attention to the strike movement in Egypt, which was mainly ignored by the bourgeois commentators, we were able to predict the imminence of a revolutionary explosion. While other so-called Marxists ran after the Muslim Brotherhood, the International Marxist Tendency (IMT) has consistently emphasized the role of the Egyptian proletariat. Everything that is happening is a striking confirmation of the perspectives of the IMT. It is sufficient to point to the articles in In Defence of Marxism covering the strike movement in Egypt over the last few years to prove this assertion.

On Thursday, October 28, 2010, we published an article written by Hamid Alizadeh and Frederik Ohsten, with the title "Egypt, the Gathering Storm". It opens with the following words:

The tensions in Egypt are reaching boiling point. The crisis of the regime is reflected in a number of splits and growing opposition. The emergence of Mohamed ElBaradei on the political scene signifies an important change in the struggle against the regime. Until now, the masses have lacked a national point of reference to connect up the different struggles, but this is now changing. Revolution is developing just beneath the surface.

In the Middle East, Egypt is a key country. Not only is it the most populated Arab country and a strategic pillar of support for imperialism, it also has a strong working class with militant traditions. Over the last few years, the Mubarak dictatorship has been shaken by strikes and protests, but it has become increasingly clear that all factors are pointing in the direction of revolution.

This was written two months before the upsurge in Tunisia and three months before the commencement of the Egyptian Revolution. Although the authors perhaps attach too much significance to ElBaradei as a factor in the equation, their general analysis of the situation in Egypt was one hundred per cent correct. In any case, it is infinitely superior to anything the bourgeois "experts" have written before or since.

What the bourgeois wrote

The aforementioned article concludes with the following prediction:

The events looming in Egypt will shake the entire region. They will have a big impact throughout the entire Middle East where a revolutionary dynamic has already started. The period up to the presidential elections will be one of preparation for the revolutionary events which are to come. The Egyptian revolution will dramatically change the course of events in the Middle East, North Africa and on a world scale.

That is what we wrote in October 2010. Let us now compare this to the statements of the leading analysts of the bourgeoisie written several months later, that is, *after* the Revolution had begun. As late as January 6, 2011, *The Economist* wrote: "Tunisia's troubles are unlikely to unseat the 74 year-old president or even to jolt his model of autarchy." A few weeks later Ben Ali had been overthrown and his regime was in ruins.

On January 25, 2011 Hilary Clinton stated: "Our assessment is that the Egyptian government is stable and is looking for ways to respond to the legitimate needs and interests of the Egyptian people." This was when the masses had already come out onto the streets of Cairo.

The same lack of awareness was shown by other bourgeois commentators, such as the BBC correspondent in Cairo who wrote on January 17 that no revolt would happen in Egypt because people there are apathetic: "Unlike Tunisia, the population has a much lower level of education. Illiteracy is high, internet penetration is low."

The article, signed by Jon Leyne in Cairo was entitled: "No sign Egypt will take the Tunisian road." To make matters worse, these lines were also included in his report of the events on January 25, the mass demonstration which marked the beginning of the revolution.

Old Heraclitus once said: "Eyes and ears are bad witnesses to men who do not understand the language." The same facts were available to these ladies and gentlemen as were at the disposal of the Marxists. Yet the very same facts can give very different results according to what method is used to interpret them. A crash course in dialectics would be of great benefit to the bourgeois. But they show no interest in wanting to understand for the same reason a man perched precariously on the edge of a cliff finds it difficult to think straight.

Crisis of capitalism

The main failure of all these people is that they do not see the role of the working class as an agent of change. They only see history as a series of combinations at the top, of the strengths and weaknesses of individual rulers. They think that crises are the results of mistakes or of conspiracies. They cannot accept that the crises are an inevitable product of a socio-economic system that has outlived its usefulness and has become a monstrous fetter on human progress.

The events that are shaking the Arab world to its foundations are just one manifestation of the general crisis of world capitalism. Not one of the problems faced by the peoples can be solved in the narrow confines of the capitalist system. That is the root cause of the revolutionary explosions in North Africa and the Middle East. That is why the Arab Revolution cannot stop until it has tackled the root problem which is private ownership of the means of production and the nation state, which are too narrow to contain the colossal potential of the productive forces.

This book is not written for bourgeois academics but as a contribution to the class struggle. It is dedicated to those courageous class fighters who braved the bullets and batons of the repressive forces to change their lives. We are not merely observers but active participants in the worldwide struggle against oppression and exploitation. We firmly believe that this struggle can only end in the expropriation of the bankers, landlords and capitalists and the creation of a new world order – socialism.

For this reason, in place of the usual Introduction, we are publishing the Manifesto of the International Marxist Tendency on the Arab Revolution. This is the summing up of the experience of the events in Tunisia and Egypt, and draws all the necessary conclusions from this experience, which is presented in the form of programmatic demands.

We warmly commend this book for the attention of every class conscious militant, not just in the Arab world but to the workers and youth who are fighting for a better future in every country and continent.

Alan Woods, London, March 12, 2011

The Arab Revolution –
Manifesto of the International Marxist Tendency

Revolution until victory! – Thawra hatta'l nasr!

The Arab Revolution is a source of inspiration to workers and young people everywhere. It has rocked every country in the Middle East to their foundations and its reverberations are being felt all over the world. The dramatic events in North Africa and the Middle East mark a decisive turning point in human history. These events are not isolated accidents apart from the general process of the world revolution.

What we see opening up before us is the early stages of the world socialist revolution. The same general process will unfold, albeit at different rhythms, around the globe. There will inevitably be ebbs and flows, defeats as well as victories, disappointments as well as successes. We must be prepared for this. But the general tendency will be towards a greater acceleration of the class struggle on a world scale.

The marvellous movement of the masses in Tunisia and Egypt is only the beginning. Revolutionary developments are on the order of the day and no country can consider itself immune from the general process. The revolutions in the Arab world are a manifestation of the crisis of capitalism on a world scale. The events in Tunisia and Egypt show the advanced capitalist countries their future as in a mirror.

Tunisia

Tunisia was apparently the most stable Arab country. Its economy was booming and fat profits were being made by foreign investors. President Zine El Abidine Ben Ali ruled with an iron hand. Everything seemed to be for the best in the best of all capitalist worlds.

The bourgeois commentators look at the surface and do not see the processes that are taking place in the depths of society. Hence they were blind to the processes at work in North Africa. They denied any possibility of a revolution in Tunisia. Now all the bourgeois strategists, economists, academics and "experts" make a public exhibition of their perplexity.

The country erupted after the self-immolation of the unemployed youth Mohamed Bouazizi. Hegel pointed out that necessity expresses itself through accident. This was not the only case of suicide by a desperate unemployed youth in Tunisia. But this time it had unexpected effects. The masses poured onto the streets and started a revolution.

The first reaction of the regime was to crush the rebellion by force. When that did not work, they resorted to concessions, which only served to pour petrol on the flames. Heavy police repression did not stop the masses. The regime did not use the army because they could not use it. One bloody clash and it would have broken in pieces.

The Tunisian working class launched a wave of rolling regional strikes, culminating in a national strike. It was at this point that Ben Ali had to flee to Saudi Arabia. This was the first victory of the Arab Revolution. It changed everything.

When Ben Ali fled, there was a vacuum of power which had to be filled by revolutionary committees. They took power at local and, in some places, at regional level. In Redeyef, in the Gafsa phosphate mining basin, there is no authority other than that of the trade unions. The police station was burnt down, the judge fled, and the town hall was taken over by the local union which has its headquarters there. Mass meetings are held in the main square and addressed by the trade union leaders on a regular basis. They have set up committees to deal with transport, public order, local services, etc.

The masses were not satisfied or pacified by their initial victory. They have been out in large numbers on the streets against any attempt to recreate the old order under another name. All the old parties have been completely discredited. When Ghannouchi tried to install new governors in the regions, the people rejected them. Hundreds of thousands protested and they had to be removed.

In Tunisia the lava of revolution has not yet cooled. The workers are demanding the confiscation of the wealth of the Ben Ali family. Since they controlled vast sections of the economy, this is a direct challenge to the rule of the capitalist class in Tunisia. The confiscation of the property of the Ben Ali clique is a socialist demand.

The Tunisian workers have kicked out unpopular bosses. The left-wing *14th of January Front* has called for the convening of a national assembly of revolutionary committees. This is a correct demand but so far no concrete steps have been taken to implement it. Despite the lack of leadership, the revolution continues to advance with giant strides, toppling Ghannouchi and raising the movement to new heights. Our slogan must be: thawra hatta'l nasr! – Revolution until victory!

The Egyptian Revolution

Tunisia opened up the Arab revolution, but it is a small country on the margins of the Maghreb. Egypt, on the other hand, is a huge country of 82 million, and it stands at the heart of the Arab world. Its numerous and militant proletariat has shown its revolutionary spirit many times. The Egyptian Revolution undoubtedly reflected Tunisia's influence but was also based on other factors: high unemployment, falling living standards and hatred towards a corrupt and repressive government.

Tunisia acted as a catalyst, but a catalyst can only work when all the necessary conditions are present. The Tunisian Revolution showed what was possible. But it would be entirely false to assume that this was the only, or even the main, cause. The conditions for a revolutionary explosion had already matured in all these countries. All that was required was a single spark to ignite the powder keg. Tunisia provided it.

The movement in Egypt showed the amazing heroism of the masses. The security forces could not use bullets against the main demonstrations in Tahrir Square for fear that a Tunisian scenario could develop. The regime imagined that it would be enough, as in the past, to crack a few heads. But it was not enough. The mood had changed. Quantity changed into quality. The old fear was gone. This time it was not the people but the police who had to flee.

This led directly to the occupation of Tahrir Square. The regime sent in the army, but the soldiers fraternized with the masses. The Egyptian army is made up of conscripts. The upper ranks of the army, the generals, are corrupt. They are part of the regime, but the rank and file are drawn from among the workers and poor peasants. And the lower and middle ranks of the officer corps are drawn from the middle class and open to the pressure of the masses.

Opposition parties demanded reforms, including the dissolution of the parliament installed in December after fraudulent elections, the holding of new elections, and a declaration from Mubarak that neither he nor his son would run for president in the elections scheduled for September. But in reality the leadership was lagging far behind the masses. The movement went far beyond these demands. The revolutionary people would accept nothing less than the immediate removal of Mubarak and the complete dissolution of his regime.

Beginning with such elementary demands as an end to the emergency laws, the firing of his interior minister, and a higher minimum wage, the demonstrators, emboldened by numbers, raised their slogans to a higher, more revolutionary, level: "Down with Mubarak!" "The people demand the fall of the regime!" or simply: "Go!" In this way, the revolutionary consciousness of the masses was raised by leaps and bounds.

The state and revolution

It is futile to attempt to explain the events in Egypt and Tunisia without the central role of the masses, which was the motor force of events from start to finish. Bourgeois and petty bourgeois "experts" now try to play down the importance of the action of the masses. They see only what is happening at the tops. For them it is only a question of a "coup", of "the army passing power to itself". The same bourgeois historians assure us that the Bolshevik Revolution in 1917 was "only a coup". They are not capable of looking history in the face, but instead are fascinated by its hindquarters.

Their "profound" analysis is superficial in the most literal sense of the word. For the bourgeois philosophers in general everything only exists in its outward manifestations. It is like trying to understand the movement of the waves without bothering to study the submarine ocean currents. Even after the masses had taken to the streets of Cairo, Hilary Clinton insisted that Egypt was stable. She based her conclusion on the fact that the state and its repressive apparatus remained intact. But in just two weeks it was in ruins.

The existence of a powerful apparatus of state repression is no guarantee against revolution, and may be just the opposite. In a bourgeois democracy the ruling class has certain safety valves that can warn it when the situation is getting out of control. But in a dictatorial or totalitarian regime there is no opportunity for people to voice their feelings within the political system. Therefore upheavals can happen suddenly, with no warning, and immediately take an extreme form.

The armed forces constituted the main basis of the old regime. But like any other army it reflected society and came under the influence of the masses. On paper it was a formidable force. But armies are composed of human beings, and are subject to the same pressures as any other social stratum or institution. In the moment of truth, neither Mubarak nor Ben Ali could use the army against the people.

The armies of many Arab countries are not the same as the armies of the developed capitalist world. They are, in the last analysis, also capitalist armies, armed bodies of men in defence of private property, but at the same time they are also the products of the colonial revolution. Of course the generals are corrupt and reactionary, but the rank and file conscripts are drawn from the workers and peasants. The lower and middle ranks of the officer caste reflect the pressure of the masses, as was shown with Nasser's coup in 1952.

The revolution provoked a crisis in the state. Tensions were growing between the army and the police and between the police and the protesters. This is why the army council in the end decided to ditch Mubarak. The army was clearly shaken by the events and showed signs of cracking under the pressure of the masses. There were cases of officers dropping their weapons and joining the demonstrators in Tahrir Square. Under these circumstances there can be no question of using the army against the revolutionary people.

Role of the proletariat

During the first two weeks power was in the streets. But having won power in the streets, the leaders of the movement did not know what to do with it. The idea that all that was necessary is to gather a large number of people in Tahrir Square was fatally flawed. Firstly, it left the question of state power out of account. But this is the central question that decides all other questions. Secondly, it was a passive strategy, whereas what was required was an active and offensive strategy.

In Tunisia, mass demonstrations forced Ben Ali into exile and overthrew the ruling party. That convinced many Egyptians that their regime might prove equally fragile. The problem was that Mubarak refused to go. Despite all the superhuman efforts and courage of the protesters the demonstrations failed to overthrow Mubarak. Mass demonstrations are important because they are a way of bringing the formerly inert masses to their feet, giving them a sense of their own power. But the movement could not have succeeded unless it was taken to a new and higher level. This could only be done by the working class.

This reawakening of the proletariat was expressed in a wave of strikes and protests in recent years. This was one of the main factors that prepared the revolution. It is also the key to its future success. The dramatic entry of the Egyptian proletariat on the stage of history marked a turning point in the destinies of the revolution. That is what saved the revolution and led to the overthrow of Mubarak. In one city after another the workers of Egypt organized strikes and factory occupations. They drove out the hated managers and corrupt trade union leaders.

The revolution moved onto a higher level. It turned from a demonstration into a national insurrection. What conclusion must be drawn from this? Only this: *that the struggle for democracy can be victorious only to the degree that it is led by the proletariat: the millions of workers who produce the wealth of society, and without whose permission not a light bulb shines, not a telephone rings and not a wheel turns.*

Reawakening of the Egyptian nation

Marxism has nothing in common with economic determinism. Mass unemployment and poverty are an explosive issue. But there was something else present in the revolutionary equation: something more elusive, which cannot be quantified but it is a no less potent cause of discontent than material deprivation. It is the burning feeling of humiliation in the hearts and minds of an ancient and noble people dominated by imperialism for generations.

There is the same general feeling of humiliation in all the Arab peoples, enslaved and oppressed by imperialism for over 100 years, subordinate to the dictates, first of the European powers, then of the transatlantic giant. This feeling can find a distorted expression in the guise of Islamic fundamentalism that rejects everything western as evil. But the rise of Islamism in recent years was only the expression of the failure of the Left to offer a genuine socialist alternative to the pressing problems of the Arab masses.

In the 1950s and 1960s, Gamal Abdel Nasser's dream of Arab socialism and pan-Arabism aroused the hopes of the Arab masses everywhere. Egypt became a beacon of hope to the oppressed and downtrodden Arab masses. But Nasser did not carry the programme to its logical conclusion and under Anwar Sadat it was thrown into reverse. Egypt became a pawn in the great power politics of the USA. In the three decades of Mubarak's rule these tendencies were multiplied a thousand fold. Mubarak was a stooge of the USA and Israel who shamelessly betrayed the Palestinian cause.

In the last three or four decades the Arab psyche was coloured by disappointment, defeats and humiliation. But now the wheel of history has turned 180 degrees and everything is changing. The idea of revolution has a very concrete meaning in the Arab world today. It is capturing the minds of millions and is becoming a material force. Ideas which connected with only a few are now convincing and mobilizing millions.

Revolutions are great clarifiers. They test all tendencies. Overnight the ideas of individual terrorism or Islamic fundamentalism have been swept aside by the revolutionary torrent. The revolution has reawakened half-forgotten ideas. It promises a return to the old traditions of socialism and pan-Arab nationalism, which have never completely disappeared from the popular consciousness. It is no accident that songs of resistance from the past are being revived. Images of Nasser have appeared on demonstrations.

We are witnessing a new Arab renaissance. A new consciousness is being forged in the heat of struggle. Democratic demands are fundamental for the people under such circumstances. People who have been enslaved for a long time finally cast aside the old passive and fatalistic mentality and raise themselves up to their full stature.

One can see the same process in every strike, for a strike resembles a revolution in miniature and a revolution resembles a strike of the whole of society against its oppressors. Once they get active, men and women rediscover their human dignity. They begin to take their destiny into their own hands and demand their rights: "We demand to be treated with respect". That is the essence of every genuine revolution.

The revolution is raising consciousness to a higher level. It is cutting the ground from under the feet of the reactionaries who have confused the masses and befuddled their senses with the poisonous fumes of religious fundamentalism. Despite the lying propaganda of the imperialists, the Islamists played little or no role in the revolution in Tunisia and Egypt. The revolution despises sectarianism. It cuts across all divisions and unites men and women, young and old, Muslim and Christian.

The revolutionary movement cuts across religion. It cuts across gender. It brings the Arab women onto the streets to fight alongside their men. It cuts across all national, ethnic and linguistic divisions. It defends oppressed minorities. It gathers together all the living forces of the Arab nation and unites them in common struggle. It enables the revolutionary people to rise to its full height, to recover its dignity and to rejoice in its freedom. Men and women can raise their heads and say with pride: "We will no longer be slaves".

The limits of spontaneity

The revolution in Tunisia and Egypt came from below. It was not organized by any of the existing political parties or leaders. All of them were left far behind by a movement they had not foreseen and for which they were completely unprepared. If there is one lesson to be drawn from the experience of the Egyptian Revolution, it is this: the revolutionary people can trust nobody but themselves – *trust in your own strength, your own solidarity, your own courage, your own organization.*

When we look at Egypt the historical comparison that immediately comes to mind is Barcelona in 1936. With no party, no leadership, no programme, no plan, the workers marched on the barracks with extraordinary courage and smashed the fascists. They saved the situation and could have taken power. But the question is precisely: why did they not take power? The answer is the lack of leadership. More accurately, they were let down by the anarchist leaders of the CNT in whom they placed their trust. Whoever has illusions in anarchism had better study the history of the Spanish Revolution!

At first sight the movements in Tunisia and Egypt appear to be a spontaneous revolution with no organization or leadership. But this definition is not really exact. The movement was only partly spontaneous. It was called into being by certain groups and individuals. It has leaders who take initiatives, put forward slogans, call demonstrations and strikes.

A lot of emphasis has been placed on the role of social networks as Facebook and Twitter in Tunisia, Egypt and earlier in Iran. There is no doubt that the new technology has played a role and is extremely useful to revolutionaries and made it impossible for states such as Egypt to retain the information monopoly they once enjoyed. But those who exaggerate the purely technological side of things are distorting the real essence of the revolution, that is, the role of the masses and the working class in particular. That is because they wish to portray the revolution as a mainly middle class affair, led exclusively by intellectuals and Internet enthusiasts. This is entirely false.

In the first place, only a small proportion of the population have access to Internet. Secondly, the regime practically disconnected the Internet and disrupted mobile telephone services. This did not stop the movement for a single minute. Without Internet and mobile phones the people organized demonstrations using a very old technology, which is known as human speech. The same technology was used to bring about the French Revolution and the Russian Revolution, which sadly had no access to Facebook or Twitter but did a tolerably good job anyway. An even bigger role than Facebook, however, was played by Al Jazeera.

Millions of people could watch the events as they unfolded, day by day, hour by hour.

As we have seen, it is not true to say that the Egyptian Revolution had no leaders. There was a kind of leadership right from the beginning. It consisted of a loose coalition of more than a dozen small parties and activist groups. It was they who issued a Facebook call for a "day of rage" to coincide with Police Day on January 25th. Some 80,000 Egyptian web-surfers signed up, pledging to march on the streets to voice demands for reform.

Both in Tunisia and Egypt initially the demonstrations were convened by groups of mainly young people who provided the leadership that the "official" opposition parties failed to provide. *The Economist* refers to "the emergence of loosely related groups pressing for reform, run via the internet by youths of generally secular outlook but no particular ideology. Some coalesced around labour rights. Some promoted human rights or academic freedom."

These actions, then, were carried out by a decisive minority and therefore they were not purely spontaneous. But this was just the tip of a very large iceberg. Public sympathy was on the side of the protesters. The nationwide protest turned into a general uprising against the Mubarak regime, with simultaneous mass protests all over Egypt. So in fact, there was a kind of leadership, although not with very clear ideas. However, in both Tunisia and Egypt the response from the masses took the organizers by surprise who did not dream of the extent of this support they would get. None of the organizers anticipated the huge numbers that answered the call, and fewer still expected the riot police to let them get very far.

It is true that the "spontaneous" character of the revolution provided a certain protection against the state, and in that sense it was positive. But the lack of an adequate leadership is also a serious weakness that has very negative effects later on.

The fact that in both cases the masses succeeded in overthrowing Ben Ali and Mubarak without the aid of a conscious leadership bears eloquent witness to the colossal revolutionary potential of the working class in all countries. But this statement does not exhaust the question under consideration by any means. The weakness of a purely spontaneous movement was seen in Iran, where despite the tremendous heroism of the masses, the revolution ended in defeat – at least for the time being.

The argument that "we do not need leaders" does not bear the slightest scrutiny. Even in a strike of half an hour in a factory there is always leadership. The workers will elect people from their number to represent them and to organize the strike. Those who are elected are not arbitrary or accidental elements, but generally the most courageous, experienced and intelligent workers. They are selected on that basis.

Leadership is important, and the party is important. A child of six could understand this proposition, which is the ABC of Marxism. But after A, B and C there are other letters in the alphabet. There are some who call themselves Marxists who imagine that unless and until a Marxist party stands at the head of the proletariat, there can be no question of a revolution. Such ridiculous pedantry has nothing in common with Marxism. The revolution will not unfold in an orderly manner, with the revolutionary party conducting the masses with a baton.

In 1917 Lenin said that the working class is always far more revolutionary than even the most revolutionary party. The experience of the Russian Revolution proved that he was correct. Let us remind ourselves that in April 1917 Lenin had to appeal to the workers over the heads of the Bolshevik Central Committee, which adopted a conservative attitude to the question of proletarian revolution in Russia.

The same conservative mentality, the same aristocratic distrust of the masses, can be seen in many of those who regard themselves as the "vanguard" of the class, but who, in practice, act as a break on the movement in a decisive situation. It is sufficient to refer to the sorry role of the old so-called vanguard in Iran, who had survived from the 1979 revolution, but who stood aloof from the revolutionary masses who came onto the streets in their millions to challenge the regime in 2009.

Do Marxists say that unless and until the revolutionary party is built and stands at the head of the working class, revolution is impossible? No, we have never said such a thing. The revolution proceeds according to its own laws, which develop independently of the will of revolutionaries. A revolution will occur when all the objective conditions are present. The masses cannot wait until the revolutionary party has been built. However, once all the objective conditions are present, the factor of leadership is indeed decisive. Very often it means the difference between victory and defeat.

Revolution is a struggle of living forces. Victory is not predetermined. In fact, at one point, the Egyptian Revolution came very close to defeat. Tactically speaking, staying in Tahrir Square was not the best option. This showed the limited outlook of the organizers. Mubarak almost outmanoeuvred the movement, buying off some layers, and mobilizing the lumpenproletarian thugs for vicious attacks. It could have succeeded. Only the decisive intervention of the masses and, particularly, the intervention of the working class prevented defeat.

The problem of leadership

The masses never have a finished plan at the beginning of a revolution. They learn through struggle. They may not know exactly what they want, but they know very well what they do not want. And that is sufficient to propel the movement forward.

Leadership is a very important element in war. This is not to say that it is the only element. Even the most brilliant leaders cannot guarantee success if the objective conditions are unfavourable. And sometimes it is possible to win a battle with bad generals. In a revolution, which is the highest expression of the war between the classes, the working class has the advantage of numbers and its control of key parts of the productive apparatus of society. But the ruling class possesses many other advantages.

The state is an apparatus for maintaining the dictatorship of a minority of exploiters over the exploited minority. The ruling class holds many other powerful levers in its hands: the press, radio and television, the schools and universities, the state bureaucracy and also the spiritual bureaucrats and thought police in the mosques and churches. In addition it possesses an army of professional advisers, politicians, economists and other specialists in the arts of manipulation and deception.

In order to fight against this apparatus of repression, which has been built up and perfected over many decades, the working class must develop its own organizations, led by an experienced and determined leadership that has absorbed the lessons of history and is prepared for all eventualities. To argue that it is possible to defeat the ruling class and its state without organization and leadership is like inviting an army to go into battle untrained and unprepared to face a professional force led by experienced officers.

In most cases, such a conflict will end in defeat. But even if the revolution succeeds in overwhelming the enemy in the first charge, it will not be enough to guarantee ultimate victory. The enemy will regroup, reorganize, modify its tactics, and prepare for a counteroffensive, which will be all the more dangerous because the masses will have been lulled into believing that the war has already been won. What at first appeared to be a moment of triumph and joy turns out to be the moment of extreme danger for the fate of the revolution, and the lack of an adequate leadership in such cases will prove to be its Achilles' heel, a fatal weakness.

The leadership of the protest movement contained diverse elements and different ideological tendencies. In the last analysis, this reflects different class interests. In the beginning this fact is disguised by the general appeal to "unity". But the development of the revolution will inevitably give rise to a process of internal differentiation. The bourgeois elements and the middle class "democrats" will accept the crumbs offered by the regime. They will compromise and enter into deals behind the backs of the masses. At a certain stage they will desert the revolution and pass over to the camp of reaction. This is already happening.

In the end it is the most determined revolutionary elements that can guarantee the final victory of the revolution: those who are not prepared to compromise and are willing to go to the end. New explosions are implicit in the situation. In the end one side or the other must triumph. The objective situation is ripe for the assumption of power by the working class. Only the lack of the subjective factor – the revolutionary party and leadership – has prevented this from taking place so far. The overcoming of the problem of leadership is therefore the central problem of the revolution.

Intrigues at the top

It was the national insurrection that persuaded the generals that only Mubarak's departure could calm Egypt's streets and restore "order". This was, and remains, their overriding obsession. All talk of democracy is merely a fig-leaf to disguise this fact. The generals were part of the old regime and participated in all the dirty work of corruption and repression. They fear the revolution like the plague and want only a return to "normality" – that is, a return to the old regime under a different name.

The ruling class has many strategies for defeating a revolution. If it cannot do so by force, it will resort to cunning. When the ruling class faces the prospect of losing everything they will always offer concessions. The overthrows of Ben Ali and Mubarak were a great victory, but they were only the first act of the revolutionary drama.

The representatives of the old regime remain in positions of power; the old state apparatus, the army, police and bureaucracy, is still in place. The imperialists are intriguing with the tops of the army and the old leaders to cheat the masses out of everything they have won. They offer a compromise, but it is a compromise that would maintain their power and privileges.

Defeated on the streets, the old regime is striving to strike a bargain, that is, try to fool the leaders of the opposition, so that they in turn could fool the masses. The idea was that once the initiative was in the hands of the "negotiators", the masses would become mere passive onlookers. The real decisions would be made elsewhere, behind locked doors, behind the backs of the people.

The men of the old regime are slowly beginning to recover their nerve. They have begun to feel more confident and redouble their manoeuvres and intrigues, basing themselves on the more moderate sections of the opposition. The masses feel uneasy. They do not want the movement to be hijacked by professional politicians and careerists who are bargaining with the generals like merchants haggling in a bazaar. But the question remains: how to carry the revolution forward? What needs to be done?

As the movement becomes more radicalized, some of the elements who played a leading role in the early stages will fall behind. Some will abandon it; others will go over to the enemy. This corresponds to different class interests. The poor people, the unemployed, the workers, the "men of no property" have no interest in maintaining the old order. They want to sweep away not only Mubarak but the entire regime of oppression, exploitation and inequality. But the bourgeois Liberals see the struggle for democracy as the path to a comfortable career in parliament. They have no interest in carrying through the revolution to the end or of disturbing existing property relations.

For the bourgeois liberals the mass movement is only a convenient bargaining chip, something with which they can threaten the government to give them a few more crumbs. They will always betray the revolution. No trust whatever can be placed in these people. ElBaradei now says that he opposes the constitutional amendments, but instead of demanding an immediate constituent assembly, he says that elections should be postponed, that the conditions are not present, that the time is not right, and so on and so forth. For these gentlemen the time for democracy is never right. *For the masses who have shed their blood for the revolution, the time for democracy is now!*

The IMT says:

• No trust in the generals!
• No trust for self-appointed "leaders" who call for restoring "normality"!
• Keep the mass movement in being!
• Organize and strengthen the revolutionary committees!
• For a clean out of all the supporters of the old regime!
• No deals with the old regime!
• The current "interim regime" has no legitimacy and should be removed immediately. Demand the convening of a Constituent Assembly now!

The Muslim Brotherhood

Some, including Khamenei in Iran, say that the revolutionary movement we are witnessing is about religion, that it is "an Islamic reawakening". But this is clearly not the case. Even the main clerics in Egypt admit it. They fear being swept aside if they try to portray the revolution as a religious movement. It is a movement of all religions, and therefore of no religion. There was no animosity against Christians on the demonstrations. There was not even a hint of anti-Semitism.

Religious sectarianism is a weapon used by reactionaries to confuse the people. The December attacks on the Coptic Christians were clearly engineered by the secret police in order to create a sectarian divide and divert attention from the real problems of the masses. They are resorting to the same dirty tactic now in order to divide the masses on sectarian lines, fomenting conflict between Muslims and Copts in an attempt to split and disorient the people and undermine the revolution.

The revolts in Tunisia and Egypt are largely secularist and democratic, and often deliberately excluding the Islamists. The notion that the Muslim Brotherhood was the "only real opposition" was false to the core. The basic demands of the Egyptian demonstrators are for jobs, food and democratic rights. This is nothing to do with the Islamists and is a bridge to socialism, which has deep roots in the traditions of Egypt and other Arab countries.

Some misguided people on the left have described the movements in Tunisia and Egypt as "middle class" revolutions. These same so-called left-wingers have been flirting with reactionary groups like Hezbollah, Hamas and the Muslim Brotherhood for a long time. They try to justify this betrayal of Marxism on the grounds of the so-called anti-imperialist stance of the leaders. This is false from start to finish. The so-called Islamists are anti-imperialists in words only, but in practice represent a reactionary trend. They are, in fact, the fifth wheel of the cart of the old regime.

The imperialists have tried to use the Islamists as a bogeyman to confuse the masses and conceal the real nature of the Arab Revolution. They say: "Look! If Mubarak goes, al-Qaeda will take his place." Mubarak himself told the Egyptian people that if he went it would be "like Iraq". These were all lies. The role of the fundamentalists and organizations like the Muslim Brotherhood has been grotesquely exaggerated. Such organizations do not represent a force for progress. They pose as anti-imperialists but they stand for the interests of the landlords and capitalists. In the last analysis they will always betray the cause of the workers and peasants.

It is frankly a scandal that certain European left groups, and even some who call themselves Marxists, have supported the Islamists. This is nothing less than a betrayal of the proletarian revolution. It is true that the Muslim Brotherhood is divided along class lines. The leadership is in the hands of conservative elements, capitalists and wealthy businessmen, while its rank and file members include more militant sections of the youth and those who come from poorer and working class backgrounds. However, the way to win the latter over to the side of the revolution is not by making alliances with their capitalist leaders, but rather to subject them to implacable criticism, in order to expose their hollow claims at being anti-imperialist and pro-poor.

This is precisely the opposite of what these groups did when they made an alliance with the leaders of the Muslim Brotherhood in organising the Cairo anti-war conference. In effect, these left organisations were providing the Muslim Brotherhood leaders with a left cover, approving their false anti-imperialist credentials and thus strengthening their grip on their own membership.

In the past the Muslim Brotherhood were backed by the CIA to undermine the leftward moving nationalism of Gamal Abdel Nasser. Islamic fundamentalism was a creation of John Foster Dulles and the US State Department, to cut across the left after the 1956 Suez War. But when Sadat and Mubarak became American stooges their services were no longer required. Hilary Clinton and others have said that the Muslim Brotherhood are not a threat, that they are people who can be worked with. This is a clear indication that the imperialists will once again try to use the Islamists to head off the revolution.

Similarly, Hamas and Hezbollah were originally set up to cut across the PFLP and other left tendencies in Palestine. Later, the CIA created Osama bin Laden as a counterweight to the Soviet forces in Afghanistan. And now they are again intriguing with the leaders of the Muslim Brotherhood to head off the revolution in Egypt and deceive the people. But the Muslim Brotherhood is not a homogeneous movement and is now splitting into different factions along class lines.

The poor people who support the Brotherhood are one thing. The leaders are another thing altogether. In the 1980s leaders of the Brotherhood were key beneficiaries of economic liberalization – the programme of *infitah* or "opening" – under which Sadat and then Mubarak dismantled the state sector, favouring private capital. One study of Brotherhood businessmen suggests that at this point they controlled 40 per cent of all private economic ventures. They are part of the capitalist system and have every interest in defending it. Their conduct is not determined by the Holy *Qur'an* but by class interest.

The "hard line" Islamists are as frightened of the revolutionary masses as the regime itself. The Muslim Brotherhood declared that it would not negotiate with the government until Mubarak stepped down. But the moment the regime beckoned with its little finger, they changed their minds. One of their leaders went onto Tahrir Square, where the protestors were standing firm and preventing the tanks from occupying the square with their bodies, appealing to them not to clash with the army.

Our attitude to such people was worked out long ago by Lenin who warned at the Second Congress of the Communist International:

> 11) With regard to the more backward states and nations, in which feudal or patriarchal and patriarchal-peasant relations predominate, it is particularly important to bear in mind:
>
> first, that all Communist parties must assist the bourgeois-democratic liberation movement in these countries, and that the duty of rendering the most active assistance rests primarily with the workers of the country the backward nation is colonially or financially dependent on;
>
> second, *the need for a struggle against the clergy and other influential reactionary and medieval elements in backward countries;*
>
> third, *the need to combat pan-Islamism and similar trends, which strive to combine the liberation movement against European and American imperialism with an attempt to strengthen the positions of the khans, landowners, mullahs, etc.*[1]

That is the real position of Marxism towards reactionary religious trends. It is the position that the IMT firmly defends.

The IMT says:

• Defend the unity of the revolutionary people!

---

1 Lenin, *Draft theses on the national and colonial questions*, 5 June, 1920, our emphasis.

- Down with the pogrom-mongers and hate-merchants!
- Oppose all discrimination based on religion!
- No compromise with reactionary and obscurantist trends!
- Every man and woman must have the right to hold any religious belief or none!
- For the complete separation of religion from the state!

Democratic demands

In the first instance the demands of the revolution are democratic. Of course! After 30 years of a brutal dictatorship the youth long for freedom. Naturally, their desire for democracy can be abused by bourgeois politicians who are only interested in their future careers in a "democratic" parliament. But we are obliged to take up the democratic demands and give them a sharply revolutionary content. This will inevitably lead on to the demand for an even more fundamental change in society.

During a strike or a revolution people feel like human beings with dignity and rights. After a lifetime of enforced silence, they discover that they have a voice. The interviews of people on the streets were a wonderful expression of this. Poor, illiterate people are saying: we are going to fight, we will not leave the streets; we demand our rights and we demand that we be treated with respect. This is a profoundly progressive thing. It is the very essence of a real revolution.

It goes without saying that Marxists always subordinate the democratic demands to the socialist revolution. But in practice the most consistent and advanced revolutionary demands will necessarily lead to the posing of workers' power and socialist revolution. The Russian Revolution is the best example of this. In 1917 the Bolsheviks took power on the basis of the slogan "Peace, bread and land", none of which has a socialist content. In theory, all three demands could be achieved under capitalism. In practice, however, they could only be achieved by breaking with the bourgeoisie and by power passing into the hands of the working class.

Some people say that this is nothing more than a bourgeois nationalist movement, not a real revolution. They merely reveal ignorance on the important role of democratic demands in a revolution under these conditions. The experience of the Russian Revolution itself shows the importance of the correct (revolutionary) utilization of democratic demands. The demand for a Constituent Assembly played a very important role in mobilizing the broadest layers of the population behind the revolutionary cause.

While fighting for the most advanced democratic demands, Marxists do not regard these demands as an end in themselves, but as part of the fight for a fundamental change in society. That is what distinguishes the Marxist outlook from that of vulgar petty bourgeois democrats.

The immediate task in Egypt was to carry out the overthrow of Mubarak and his rotten regime. But this is only the first step. It has opened the floodgates and allowed the revolutionary people to push their way through. They are daily discovering their strength on the streets, the importance of organization and mass mobilization. That is already a tremendous conquest. Having gone through the experience of a thirty year dictatorship, they will not allow the imposition of a new one, or any intrigue to recreate the old regime with a new name. Tunisia is sufficient proof of this.

Now they have had a taste of their own power, the masses will not be satisfied with half-measures. They know that what they have achieved they have conquered with their own hands. The struggle for complete democracy will permit the construction of genuine trade unions and workers' parties. But it will also pose the question of economic democracy and the fight against inequality.

Slogans and tactics must be concrete. They must reflect the real situation and the real concerns of the masses. The objective tasks of the Russian Revolution were democratic and national: overthrow of the tsar, formal democracy, freedom from imperialism, freedom of press, etc. We demand complete democracy, immediate abolition of all reactionary laws, and a constituent assembly.

Yes, we must overthrow the old regime, not just Ben Ali and Mubarak, but all the "little Mubaraks" and the "little Ben Alis". There must be a thorough purge of the state. And there must not be a single figure in the government who played any part in the old regime. Why should the revolutionary people, who sacrificed all in the struggle, allow those who played no part in the revolution to be in power, even in the form of an interim government? Take a big broom and sweep them all out! That is our first demand. We will accept nothing less than this.

But this is also insufficient. For decades these men robbed and looted the wealth of society. They lived in luxury while the people were reduced to poverty. Now we must get back every cent that they stole from the people. We demand the immediate confiscation of the wealth and property of these parasites, and the expropriation of the property of the imperialists who supported them.

This shows how the revolutionary democratic demands must lead directly to socialist demands. Whoever is incapable of correctly utilizing democratic demands in a revolutionary way will forever be doomed to the role of an impotent sectarian. Such a person will never be capable of connecting with the real movement of the masses.

Democracy, however, means different things to different people. The poor people of Egypt do not fight for democracy in order to provide ministerial positions for careerists but as a means of solving their most pressing problems: the lack of jobs and houses, the high cost of living, etc. These economic and social problems are too deep to be solved by any bourgeois government.

Democracy would be an empty phrase if it refused to lay hands on the obscene wealth of the ruling elite. Confiscate the property of the ruling clique! Expropriate the property of the imperialists who backed the old regime and exploited the people of Egypt! The fight for democracy, if it is pursued to the end, must inevitably lead to the expropriation of the bankers and capitalists and the establishment of a workers' and peasants' government. Under Mubarak's regime the Egyptian capitalists have favoured foreign business and assisted imperialism in looting the wealth of the country and exploiting the Egyptian workers. We demand the expropriation of the property of the imperialists for the benefit of the people.

The IMT says:

* For the immediate abolition of all reactionary laws!
* For complete freedom of assembly and the right to organize and strike!
* For a revolutionary constituent assembly!
* For the confiscation of all the money stolen by the old regime!
* For the expropriation of the property of the imperialists!

The Constituent Assembly slogan

If there was a party in Egypt like the Bolshevik Party, the question of power would be posed. But in the absence of a leadership with a clear plan, the revolution can pass through all manner of vicissitudes. At present the revolutionary wave has still not subsided. But the masses cannot remain permanently in a state of ebullition. They must work and earn money to eat. The revolutionary lava will cool for a time. Eventually the revolution will be pushed toward some form of bourgeois democracy.

In such a situation democratic demands have an immense importance. In a situation like Mubarak's Egypt, democratic demands are a powerful lever for mobilizing the broadest layers of the masses for the revolution. We must fight for the maximum democratic rights – the right to vote, strike, etc. – because it is in the interests of the workers to have the freest possible scope to develop the class struggle. It is not a matter of indifference for a worker to live under a totalitarian regime than to have these basic rights. Democratic demands must therefore occupy a key place in our programme.

Some people are puzzled by the fact that whereas we now advocate a Constituent Assembly for these countries, we opposed it in the cases of Bolivia and Argentina. The explanation is really very simple. Slogans do not exist outside of time and place. They must reflect concrete conditions of the class struggle at a given stage of the development of a particular country.

In Bolivia, during the revolutionary uprisings of October 2003 and May-June 2005 the slogan of a constituent assembly was counterrevolutionary. Why? At the time, the Bolivian workers had staged two general strikes and two insurrections. They had set up soviet-like bodies in the form of the Neighbourhood Juntas, the Popular Assemblies and the *cabildos abiertos* (mass meetings).

The Bolivian workers could have easily taken power. It would have been sufficient for the leaders of the COB (trade unions) to proclaim themselves as the government. Under these concrete conditions, to advance the slogan of a constituent assembly was a betrayal. It diverted the attention of the workers from the central task – the seizure of power – and into parliamentary channels.

The counterrevolutionary nature of this slogan was confirmed by the fact that the World Bank and the US funded Office for Transition Initiatives promoted the idea of a constituent assembly. One might add the small detail that at this time Bolivia was already a bourgeois democracy. In the case of Argentina, the slogan was raised by certain left groups after the *Argentinazo* uprising in December 2001. In the context of an already existing bourgeois democracy, the slogan of a constituent assembly was completely wrong and it amounted to saying: "We don't like the bourgeois parliament that we have. We want another bourgeois parliament instead."

One has to be completely blind not to see that these cases have nothing at all in common with the situation in Tunisia and Egypt. After decades of dictatorship, there will inevitably be big illusions in democracy, not just in the petty bourgeoisie but among the masses. This conditions our attitude. We are for democracy, but it must be complete democracy. One of the democratic demands is, "we need a new constitution, and therefore a constituent assembly, but we don't trust the Egyptian army to convene it and therefore the struggle must go on in the streets."

Of course, Marxists cannot have a mechanical attitude to democratic slogans, which are always subordinate to the general interests of the socialist revolution. We do not share the superstitious attitude of the petty bourgeois towards formal democracy. The deepening of the revolution will expose the limitations of bourgeois democracy. Through experience the workers will come to understand the need to take power into their own hands. But in order to understand the limits of bourgeois democracy, the workers must first pass through the school of democracy. This presupposes a serious fight for the most advanced democratic slogans.

After decades of authoritarian rule in Egypt, we cannot be indifferent to the question of the Constitution. The current proposal by the Army Council is that some constitutional amendments, drafted by experts appointed by the Army, will be put to a referendum. This is completely undemocratic. Mubarak's constitution cannot be amended, it should be thrown out and a democratic and revolutionary Constituent Assembly convened in order to discuss a completely new constitution. The reactionary role of the generals was shown by the army's violent disbanding of the Tahrir Square camp.

Having overthrown a dictatorship through struggle, the revolutionary people cannot hand power to the same generals who supported Mubarak till the very last minute. The workers cannot trust the army chiefs or any council of "experts" appointed by them to write a genuinely democratic constitution. We are for a constituent assembly: a democratically elected body to work out the constitution. This is an elementary democratic demand.

But the question remains: who will convene the Constituent Assembly? We cannot entrust this task to the Egyptian Army, either. Therefore, the struggle must continue on the streets, in the factories, in the youth, among the unemployed, until the battle for democracy is complete.

The situation in Egypt is analogous, not to Bolivia in 2003 and 2006 or to Argentina in 2001, but to Russia in 1905 or 1917. We must make use of the most advanced democratic slogans to pose the central question of workers' power. We say to the workers and youth: "You want democracy? We do too! But don't trust the Army or ElBaradei – let's fight for real democracy!" In Egypt, Tunisia and Iran today, the slogan of a Constituent Assembly is very relevant indeed.

The workers of Egypt have already drawn the correct conclusion. This is strikingly revealed in the statement of the Iron and steel workers in Helwan, who, during the struggle, advanced the following demands:

1) the immediate stepping down of Mubarak and all the figures of the regime and its symbols;
2) the confiscation of wealth and property of all the regime's symbols and all those to be proven to be corrupt, on behalf of the interest of the masses;
3) the immediate resignation of all workers from the trade unions controlled by or affiliated to the regime and declaring their independent unions now preparing their general conference to elect and form their syndicate;
4) the acquisition of public sector companies that have been sold or closed and the declaration of nationalizing them on behalf of the people and the formation of a new administration to run it, involving workers and technicians;
5) the formation of committees to supervise workers in all work sites and monitor the production and distribution of prices and wages;
6) call for a constituent assembly of all classes of people and trends for the drafting of a new constitution and the election of people's councils without waiting for the negotiations with the former regime.

These demands are absolutely correct. They show a very high level of revolutionary consciousness and coincide completely with the programme advanced by the Marxists. This programme provides the Egyptian Revolution with all it needs to succeed.

Trade unions

The revolution poses the need for organization. The trade unions are the most basic form of organization for the workers of all countries at all times. Without organization the working class will always be only raw material for exploitation. The task of building and strengthening the unions is therefore an urgent priority.

In Egypt and Tunisia the unions were closely linked with the old oppressive regime. To all intents and purposes they were part of the state. Their upper levels were corrupted and in many cases members of the ruling party. Their main role was to police the workers. However, at rank and file level they consisted of workers and honest militants.

Even in bourgeois democracies there is an organic tendency of the union tops to fuse with the state. But history shows that when the working class moves even the most corrupt and bureaucratized trade unions can come under the pressure of the working class and become transformed in the course of struggle. Either the old leaders will change and begin to reflect the pressure of the workers or they will be removed and replaced by others who are prepared to put themselves at the head of the movement.

In Tunisia the UGTT leaders were compromised with the Ben Ali regime. The old leaders were prepared to participate in a provisional government formed by Ghannouchi but were forced to resign under the pressure of the workers. But at local and regional levels the UGTT played a leading role in the revolution. In some areas, like in Redeyef, the UGTT actually took over the running of society. In others, the local unions played a key role in the organisation of the revolutionary movement through revolutionary committees. This shows the vital role of the unions as a vehicle for revolution.

What is needed is a through cleansing of the UGTT at all levels, removing all those bureaucrats which are linked to the old regime, starting with its general secretary Abdessalem Jerad, who is playing an openly strike-breaking role. The regional structures and national federations which are under the leadership of the left and democratic activists and which represent a majority of the membership of the UGTT should convene immediately an emergency national congress. A move to democratise the union and bring it in line with the revolutionary movement would have massive support amongst ordinary workers. If the workers and youth were able to remove Ben Ali and then Ghannouchi, it should be even easier for them to remove the corrupt trade union leaders who supported them.

In Egypt the corrupt union leaders were unable to prevent the wave of strikes that was a preparatory school for the revolution. The Egyptian workers have moved against the old corrupt leaders and are fighting to create unions which are genuine democratic and militant organizations of the class. In so doing they have shown an unerring revolutionary class instinct. The fight for democracy is not confined to the political arena. It must enter the trade unions and the workplaces also.

The struggle seems to be moving in the direction of setting up a new Egyptian Federation of Independent Trade Unions. In revolutionary conditions like the ones which exist now, this can become the main organisation of Egyptian workers. However, it would be a mistake to abandon altogether the struggle within the old official unions, which still claim to represent millions of workers. In some instances, whole workplaces and sectors will be unionised anew. In some other cases, democratic and militant unions will emerge through the workers taking control of the official structures.

The bourgeoisie and the imperialists understand the central importance of the unions. They will send their paid agents to corrupt and deceive workers in order to prevent them from drawing revolutionary and socialist ideas. The CIA has close links with the leaders of the AFL-CIO and the European Social Democracy and so-called International Trade Union bodies. They will try to bring the militant trade union movement under their control.

The workers must beware of such "friends" who come to corrupt them and undermine the revolution from within. They must also beware of the so-called NGOs that are a disguised agency of imperialism. The role of the NGOs is to divert the workers from the revolutionary path, entangling them in a thousand trivial tasks, charities, etc., turning former revolutionaries and militant workers into paid lackeys, office boys and bureaucrats. This is a poison that can corrode the workers' movement.

The task of the unions is not to prop up capitalism but to overthrow it. Our first aim is to fight for improved living standards, better wages and conditions. We must fight for every improvement, no matter how small. But we must also understand that it will be impossible to obtain our basic demands as long as a parasitic oligarchy is the owner of the land, the banks and the major industries.

In the struggle against the old regime, the unions have linked up with other layers of society: the unemployed, the women, the youth, the peasants, the intellectuals. That is absolutely necessary. The working class must aspire to place itself at the head of the Nation and to lead the fight against all forms of injustice and oppression.

The revolutionary people are setting up popular committees of all sorts. That is a necessary step to provide the revolutionary movement with an organized and coherent form. Such broad committees do not, however, replace the trade unions, which must remain the basic organizational form of the workers' movement.

The trade unions are a school of revolution that will play a key role in overthrowing the old regime and establishing a new, socialist society, in which the role of the unions will be expanded a thousand fold, playing a major part in the running of the nationalized industries, planning production and running society.

The IMT says:

• Build the trade unions and turn them into genuine fighting organizations!
• Purge the unions of all corrupt elements and bureaucrats!
• For democratic unions: elections at every level and right of recall of all officials!

- Against corruption! No union official must receive a wage higher than a skilled worker!
- No to state control of the unions! The unions must be in the hands of the workers!
- For workers' control of industry! For the expropriation of the bankers, landlords and capitalists! For a democratic socialist plan of production!

Role of the youth

Karl Liebknecht, the great German revolutionary and martyr once said: "The youth is the flame of the Socialist Revolution". These words could be emblazoned on the banner of the Arab Revolution. At every stage the youth has played the key role. The protestors who poured onto the streets of Tunisia and Egypt were mainly young people, unemployed and without any future. Some were university graduates, others poor people from the slums.

In all the countries of the Middle East and North Africa, the majority of the population are young people. They are suffering the worst effects of the crisis of capitalism. Seventy per cent of youth under the age of 25 in Tunisia are unemployed. The figure is 75 per cent in Algeria and 76 per cent in Egypt. A similar situation exists in other countries.

University graduates have no jobs and therefore have no prospect of marriage, no home and no future. These facts show the impasse of capitalism. These countries need doctors, teachers, engineers, but there are no jobs. Millions of young people are unable to find work, and are therefore unable to marry and raise a family. They are motivated by a deep sense of injustice and a burning anger and resentment towards a system that denies them a future and a corrupt regime that has enriched itself at the people's expense.

The only hope these young people have is to fight for a fundamental change in society. They have cast aside all fear and are prepared to risk their lives in the fight for freedom and justice. In Tunisia the revolutionary youth organised themselves and called a mass rally in Tunis, marching on the Prime Minister's office and camping in front of it, in the Kasbah esplanade. Mass movements of the school students raised the demand for a constituent assembly, and demonstrated shouting "down with government". They provided the catalyst for a movement which finally brought down the government of Ghannouchi at the end of February. In Egypt we again see the same thing. The protestors who led the way were mainly young Egyptians, unemployed and without any future.

History is repeating itself. In 1917 the Mensheviks accused the Bolsheviks of being just a "bunch of kids", and they were not entirely wrong. The average age of the Bolshevik activists was very low. The first section to move is always the youth, who are free from the prejudices, fear and scepticism of the older generation.

The youth of every country are open to revolutionary ideas. We must go to the youth! If we go to the youth with the ideas of revolutionary Marxism and proletarian internationalism, we will get an enthusiastic response.

The IMT says:

- Jobs for all!
- Every young person must be guaranteed either a full-time job or free full-time education.
- Equal pay for work of equal value!
- An end to police harassment!
- Full democratic rights and votes at 16!

The role of women

The decisive factor is that the masses have acquired a sense of their collective strength and are losing their fear. Beginning with the youngest, most energetic and determined elements, the mood of defiance has transmitted itself to the older, more cautious and inert layers of the population.

One of the most inspiring aspects of the revolutions in Tunisia and Egypt, however, was the active participation of the women. The old submissiveness is disappearing. In Alexandria elderly housewives threw pots and pans onto the police from the balconies of their flats. On the demonstrations young female students in jeans fought side by side with other women wearing the hijab. It was the women workers played a key role in the massive strikes of textile workers in Mahalla al Kubra in recent years, strikes which prepared the present revolutionary upheaval.

Women have been to the forefront of every revolution in history. The images of the women of Bahrain, demonstrating fearlessly, some with veils, some without, are an inspiring picture of the revolution in action. They are repeating the experience of the heroic women of Paris in October 1789 and in Petrograd in February 1917.

The awakening of the women is a sure sign of revolution. Society cannot advance and prosper as long as women are enslaved. It is not by chance that reactionaries in Egypt, as well as fomenting religious pogroms, attacked the March 8th demonstration in Tahrir Square. The Arab Revolution will recruit its most determined and courageous fighters from the ranks of the women, and the complete emancipation of women is the first duty of the revolution. The place of women is not in the kitchen but on the streets fighting alongside the men. They are the most fearless elements. And they have most to fight for.

The IMT says:

- Down with discrimination and inequality!
- Full recognition of women as equal citizens and human beings!
- Full social, political and economic equality for women!
- An end to all discriminatory laws!

- Organize the women workers in free and democratic trade unions, independent of the state!
- Equal pay for work of equal value!

The revolution is not finished

To say that a revolution has begun is not to say that it has been completed, much less that victory is assured. It is a struggle of living forces. Revolution is not a one-act drama. It is a complicated process with many ebbs and flows. The overthrow of Mubarak, Ben Ali and Ghannouchi marks the end of the first stages, but the revolution has not yet succeeded in completely overthrowing the old regime, while the latter has not yet succeeded in re-establishing control.

In Russia in 1917 the revolution lasted for nine months, from February to October, when the workers finally took power under the leadership of the Bolshevik Party. However, the Russian Revolution was not a straight line and proceeded through all kinds of vicissitudes and contradictions. There was a period of open reaction in July and August. Lenin had to flee to Finland and the Bolshevik Party was virtually illegalised. But this merely prepared the way for a new advance of the revolution, culminating in the October insurrection.

In Spain we saw a similar process, starting with the fall of the monarchy in 1931, followed by a big upsurge of the class struggle. But the defeat of the Asturian Commune in October 1934 led to a period of reaction, the *Bienio Negro*, or two black years in 1935-36. But this proved to be only the prelude to a new upsurge of the revolution, starting with the victory of the Popular Front in the elections of 1936, leading to the Civil War and ending in defeat and fascism.

After the fall of Mubarak, the Egyptian Revolution is like a big carnival. But the masses are fighting for things no bourgeois government can give them. Like the Russian workers in February 1917, the workers of Egypt have succeeded in overthrowing a tyrant but they have not won their main objectives. The real struggle is still ahead. What has been solved by Mubarak's overthrow? What was achieved by Ben Ali fleeing to Saudi Arabia? Nothing fundamental has been solved. The workers are fighting for bread, jobs and houses, not for some kind of charade of formal bourgeois democracy in which everything changes so that everything can remain the same.

Through painful experience the masses are learning some serious lessons. Sooner or later they will draw the conclusion that the working class must take power. There will be an extended learning process, a process of inner differentiation. This has already begun. In the revolutionary committees the more moderate elements who led the movement in its early stages, and who have illusions in the army, are being challenged by new layers of workers and youth who are opposed to compromise. They fear that what they have conquered with their blood can be taken away from them by subterfuge. This suspicion is well founded.

With the fall of Mubarak the Egyptian Revolution won its first great victory. But none of the fundamental problems of Egyptian society have been solved. Prices continue to rise, homeless people sleep in cemeteries and about 10 per cent of the workforce is unemployed according to official statistics, though the real figure is much higher.

There is a burning anger against inequality and the all-pervading corruption that is the chief characteristic of the old regime. Billions of dollars of public money have gone missing. The amounts looted by the Mubarak family alone are estimated at between US$40 billion and $80 billion. This has provoked anger and disgust, in a country where 40 per cent of the people are living below the poverty line.

It is impossible to say for sure what will follow. However, we can say that the revolution will be protracted in time and will experience all manner of ups and downs. At the present time, the masses are intoxicated with the idea of democracy. The feeling of euphoria affects even the most advanced and revolutionary elements. This period of democratic and constitutional illusions is an inevitable phase but it will not last. The revolution stirs society to the bottom. It awakens new, previously inert and "backward" layers to political life. They are demanding their rights. When these people say "thawra hatta'l nasr" (revolution until victory), they mean it.

All attempts to restore the political equilibrium will come to nothing because the crisis of capitalism does not permit any solution to the most basic needs of the population. There will be a series of unstable bourgeois regimes. One unstable ministry after another will fall. This presents a danger. When the class struggle reaches the point of deadlock, the state tends to rise above society and acquire a relative independence. The result is an unstable military regime, or, to give it its correct name, a Bonapartist regime. The very fact of the existence of such a regime indicates that the revolution that began on 25 January is not finished. It will experience many new turns before the final denouement can be written.

Despite all the appeals for "national unity", Egyptian society is becoming sharply polarized. The revolution still has considerable reserves of support in the population. Students are agitating on the campuses. Workers are staging strikes and factory occupations, driving out hated managers and corrupt trade union leaders. The strike of the Egyptian oil workers won all their demands, including the resignation of the oil minister, in just three days. This shows where the real power lies.

The military regime in Egypt cannot maintain itself for long. All the attempts to restore "order" (that is, the rule of the rich and powerful) have failed. The army has tried to stop strikes, but the strikes continue. Far from subsiding, the movement of the workers is increasing. What can the generals do? If they were unable to use their tanks to crush the insurrection, still less can they use them to crush strikes in what is supposed to be a democratic regime.

The generals will have to pass power to a civilian (i.e. bourgeois) government. *This will be counterrevolution in a democratic disguise.* But it will not be easy for to the counterrevolution to restore stability. For the workers, democracy is not an empty word. If it does not lead to an improvement in living standards, jobs and houses, what was the point of fighting in the first place?

If all this had happened ten years ago, they might have been able to consolidate some form of bourgeois democratic regimes. The boom in world capitalism would have given them some margin for manoeuvre. But now there is a profound crisis on a world scale. This is both the reason for the revolutionary ferment and the reason why it cannot easily be brought to an end. The capitalist system cannot offer anything to the masses. It can't even provide jobs and a decent living standard in the USA and Europe. How can they hope to do it in Egypt?

The actions of the workers striking, occupying the factories and kicking out the managers are of tremendous importance. They mean that the revolution is entering the factories and workplaces. They signify that the workers of Egypt are proceeding from the struggle for democracy in society to the struggle for economic democracy in the workplace. It means that the Egyptian working class is beginning to participate in the revolution under its own banner, fighting for its own class demands. This is a decisive factor for the future of the revolution.

The workers are protesting against corruption and low salaries. They are rebelling against state-appointed managements and setting up revolutionary committees to run factories and other workplaces. That is the correct line to take.

Bourgeois commentators have emphasized that many of these strikes are of an economic nature. Of course! The working class is pressing its immediate demands. That is to say, they see the revolution as a means of fighting not just for formal democracy but for better wages, for better working conditions – for a better life. They are fighting for their own class demands. And this struggle cannot cease just because Hosni Mubarak is no longer sitting in the Presidential Palace.

For a workers' democracy!

In Suez, the state collapsed completely for four or five days. Like in Tunisia earlier, revolutionary committees and armed checkpoints were established to defend the people. These facts demonstrate beyond question that soviets (i.e. workers' councils) are not an arbitrary invention of the Marxists but emerge spontaneously in any genuine revolution.

This poses the central question, that of the state. The old state power has been brought to its knees by the revolution. It must be replaced with a new power. There is a power in society that is stronger than any state. That power is the revolutionary people. But it must be organized. In both Egypt and Tunisia there are elements of dual power in the revolutionary committees. Entire cities and regions were taken over by these committees.

In Tunisia, the revolutionary organisation of the people went even further than in Egypt. These bodies, in many cases organised around the local structures of the UGTT trade unions, took over the running of all aspects of society in towns and cities and even in whole regions, after expelling the old, RCD regime, authorities. For all the talk of "chaos" and "lack of security" on the part of the ruling class, the fact is that working people organised themselves to guarantee order and safety, but this was a different type of order, a revolutionary order.

In Egypt, following the collapse of the police force on January 28th, people stepped in to protect their neighbourhoods. They set up checkpoints, armed with knives, swords, machetes and sticks to inspect cars that were coming in and out. In some areas, the popular committees virtually took over the running of the town, even organizing the traffic. Here we have the embryo of a people's militia – of an alternative state power.

And just as the people set up committees to protect their areas from criminal elements when the police were taken off the streets in order to cause chaos and disorder, now in order to organize the revolution in the most effective manner, the same idea must be taken up and generalized. *In order to defend and extend the revolution, we must form defence committees everywhere!*

Elected Committees for the Defence of the Revolution, which already exist in some areas, should be established in every factory, street and village. The revolutionary committees should link up on a local, regional and national level. This would be the starting point for a future democratic workers' and peasants' government – a real alternative to the rotten dictatorial regime.

The IMT demands:

- A complete purge and democratization of the army!
- For the setting up of soldiers' committees and committees of revolutionary-minded lower ranking officers!
- Out with the corrupt and reactionary generals!
- Immediate disbandment of all repressive bodies!
- All those guilty of acts of terror against the people must be put on trial and punished!
- The general arming of the people!
- The establishment of a people's militia!
- For a workers' and peasants' government!

Revolution knows no frontiers

The international character of the revolution has been clear from the very beginnings. Other Arab countries face many similar problems to those in Tunisia and Egypt: rising food prices, sharply deteriorating economic conditions, unemployment and rampant official corruption. Many millions of people are struggling to exist. And in society as in nature, similar conditions produce similar results.

What has happened in Tunisia and Egypt can happen in many other countries, and not only in the Arab world.

The imperialists have been trying to console themselves with the thought that there is no domino effect. But the dominoes are already beginning to fall: Libya, Morocco, Sudan, Iraq, Djibouti, Yemen, Bahrain and Oman – all are entering the revolutionary maelstrom. As in Tunisia and Egypt, the people of Algeria, Jordan and Yemen were living in poverty under dictatorial ruling elites which lived a luxurious life by plundering the nation.

In the case of Iraq, the revolution is linked to the struggle against imperialism and foreign domination and the right to self-determination of the Kurdish people. At the same time, one characteristic of the protest movement in Iraq is that it has cut across the sectarian divide between Shiites and Sunnis, between Arabs, Kurds and Turkmens, which has been the basis for the domination of reactionary politicians.

Among the main issues raised by the protesters are rising living costs, partly caused by the government's withdrawal of subsidies for petrol and sugar – an explosive issue across the Arab world. The leaders of Jordan, Algeria and Libya all reduced taxes on imported food or lowered the prices of staples in an attempt to avoid unrest. In Algeria the regime has made concessions in an attempt to prevent an explosion that would be even bigger than the insurrection in the Berber areas in 2001.

Even the oil-rich monarchs of the Gulf are worried. Kuwait has distributed £4,000 (€4,600 or US$6,500) to all its citizens to keep the population quiet. But such measures can at best succeed only in postponing the inevitable revolutionary upsurge.

The Western media shamelessly portrayed the movement in Bahrain as a religious-sectarian struggle of the Shiite majority and the Sunnis. That is a lie. The Bahrainis are fighting against corruption, for free elections, against discrimination and for rights for immigrants and women, for equitable distribution of wealth and against unemployment. Everywhere we see the same courage of the masses in face of fire. In Bahrain the army was forced to withdraw from Pearl Square. Once again, the role of the working class was crucial, as it was the threat of a general strike on the part of the Bahraini trade unions which forced the regime to make some concessions

In all the Gulf Sates there is brutal exploitation of labour, largely immigrant labour. There are 1.1 million Pakistanis working in Saudi Arabia alone. A similar situation exists throughout the Gulf. There have been strikes and uprisings there in the past that have not been reported, such as the strike of 8,000 building workers in Dubai.

The Saudi regime itself, that bastion of reaction in the Middle East, resembles a pressure cooker without a safety valve. In such a regime, when the explosion comes, it will occur without warning and with extreme violence. The Saudi royal family is corrupt, degenerate and rotten to the core. It is split over the succession and there is growing resentment and discontent in the population. When the moment comes, all the oil in the kingdom will not save them. It is significant that now even the Wahhabi clergy is turning against them.

The Arab Revolution has revived the revolutionary movement in Iran, where officers in the Revolutionary Guard have said they are not prepared to fire on the people and warned the Basij to leave their truncheons at home. Rifts in the state apparatus reveal the deep crisis of the regime which is split from top to bottom.

Because each case is somewhat different, it is hard to say what kinds of regimes will emerge in each case. What kinds of political tendencies and regimes will emerge depends on many factors and will differ from one country to another. The processes in Tunisia and Egypt were almost identical. But in Libya the situation is different. The regime had more of a base, particularly around Tripoli. The uprising was largely confined to the eastern part and the revolution has been transformed into a civil war, the outcome of which is still uncertain.

Gaddafi doesn't care if the whole country goes down with him. Having lost control of the whole of the east including the second biggest city, Benghazi, he decided to fight to the last, plunging Libya into a bloody conflict. There have been wide ranging defections in the Libyan army, even at the top level. But it did not have the same effect as in Egypt because of the different nature of the army and the regime.

One thing is clear: everything has been thrown into the melting pot. Not one of these regimes will survive in the end. There are different possibilities, depending on the class balance of forces and a whole series of internal and external factors that are impossible to foresee. But one thing is clear: no matter what regime is installed, it will not be able to satisfy even the most minimal demands of the masses.

Impotence of imperialism

The imperialists are worried about where all this will go, and how far it will spread. They did not expect these events and do not know how to react. Obama did not dare call on Mubarak publicly to resign because of the effects in these other states. He was obliged to speak in carefully calculated code. The very words "democracy" and "human rights" in the mouth of Obama and his European counterparts stink of hypocrisy.

The cynicism of Western governments stands exposed in all its crudity. After decades of backing the vicious dictatorship in Tunisia, suddenly they are all in favour of democracy and human rights. Yet Sarkozy had praised Ben Ali as a friend of democracy and human rights even when he was torturing his opponents in the prisons. And Washington covered up the barbarous acts of all the other pro-western dictators. Now they are getting their just reward.

Politics affects the economy and vice-versa. Oil prices have climbed on fears the unrest could spread to other Arab states including oil giant Saudi Arabia or interfere with oil supplies from the Red Sea to the Mediterranean through the Suez Canal. Brent crude surpassed the US$120 a barrel mark and is still hovering over the $110 mark. This threatens to undermine the weak and fragile recovery of the world economy.

For economic, political and military reasons the imperialists need stability in the Middle East. But how are they to get it? That is the question! From the beginning the US has been struggling to find a coherent response to events that are changing by the day, even by the hour. In reality the strongest power in the world has been reduced to the role of a helpless onlooker. An article in *The Independent* by their correspondent in Washington, Rupert Cornwell, carried the interesting title: *Washington's strong words underline US impotence*. That expresses the real position.

Some "clever" people, however, think that the Arab Revolution is all part of an imperialist conspiracy. Nothing could be further from the truth. The bourgeoisie was taken completely by surprise by all this. These revolutions are completely destabilizing one of their most important regions. This is far from welcome to them. And it has repercussions far beyond the Arab world.

The Middle East is a key area for the imperialists. The Americans have spent four decades establishing their position there. Egypt was a key piece in their calculations. Now all this has been swept away before their eyes in a few weeks. The richest and most powerful state on earth was completely paralyzed. Obama could not intervene, and even found it difficult to say anything about it for fear of offending their Saudi allies.

Eight per cent of world trade passes through the Suez Canal, and the Americans were terrified that would be closed, but they could do nothing about it. All that Obama could say was that it was the Egyptian people's choice. The Americans did not say that when it came to Iraq or Afghanistan, where US imperialism did not think twice about invading.

US warships were in fact sent to Suez but did nothing. This was intended to reveal the mailed fist that is concealed within the velvet glove of Obama's "democracy". But in reality it was an empty gesture. The US burned its fingers in Iraq. A new military adventure in Egypt would have provoked a storm in the USA and on a world scale. There would not have been a single US embassy left standing in the Middle East and all the other pro-US Arab regimes would be faced with overthrow.

The USA has a special interest in Bahrain because of its important strategic position next door to Saudi Arabia and Iran. It is the base of the Fifth Fleet, the most important US naval base in the whole region. Yet they were powerless to intervene against the revolutionary movement in Bahrain. If this was all part of an imperialist plan, nobody told Obama about it!

In the case of Libya they did not hesitate to denounce Gaddafi and call for his overthrow – which they signally failed to do in the case of Mubarak. This is yet another example of their duplicity, cynicism and double standards. But although they hinted that military action was not ruled out, they hesitated to act. In the moment of truth they could not summon up the courage to intervene. Hilary Clinton said that a no-fly zone would have to be approved by the UN – knowing full well that it would be vetoed by Russia. This is a complete contrast to the conduct of the USA in Iraq.

In reality, the imperialists are trapped. They know that any hint of American troops on the soil of Libya or any other Arab country would provoke a backlash all over the Arab world. However much they hate Gaddafi, the people of Libya do not want to see their country "liberated" like Iraq and Afghanistan.

The IMT says:

• No to foreign intervention!
• End the occupation of Iraq and Afghanistan!
• Down with imperialism!
• Hands off the Arab Revolution!

Israel and the Palestinians

Nowhere has the Arab Revolution caused greater panic than in Israel. The strongest military force in the region was paralysed in the face of the events in Egypt. The Israeli ruling clique even had to be careful about what they said about the situation in Egypt. Binyamin Netanyahu ordered ministers not to talk about it in public. Israel called on the United States and a number of European countries to curb their criticism of President Hosni Mubarak. Jerusalem tried desperately to convince its allies that it was in the West's interest to back Mubarak in order to maintain the stability of the Egyptian regime. This flew in the face of the efforts of the United States and European Union to remove him so that they could guarantee an "orderly transition" and avoid a revolutionary overthrow.

Marx pointed out that no people could ever be free if it enslaved another people. Israel rules over a large and disaffected population of Palestinians who are learning on their televisions how to overthrow tyranny. On the West Bank the Palestinians are held down with the help of the Palestinian Authority's police. But it is open to question whether Palestinian police units, or Israeli security forces, would be able to crush a mass democracy movement, after Egypt's powerful army refused to fire on the people.

The separate peace signed by Israel and Egypt in 1979 was a betrayal of the Palestinian cause and is deeply unpopular in most of the Arab world. The backing of Egypt has been an important element in helping the continuing Israeli occupation of the Palestinian territories conquered in 1967.

The Oslo agreement between Israel and the Palestinians in 1993 was a new betrayal. The so-called Palestinian territories are nothing more than a version of the South African Bantustans. It was a cruel mockery of a homeland and none of the basic demands of the Palestinians were conceded. Israel continued to rule the roost. Since then things have gone from bad to worse.

Now the fall of Israel's most powerful regional ally has radically altered the whole equation. It has shaken the Israeli government and called into question the deep-seated belief that the occupation of the Palestinian territories can be sustained indefinitely. Overnight the carefully prepared plans of the imperialists are in ruins.

Decades of so-called armed struggle and negotiations have led nowhere. But the revolutionary movement poses the Palestinian question in a completely different light. The ruling clique in Israel is not at all worried about Hamas' rockets and suicide bombers. On the contrary, every rocket that falls on an Israeli village serves to push Israeli public opinion behind the government. But a Palestinian Intifada, combined with the Arab Revolution in Egypt and Jordan, is another matter altogether.

As a military power, Israel may be unbeatable. In the event of a war with Egypt, Israel would probably win again. But could it win against masses of protesters in town squares across the West Bank, Gaza and Israel too, demanding political rights for Palestinians? This is a question that must keep the Israeli generals and politicians awake at night.

The fall of Mubarak has very serious implications for Israel. In the best case, Israel's defence spending will have to rise still further, as its rulers contemplate the threat of a war in the south. This will put further strains on an economy that was already in crisis. New cuts and attacks on living standards will be the result, putting an intensification of the class struggle on the order of the day in Israel.

Netanyahu imagined that his country was an island of stability and democracy that could not be affected by revolution. But basically, Israel is just another Middle Eastern country that is threatened by the revolutionary wave emanating from Tunisia and Egypt. There are new contradictions inside Israel. The increase in fuel and water has made Israel one of the most expensive countries to live in the world. The Histadrut (Israeli trade unions) leadership has been playing with the idea of a national strike.

The events in Tunisia and Egypt will have profound consequences for the Palestinians. The Palestinians have been betrayed by everyone they put their trust in, beginning with the supposedly friendly Arab regimes and ending with their own leaders. The latest revelations by WikiLeaks had exposed the scandalous collusion of Abbas with the Israelis and Americans. This will have a big effect on the psychology of the Palestinian masses.

For forty years, the PLO leadership has betrayed the Palestinian cause. The PLO could have taken power in Jordan in 1970 and then the whole history of the region would have been different. But the petty bourgeois nationalist leadership refused to attack their "Arab brothers", so the Jordanian monarch mobilized the

Bedouins who (with the help of the Pakistani Army) slaughtered thousands of Palestinians. It is a fact that many more Palestinians have been killed by Arab "brothers" than by the Israelis.

The same Bedouins who attacked the Palestinians in 1970 are now protesting against the King. Former army officers are warning the regime that unless it makes concessions it will face the same fate as that of Ben Ali and Mubarak. This shows that the Hashemite monarchy is fast losing its base and is hanging by a thread. The movement has spread from the Bedouin areas to Amman and the Palestinians, who make up the majority of the population of Jordan.

It is time to reassess the tactics and strategy of the Palestinian struggle. The WikiLeaks revelations have exposed the Palestinian leaders as little more than Israeli stooges. The mood of the Palestinians is angry and bitter. There have been a number of attempts to organise mobilisations both against Abbas in the West Bank and against Hamas in the Gaza Strip, which have been met with heavy repression. Even demonstrations in solidarity with the Egyptian and Tunisian revolutions have been banned by both Hamas and the Palestinian Authority.

Now a united movement against the current leadership of the Palestinian movement, against Israeli occupation and for the unity of the Palestinian struggle has been set up, attracting the support of tens of thousands on Facebook and calling for demonstrations and protests. For Palestinians, an Intifada in Egypt was part of their dreams for decades. Now it is a reality. The overthrow of the reactionary Arab regimes by the masses will deal a serious blow against Israel and US imperialism and transform the whole situation. Now for the first time the Palestinians can see who are their only real friends: the workers and peasants of the whole Arab world.

This represents a fundamental turning point. The Palestinians have seen how it is possible to fight against the oppressors, not with bombs and rockets, but by revolutionary mass action. The whole mood will be different now. There will be new stirrings in the youth, movements against Hamas in Gaza, and against the PLO leaders in the West Bank. There is growing pressure for something different than what has existed heretofore. The idea of a new Intifada will rapidly gain ground among the Palestinians. This would change everything.

For a Socialist Federation!

After the First World War the so-called Arab nation states were created artificially by imperialism. This division was not based on any natural or historical criterion but purely on the interests of imperialism. The Sykes-Picot agreement divided Iraq, Lebanon, Syria and Jordan between Britain and France. Under the Balfour Declaration in 1918, the British gave permission for the establishment of a Jewish homeland in Palestine.

In the Gulf, small states with huge reserves of oil were established so they could be controlled by imperialism easily, for access to resources. The Saudi monarchy consisted of desert bandits, raised to power by the British agent Wilson Cox. Imperialism has divided the living body of the Great Arab Nation.

The Arab Revolution can never succeed until it has put an end to the shameful Balkanization of the Arab world. The only way to break the chains forged by imperialism is to place on our banner the slogan of a Socialist Federation of the Arab world. This would create a mighty Socialist Commonwealth, stretching from the Atlantic Ocean to the Euphrates.

On the basis of a nationalized planned economy, unemployment would be immediately abolished. A vast reservoir of unused labour power would be mobilized to solve the problems of housing, health, education and the infrastructure. By pooling the huge resources of all these countries on the basis of a common plan of production, deserts could be made to bloom and a new cultural revolution would put all the gains of the past in the shade.

A Socialist Federation, with full autonomy for all the peoples, is the only way to solve the national and religious strife that has poisoned the lives of the peoples for decades, leading to one war after another. Muslims and Copts, Sunnis and Shiites, Palestinians and Jews, Arabs, Amazigh (Berbers), Maronites, Kurds, Turkmens, Armenians, Druzes – all will find a place in a Federation based on the principle of absolute equality.

The IMT says:

• Defend the rights of the Palestinian people and all oppressed nationalities to self-determination!
• Down with the imperialist and Israeli aggressors!
• End the occupation of Iraq, Afghanistan and Palestine!
• Drive out the collaborators!
• For the revolutionary overthrow of all the Arab puppets of imperialism!
• Expropriate the property of the imperialists and their Arab stooges!
• The wealth of the Arab lands must be returned to the people!
• For the revolutionary unity of the peoples!
• For the Socialist Federation of the Middle East and North Africa, on the basis of a free, equal and fraternal union, with full autonomy to every nationality!

Leaps in consciousness

The Egyptian Revolution is the final answer to all those sceptics and intellectual snobs who constantly harp on the alleged "low level of consciousness" of the masses. Those western "experts" who talked contemptuously of the Egyptians as "apathetic" and "passive" and "indifferent to politics" must eat their words.

Marxists understand that human consciousness in general is not progressive or revolutionary but profoundly conservative. Resistance to change is deeply rooted in the human mind as part of a survival mechanism that comes from the remote past of our species. As a general rule, therefore, consciousness lags behind events. It does not change gradually, today more revolutionary than yesterday and tomorrow more than today, any more than water that is cooled from 100 to 0 degrees first becomes a paste, then a jelly and finally a solid.

This view of consciousness is metaphysical and mechanical, not materialist and dialectical. Dialectics teaches us that things change into their opposite, and that small, apparently insignificant changes can at a certain point, known in physics as a critical point, produce explosive transformations on a gigantic scale. The change in consciousness happens suddenly, when it is compelled by great events to change. When this occurs, consciousness is swiftly brought into line with reality. This leap of consciousness is precisely what a revolution is.

The masses, whether in Egypt, Iran, Britain or the USA, do not learn from books but from experience. In a revolution, they learn much faster than in other circumstances. The Egyptian workers and youth have learnt more in a few days of struggle than in thirty years of "normal" existence. On the streets the masses developed a sense of their own power. They lost the deadening fear of the uniformed riot police backed up by water cannons and thousands of plain-clothes thugs, who they pushed back and defeated.

In a revolution the learning process is enormously speeded up. We see exactly the same process in Egypt and Tunisia. Here is a vast laboratory where the different vague, competing lists of demands issued by different organisers are put to the test. On the streets the masses decide which slogans are appropriate and which are not. We will see the same process repeated time and time again, and not just in the Middle East and North Africa but everywhere.

From Cairo to Madison

In 1917 it took about a week for people in India to learn that there had been a revolution in Russia. Today everyone can see the revolution live on their television screens. The situation in the Middle East is having a tremendous effect around the world. In India, for the first time in 32 years, the unions and left parties recently organised a general strike over wages and prices. There was a march of 200,000 on the streets in New Delhi, over food price rises. Although India is growing at an annual rate of nine per cent, this increases inequality by concentrating wealth at the top.

In Tunisia and Egypt the capitalist system is beginning to break at its weakest links. The bourgeois will tell us that such things cannot happen in the advanced capitalist countries, that the situation is different and so on and so forth. Yes, the situation is different, but only in degree. Everywhere the working class and the youth will be faced with the same alternative: either we accept the systematic destruction of our living standards and rights – or we fight.

The argument "it cannot happen here" is without any scientific or rational basis. The same thing was said of Tunisia only a couple of months ago, when that country was considered to be the most stable in North Africa. And the same argument was repeated in relation to Egypt even after Ben Ali was overthrown. Just a few weeks were sufficient to expose the hollowness of those words. Such is the speed of events in our epoch. Sooner or later the same question will be posed in every country in Europe, in Japan, in Canada, and also in the United States.

Inflation is rising. Food prices are rising. This will have the most serious effects everywhere, particularly in poor countries. According to the World Bank, 44 million more people will be thrust into extreme poverty in the coming period, pushing the figure to over one billion worldwide. Millions of people are fighting for food, jobs and housing – that is, for the most basic conditions of a semi-civilized existence. These conditions ought to be freely available to everybody in the first decade of the 21st century. But the decrepit capitalist system is no longer able to guarantee these things even in Europe and North America. This is why there are riots and uprisings. It is a life and death question.

The present crisis is not a normal cyclical crisis of capitalism. The recovery also is not normal. The capitalists are trying to squeeze the workers more than ever in an attempt to re-establish the economic equilibrium: to pay off their debts, reduce cost of labour, etc. But by so doing, they destabilize the entire situation. This partly explains both the Arab revolution and the upsurge of the class struggle in Europe

Every country in the world has been affected. It is no accident that China added its voice to the chorus calling for a return to "order" in Egypt. In part it is a question of economic interest. The Chinese regime is interested in global economic stability because it wants to continue to earn a lot of money from exports. But above all, Beijing is afraid of anything that could provide an impetus for strikes and protests in China itself. They have clamped down on all protest and blocked any reference to Egypt on the Internet.

By contrast, every class conscious worker in the world will rejoice at the marvellous movement of the workers and youth in Tunisia and Egypt. The psychological effects of this cannot be underestimated. For many, especially in the advanced capitalist countries, the idea of revolution appeared as something abstract and remote. Now the events that have unfolded before their eyes on television show that revolution is not just possible but necessary.

In Europe and the USA there is a seething hatred of the bankers and fat cats who are rewarding themselves obscene bonuses while the rest of society suffers continuous attacks on their living standards. This fact is strikingly reflected in the dramatic events in Wisconsin. It is no accident that the workers of Madison, Wisconsin, chanted things like "fight like an Egyptian". This is the effect of the vicious policies being imposed on the working class during an economic recovery in the US.

Suddenly the world has woken up to the fact that there has been an explosion of the class struggle in Wisconsin, with 100,000 people on the streets. We see images of workers holding placards calling the governor Hosni Walker and chanting: "Wisconsin Dictator Must Go". Egyptian workers even sent solidarity messages to the Wisconsin workers. There have been student walkouts, campouts at the state Capitol and spontaneous rallies. The police who were sent to disperse the demonstrators went over to the people, joined the occupation wearing jackets that carried slogans like "cops for labour". This is an extremely important development.

In Europe we have seen big movements of the workers and youth: eight general strikes in Greece in the last twelve months; a huge strike movement in France bringing three and a half million workers out onto the streets; the movement of the British students; a general strike in Spain; in Italy the movement of the metal workers. Recently there was the biggest general strike in Portugal since the fall of the dictatorship in 1974. Even in the Netherlands there were 15,000 students protesting at The Hague. In Eastern Europe as well we have seen big movements in Albania and Romania. In Bulgaria, even the police have been out on strike.

Twenty years ago, the bourgeoisie was overjoyed at the overthrow of "communism". But their rejoicing was premature. In retrospect the fall of Stalinism will be seen as only the prelude to a far more dramatic development: the revolutionary overthrow of capitalism. Everywhere, including the United States, the system is in crisis. Everywhere the ruling class is trying to place the full burden of the crisis of its system on the shoulders of the poorest layers of society.

These movements have striking similarities to the mass movements that led to the overthrow of the regimes in Eastern Europe. On paper these governments had a powerful state apparatus, big armies, police, and secret police. But that did not save them. Nor will all the money, police and armies in the world save the rulers of Europe and the United States once the workers move to change society.

The masses have shown again and again determination and willingness to struggle. In order to achieve victory they need to be armed with a clear programme and leadership. The ideas of Marxism are the only ones that can provide it. The future is ours.

- Long live the Arab Revolution!
- Workers of the world unite!
- Long live socialism, the only hope for the future of humankind!
- Thawra hatta'l nasr!

London, March 14, 2011

TUNISIA

TUNISIA

THE TUNISIAN SPRING

Editorial Board of Marxy.com Arab website of the IMT

In the last two weeks, the streets of Tunisia have been the scene of clashes between protesters and the forces of repression. The direct cause behind the outbreak of these events is the solidarity shown by the masses with a young man who immolated himself in the town of Sidi Bouzid on the 17th December. After this incident, another young man (Hussein Falahi) committed suicide by jumping off an electricity pylon to protest against his unemployment. After this, a third young man, aged 34, committed suicide by jumping into a well in the Gdir region. These acts reflect the deep frustration that young Tunisians are experiencing.

The young Mohamed Bouazizi, 26 years of age, who is an unemployed graduate, burned himself in protest against the confiscation of his small fruit stall under the pretext of selling without a license. The police did not allow him to meet with the governor and he was attacked violently by the local state officials. He was transferred to the local hospital in critical condition. Thereafter, a crowd of young people protested outside the headquarters of the municipality to denounce oppression and exploitation, demanding the right to employment for young people in the region. Thousands of people were present in these events; most of them are unemployed, and they raised slogans condemning the policy of the ruling class and demanding revenge.

Soon after, a wave of protests spread to other cities. The reports are already talking about the death of a demonstrator, the young Mohamed Bashir Ammari (18 years), who was shot while he was protesting in the town of Menzel Bouzaiane for the right to work, for a decent life, and against corruption. According to recent reports another martyr, the 44 year old Chawki Belhoussine El Hadri, fell dead after being wounded by police bullets in his back during the protests in Menzel Bouzaiane.

In the village of Zanoch, located in the municipality of Gafsa, mobilisation increases day after day. Two unemployed graduates organized a sit-in outside the village council on the morning of the 23rd December. The evening before, another unemployed young person, Aliani Hashemi, tried to commit suicide by self immolation. Reports indicate that repressive forces were sent there by the thousands.

The scale of protests has expanded to other cities like Meknassi, Menzel Bouzaiane, and Regueb. Clashes with the forces of the state, which encircled the town of Sidi Bouzid, continued into the night of Sunday 19th and Monday 20th December. The clashes did not stop until 3am on the Monday. The state forces have used tear gas and bombs, and have raided houses and arrested youth.

The town of Sidi Bouzid is still under police control and is sealed off behind a wall of silence by the official and semi-official media.

On Saturday 25th December, the region of Souk Jedid near Sidi Bouzid has seen violent clashes in which the forces of repression used live ammunition. Something similar took place in the area of Sidi Ali Ben Aoun, where the repressive forces fired live ammunition and tear gas on unarmed protesters, and they cut the electricity. This did not stop the masses, leading to new clashes between protesters and the repressive forces.

In the city of Bouzaiane, the intervention of the army and police were needed to impose a state of siege and curfew on the city, and to impose complete control over the Azaafor district. On the same day, Saturday 25th December, the city of Fernana in the municipality of Jendouba experienced disruption to traffic on the road between Aïn Drahem and Jendouba when protesters lit a bonfire. According to trade union sources from Jendouba, a number of demonstrators in the town of Fernana had poured gasoline on the main road between Fernana and Jendouba during Saturday evening and set it on fire.

The dictatorship responds

Faced with these protests, the dictatorship has spared neither bullets nor tear gas, and has done everything possible to transform Tunisia into a one-sided war zone against the oppressed and the poor who have risen to demand freedom, the right to decent work, and bread. There have been at least two deaths: Mohammed Bashir Ammari and Chawki Belhoussine El Hadri, along with an unknown number of demonstrators who were wounded, whilst others have been imprisoned and even abducted.

The reports reveal cases of torture among prisoners, for instance by the police in the town of Sidi Bouzid, which has caused even more anger among the masses.

Parallel to this brutal repression, the authorities have issued a statement expressing their "full regret" for the incident with the young Mohamed. But they condemned what they called a "group of deceivers" who want to distort "the achievements of change". The Interior Ministry also issued a statement on this occasion that tried to justify the use of live ammunition against unarmed citizens.

Zine El Abidine Ben Ali, the dictator who has controlled Tunisia with an iron fist for 23 years, made a speech on Tuesday 28th December, in which he stated that, "these riots will damage the reputation of Tunisia with investors", and he pledged to strictly enforce the law against what he called a minority of "extremists" and "paid troublemakers".

He also said that, "the use of violence and riots in the streets by a minority of extremists and provocateurs against the interests of their country is an unacceptable means of expression. It gives a negative and uncivilized image that distorts the picture of our country and hinders the enthusiasm of investors and tourists, which prevent the creation of jobs, which we need to reduce unemployment; therefore, the law will be applied firmly".

This is the logic of a brazen dictatorship: protests against injustice are presented as actions against the interests of the country and "damaging the image of Tunisia amongst investors". The brutal repression, meanwhile, seems to be very much in the interest of the country and helps the image of Tunisia! Demonstrations in demand of jobs "are unacceptable, negative, and non-civilized". Looting the country's wealth for decades and depriving the people of all they need is quite acceptable and a proof of civilized existence.

Zine El Abidine Ben Ali did not fail to condemn those who "do not want the good of their country" – the "foreign television stations that broadcast lies without investigation, and that adopt an attitude of intimidation and hostility towards Tunisia". In reality he wants to continue to kill, arrest, and punish quietly without being disturbed.

Reports say that the dictatorial regime in Tunisia has used fascist methods to quell the demonstrations, using extreme violence against demonstrators in the streets and public places. Police conducted random arrests and have initiated a campaign of kidnapping under the cover of night with the help of police checkpoints. The regime also used groups of criminals organised into militias to attack citizens. Dozens of reactionary militias, backed by police, also violently attacked demonstrators with sticks and stones.

The crackdown has spared no-one. The leader of the Tunisian Communist Workers Party (PCOT), Ammar Amroussia, was arrested along with an unknown number of young people and party activists. In an amusing gesture from the authorities, they have announced a total ban on all forms of protest and demonstrations! As if these were legal forms of expression before. Again we see what level of repression this regime is willing to resort to in order to defend its rotten parasitic privileges.

This repression, however, is not a sign of strength; on the contrary it is proof of the weakness of the regime and of its total bankruptcy. The level of terror the regime tries to exercise shows that it is aware that it can be overthrown by this mass movement. Trying to retake the initiative and win new support, it has also recently conducted a manoeuvre by reshuffling its government.

The reasons behind the mobilization

Besides the direct and the immediate trigger of these movements we find more profound reasons. Tunisia, from the point of view of capitalist imperialism, has been considered a haven for private investment in tourism and the service sector. Tourism was the largest source of foreign money. The country hosts seven million tourists per year. The annual income of the tourism sector is estimated at about 5.2 billion dollars, employing approximately 350.000 people. Tunisia has also been touted as the most stable country in the region; an attractive destination for foreign investment from Europe and the Gulf countries thanks to the "opening" of its economy and its commitment to fully liberalise the Tunisian Dinar.

However, the country is now experiencing crisis, having been ruined by a terrible exploitation of the productive forces. The regime and the imperialists have always praised its economic model, as it gave the best results and relatively high growth rates. This was used by the regime to justify any acts of repression and persecution – but all of this has come to an end. The yearly growth figures of 5 per cent over the last decade fell to 3 per cent by the end of 2009.

Even this long period of growth had no positive effect on the living standards and working conditions of workers. The unemployment rate in 2004, according to official figures, was 13.9 per cent of the workforce. At the end of 2009 this rate peaked to at least 22 per cent. Offers of employment and vacancies are precarious and temporary; this is especially the case in the free trade zones. To keep the Tunisian industry competitive in textiles and mechanical and electronic industries, poverty wages have been imposed on workers, which do not meet the minimum living standards, since the minimum wage in Tunisia is 250 dinars (130 euros). Since 80 per cent of trade in Tunisia is with the European Union, which in turn is experiencing a deep recession, we can expect a greater decline in the next period.

On top of these economic factors that are fuelling the struggle of the masses, there is also the dictatorship, the stifling of all forms of freedom, and the brutal repression by the police.

The working class is mobilising

What is more crucial in this movement is the attitude of the working class and its ability to enter the fight under its own independent banner and organisation, to take the lead for all the oppressed layers of society. We are have seen the embryo of this developing in the recent struggles.

On Wednesday 22nd December, the trade unions officially entered the protest movement. In Bizerte, a meeting of workers and trade unionists was organised at the headquarters of the Regional Union to express the solidarity of the union of Bizerte and their members with protests in Sidi Bouzid. This was the first attempt made to mobilise union members from outside the region of Sidi Bouzid. This meeting had a large presence of students as well.

Later on Friday 24th December a large number of trade unionists and activists from civil society met in the headquarters of the regional union in Bizerte, again to express their support for the movement of popular protest in Sidi Bouzid. The protesters also staged a sit-in outside the headquarters of the regional labour union, during which they chanted slogans such as "the right to work is a duty; protest is a duty; lifting the state of siege is a duty"; "employment is a right"; "Employment! Freedom! Dignity!" and calling the Tunisian rulers a "group of thieves".

The regional branches of the labour unions in Mahdia, Kairouan, and Jendouba have expressed their support with the protest movement in the region of Sidi Bouzid. On top of that a large number of union officials issued a statement expressing their unconditional solidarity with the masses of Sidi Bouzid, their willingness to provide all forms of legal aid, demanding the immediate release of all detainees and the lifting of the siege imposed on the city, and asking the government to meet all the demands of the of the protesters for employment and development.

The union of secondary education also expressed its full support to the protesters in Sidi Bouzid and rejected the "option of force" to solve social problems. In addition it announced a regional strike in Sidi Bouzid on the 12th January for the release of all detainees.

These movements are a great step forward and are the best way to show class solidarity with the demonstrators. Unions must assume their responsibilities as organisations of struggle to unite workers against exploitation, oppression, dictatorship, and repression. In order to achieve this most effectively, unions must call for a nationwide general strike, demand an immediate end to repression, condemn those responsible for the repression of protesters, and call for political freedoms.

The limits of the movement

The movement of the Tunisian masses has demonstrated the depth of discontent accumulated under the surface. More importantly it has revealed the enormous magnitude of revolutionary energy amongst the masses of workers, unemployed youth, and the rest of the oppressed strata, and their overwhelming desire to change society.

Despite the use of live ammunition and tear gas against unarmed demonstrators, the Tunisian dictatorial capitalist regime could not stop the movement of the masses. On the contrary repression has only led to more demonstrations. The Tunisian people have shown the highest degree of bravery in their challenges against the barbarism of the state.

This movement indicates, from our point of view, the end of an era characterised by an apparent stagnation of the class struggle, and is an expression of the accumulation of many explosive factors. It is the beginning of another stage of mass movements that sooner or later will overthrow the regime of tyranny and exploitation in Tunisia once and for all.

But despite everything, it is a "spontaneous" movement, a movement that is not guided by a scientific program and clear prospects. But this is not the fault of the masses; the masses have done all they should do, they have demonstrated against repression and have made all sorts of sacrifices. What more can we ask for?

The masses know exactly what they do not want: they do not want oppression or exploitation, or unemployment, or famine, or poverty, or exploitation – and they have mobilized to reject it all! But they do not know exactly what they do want. They do not know what the alternative is. This is understandable. The question of the alternative is the task of Marxists and revolutionary workers.

If a revolutionary Marxist party existed in Tunisia, rooted in the working class and oppressed masses in general – a party with a transitional program and a clear scientific socialist internationalist perspective – the working class in Tunisia would be able to transform this wonderful movement in to a successful revolution that could throw the capitalist dictatorship regime in to the dustbin of history and build the system of socialism, justice and equality. But such a leadership is exactly what is missing today.

The alternative

We Marxists, members of the IMT, propose some ideas for discussion amongst left activists, the working class in general, and the young rebels in the streets of Tunisia, as part of our contribution to the developing of an alternative that can direct the movement towards revolutionary horizons.

We Marxists, call upon the left activists and workers to organise the mass movement by launching the initiative to set up democratically elected committees of struggle in working class neighbourhoods, factories, and universities, aiming at organising and giving leadership to the movement. These committees will be the embryo of peoples' and workers' councils. They should be coordinated at local, district, and at the city level, and should form regional and national coordination.

We call for the defence of workers' neighbourhoods, the headquarters of unions, and demonstrations against the attacks of reaction and repression by forming militias for self-defence, controlled by elected bodies and committees of struggle. The dictatorship has a system of repression and organizes fascist militias to attack the masses; we must form our own militia to defend ourselves!

We call for mobilisation in the labour unions, amongst workers in poor neighbourhoods, universities, and in the ranks of left-wing parties for a general strike against the dictatorship, oppression, and exploitation.

We call for an end to repression and for the prosecution of any perpetrators of violence against the masses. We demand the imposition of all forms of democratic freedoms: the right to strike, the right to demonstrate, and the right to take collective action.

We must organize the strike on a platform of popular demands, such as the immediate increase of the minimum wage to meet all the needs of daily life, and cultural and recreational activities for workers and their families.

We must demand the end to privatisation and for the nationalisation of all the vital economic sectors under workers' control, destroying the dictatorship of Ben Ali, and the construction of a democratic regime based on the democratic control of workers and poor masses through democratically elected councils.

We also need to win our brothers and sons in the apparatus of repression: the ordinary soldiers and policemen, who live under the same conditions as us, through a fraternal call to turn their arms against our common enemy – this system of exploitation and oppression. We must maintain a firm stance against all acts of repression and at the same time invite them to join the ranks of their fellow workers, peasants, and the poor.

We propose to issue an internationalist call to the North African working-class to show international solidarity with Tunisian workers in their struggle against the brutal repression to which they are exposed. We have already seen the first step in this direction in Jordan, Lebanon, and Europe, where different solidarity activities have been organized. We must bring back to life the traditions of militant solidarity that characterised the struggle against colonialism in the Maghreb region, especially since this region is going through important social and political struggles, such as the heroic struggles in Algeria against unemployment and for the right to housing, or the heroic struggles in Morocco and Western Sahara against unemployment and privatisation, and for the right to housing.

We call on young workers and Marxist militants to establish Marxist groups amongst the ranks of the revolutionary fighters in the streets. Tens of thousands of young people rebelled against the dictatorship of Ben Ali in Tunisia, but the Tunisian youth and workers need much more than heroism and determination. They need a mass revolutionary party to assist them. This party does not exist yet, but we must aim to form it out of the most advanced youth and workers who are today protesting in the streets of Tunisia.

The only real way to achieve democratic rights and freedoms, and to end exploitation and submission to imperialism, is to establish a socialist Tunisia as part of a socialist federation of the Middle East.

December 30, 2010

THE TUNISIAN UPRISING

In Defence of Marxism, Middle East Correspondent

Mohamed Bouazizi, a young Tunisian from the central rural city of Sidi Bouzid, attempted to end his life by setting himself on fire. He has been unemployed since he graduated from university five years ago. A few days later another unemployed youth tried to electrocute himself in protest against the poor prospects for Tunisian youth.

In the city of Sidi Bouzid, 25 per cent of male graduates have no job. This figure increases to 44 per cent for female graduates. Meanwhile five other youths have tried to kill themselves but were saved in time. Those acts of despair have provoked a chain reaction of riots and protests all over the country.

The clashes started in the inner cities of the country but have now flared up in the capital Tunis and other important cities. This spontaneous outburst of anger against unemployment is turning more political, with demonstrators demanding the end of the power wielded by the greedy and corrupt Trabelsi family over government, state institutions and the economy.

The Trabelsi family, starting with the dictator president Zine El Abidine Ben Ali and his wife Leila, dubbed as the 'regent of Carthage', has been holding Tunisia with an iron grip for the last 23 years. This is the first time since the 1984 bread riots that Tunisia has witnessed such a widespread, tireless and stubborn protest movement. For two weeks the whole nation was almost paralysed by this movement.

Gulf News, a Middle Eastern newspaper has understood the real meaning of these events when it wrote on 1st January 2011: "No one thought [Tunisia] susceptible to the kind of social and political unrest it has witnessed recently". Tunisia was until recently thought to be a model country in this troubled region. A haven of stability, this darling of the West combined economic growth (as a popular tourist destination and a very cheap subcontractor for European industries) with so-called enlightened dictatorship, a secular bulwark against Islamic fundamentalism.

Tunisia is probably the best friend of the European imperialist countries and its economy depends almost 80 per cent from revenues and investment from EU countries and companies. The new troubles in Tunisia are sending shivers down the spines of neighbouring dictatorships and of imperialism.

Tunisia was recently congratulated by the IMF and the World Bank because of the way it resisted to the effects of the world recession. If Tunisia can explode, imagine what can happen in other countries in the North of Africa or the Middle East. Al Jazeera, the popular Qatari television network, recently published an article about the "rebirth of Arab activism". But it was not referring to Islamic fundamentalism or a spate of terrorist attacks. It explains how "Mohamed Bouazizi, the young Tunisian who set himself on fire on December 17, is emerging as a symbol of the wider plight of the millions of young Arabs who are struggling to improve their living conditions."

"The roots of this Tunisian 'uprising' are to be found in a lethal combination of poverty, unemployment and political repression: three characteristics of most Arab societies". So Tunisian uprisings, mass movement, strikes and mass clashes with the state apparatus are on the agenda in all of the Arab countries. This is not really a prediction about the future. This is already happening now in Egypt, Algeria and Jordan!

The Arab regimes and their imperialist friends are following these events very closely. Neighbouring Libya has even decided to open its borders with Tunisia so that unemployed youth can look for a job in the country of Colonel Khadafi. Germany has pledged to invest in the poor central rural region of Sidi Bouzid.

Meanwhile, "democratic and human rights-loving Europe" keeps very silent on the brutal repression of the decaying Trabelsi dictatorship. Not a word of condemnation has even been whispered by any government of the European Union or the United States.

In an unsuccessful attempt to defuse the protests the government has already sacked two ministers, three governors and has made (again) plenty of promises of investment and employment schemes. The regime combines those measures with brutal repression, which has already claimed the lives of two demonstrators, injured hundreds of others and put many others behind bars.

But the fear of the Tunisian youth has disappeared. Significantly, in the recent days the protests have been joined by the workers' unions. Today the university students resume their courses all over Tunisia. This could be a crucial turning point for the movement.

January 3, 2011

THE PROTESTS CONTINUE

Editorial Board of Marxy.com Arab website of the IMT

The earthquake!

For the fourth week straight, Tunisia is continuing to witness a popular mass movement. The uprising began in the region of Sidi Bouzid in the centre of western Tunisia on December 17th, in solidarity with young Mohamed Bouazizi, who set himself on fire in protest against the confiscation of his fruit stand. Since then, the movement has spread like wildfire to the rest of the cities and regions of Tunisia, and raised multiple demands, first among them the right to work and liberty. These protests have included setting fire to a number of government buildings, as well as the headquarters of the governing party and police stations. The movement has acted as a pole of attraction for various groups in society dissatisfied with the existing system: the unemployed, political and human rights activists, trade unionists, students, professors and lawyers. This proves the seriousness of the movement and its enormous potential.

How similar this glorious mass intifada is to an earthquake! For it has remained under the surface, preparing its arrival slowly and silently over decades of apparent calm, and then it exploded. The epicentre was the town of Sidi Bouzid, but its aftershocks, which will open the door to the fall of all the crumbling castles of tyranny, spread rapidly to many other areas.

The repression was unable to stop the movement. On the contrary: the more intense the repression became, the more the popular anger flared up and fresh layers joined the movement as its struggle evolved. In the city of Ouled Haffouz (in the province of Sidi Bouzid), students from several campuses organized a demonstration which was joined by many unemployed youth, teachers and workers, and started from the headquarters of the local labour union to reach the headquarters of the government of the department. The protesters demanded the right to work, the equitable distribution of wealth, and general freedom. They also raised slogans in solidarity with the people of Sidi Bouzid and Thala. Reports indicate that demonstrators attacked an office of the forces of repression in the Saeeda area in the Regueb department in southern Tunisia (37 km from the town of Sidi Bouzid), and the authorities responded by firing live rounds, wounding at least five people.

As protests escalated on Friday, January 7th, the teachers joined the strike call following the earlier strike call issued by the lawyers. The website of the Tunisian Communist Workers' Party (www.albadil.org) published a report about the spreading of the protests to Jerissa, Kalaa Kashbat and Tajerouine in the Kef province. It also reported protesters in the city of Makthar (in the north-western province of Siliana, 160 km from Tunis, the capital) blocking the main streets of the city with tyres and rocks and continuing confrontations with the police. The demonstrators also set fire to the city hall and destroyed the adjacent building, a government registrar, as well as a number of other government offices.

The city of Bouruois (in the north-western province of Siliana) also saw protests break out on the initiative of the students of secondary and preparatory schools, during which there were clashes between the protesters and the forces of repression who attacked them. There were intense clashes on the night of Thursday the 6th of January, between the unemployed youth and the security forces that used tear gas grenades and rubber bullets. This drove the demonstrators to burn tires and set fire to the mayor's office, the building of the ruling party, a branch of the official "peasants' union", a part of the city hall, and one financial institution, as well as to deface the November 7th monument (which commemorates the day Ben Ali came to power). A crowd of unemployed youth continues to occupy the provincial headquarters, demanding their right to work. The same thing was experienced in the city of Kairouan, which is considered one of the most important Tunisian cities (about 160 km from Tunis), where protests broke out on the initiative of the students and teachers at the Aqaba institute in Kairouan.

Protests also spread to Sousse province (70 km south of the capital, and 300 km north of Sfax), where in the city of Enfidha the students from the secondary and preparatory schools came out to the street last Friday morning to support the people of Sidi Bouzid and the city of Thala, and trade union sources stated that major security reinforcements had arrived from Sousse to control the situation.

In the province of Jendouba (far north-west, 200 km north of Tunis), in the border city of Ghardimaou, a mass rally was organized with the participation of the students of the Youth institute and the Ghardimaou institute and the other preparatory schools. The procession witnessed the intervention of the police forces, and the students responded by pelting them with rocks. Trade union sources reported that the security forces used tear gas grenades against the protesters.

In the city of Bousalem, students from the Shareh Al-Bi'a institute came out in a demonstration after the strike that the teachers carried out on Friday morning, which brought out a significant section of Shareh Al-Bi'a. Students from the Bousalem secondary school, however, were banned from leaving their school, with the gates of the institute being locked.

In the province of Kasserine (in the centre of western Tunisia, at a distance of about 228 km from the capital) a student protest which began from the city's schools took over the streets and turned into clashes between the police (who used their batons and tear gas grenades) and the unemployed youth and students. Eyewitnesses said that in the city of Feriana a massive march was held on Friday morning which took over the streets of the city, punctuated by confrontations with the forces of repression, with the demonstrators burning the offices of the ruling party and the municipality.

The working class city of Sfax (275 km south of Tunis) also witnessed a mass march which began from the Ali Al-Nouri preparatory school and went to the Mustafa Al-Fourati secondary academy before ending at the Abul Hasan Alakhmi Biskra institute, despite the road blocks set up by the forces of repression.

In the city of Jebeniana (Sfax), for the fifth consecutive day, there have been clashes between students of the January 18 academy and the forces of repression that are surrounding the campus to prevent the students from coming out onto the street, but the latter have failed in attempts to storm the school and arrest student activists.

According to a statement of the Union of Communist Youth of Tunisia, on the 7th of January:

> Many colleges in the capital Tunis and other cities have witnessed, since the return to classes on Monday, January 3rd, a series of movements in solidarity with the social movement in Sidi Bouzid and elsewhere in the country, coming from the General Union of Tunisian Students through the general assemblies, slogans and red symbols graffitied on the walls, and protests in front of the centre of the 'campus security' which have led to clashes with the political police in more than one location, the most serious of which is the clash at the April 9 college in the capital and in the arts college in Sousse beginning on the 4th of January.

> The police faced down every outbreak of the movement with total brutality – using tear gas and batons and all manner of abuse from which no one was spared amongst the students, faculty and staff. As happened in the arts college in Sousse, where after the blind police repression, amongst the number of wounded we are told of Wael Nawar, Munther Aqiq, Iman Malih, Qais Al-Bazzouzi and Mourad Ben Jeddom who had to be taken to the emergency room, where they continued to be surrounded in the confines of the hospital, despite the presence of many civil society activists who were there to break the siege around them.

> On the other hand, the police arrested some freedom fighters, amongst them a union leader of the General Union of Tunisian Students (UGET), Wael Nawar whom police violence left with a broken leg and who was abducted from his house on the morning of January 6. He was held in custody in the police station where he was once again subjected to beatings and torture before being referred quickly to be tried without the knowledge of his family and lawyer on multiple charges. Some of the charges date back

to two old cases that have been following him for a while, now plastered with new charges against the backdrop of the latest developments.

It is worth remembering that these latest developments are not isolated, neither at the domestic nor regional level. From the point of view of the domestic situation, this intifada comes in the context of a mighty rise of conflict in the class struggle in Tunisia. The country has experienced a series of outbreaks of heroic struggles over the past three years, which faced violent repression, the most notable of which was an uprising in the mining area of Gafsa in 2008, which broke out spontaneously against the results of a skill test required to obtain a job in one of the big companies and developed to become a protest against corruption and the lack of job opportunities. These protests continued for many months through rallies, sit-ins and strikes, during which two were killed and an unspecified number were wounded as a result of barbaric repression, in addition to dozens of arrested who are facing unjust sentences after sham trials.

In August 2010 the situation exploded again in the south-east in protest against the closure of the "Ras El Jadir" commercial border crossing which is shared with Libya. There were violent clashes in Ben Guerdane during those protests which resulted in many injuries amongst the demonstrators and the repressive apparatus arrested more than 150 people.

At the regional level, specifically in the Maghreb region, these movements follow the overwhelming mass struggle of the working class and toiling masses in Morocco and Western Sahara and Algeria.

Tunisia and the Maghreb region as a whole have entered the stage of revolutionary storms. These movements in which the leading role is being played by the unemployed youth, the teachers and students, are an anticipation of the rising of the workers which Tunisia and the region in general will experience sooner or later. The movements of the youth are an accurate barometer of the extent of the pressures which are building up in the depths of society. The winds of change have begun to blow the leaves of the mighty tree: the unemployed youth, the students and the teachers, and it will inevitably shake the roots: the working class. The time has come where the old mole of the revolution which has been digging underground for decades shall pop his head up, and the whole world will leap to their feet and shout with joy: "well dug old mole!"

Forms of the struggle

The movement broke out, as we noted above, against the backdrop of the young Bouazizi setting himself on fire, and this incident was followed by the attempts of other youths to commit suicide themselves, in separate regions of Tunisia. This tragic incident is evidence of the extent of the frustration and discontent that is accumulating in the depths of the youth, because of the reality of terrible poverty, unemployment, exploitation, and of being gagged for decades by a blood sucking ruling layer. Just as it is also evidence of the barbarism of the capitalist system which imposes on young people miserable and unbearable conditions, pushing them to prefer death by drowning in the sea in a desperate attempt to escape to Europe, or suicide, or drowning in the swamp of crime and drug addiction.

And when they rise up for their political rights, the dictatorial regime does not hesitate from firing live rounds at the chests and backs of the protesters, and many victims have fallen so that the system of private property and capitalist exploitation is defended.

To the families of these youth, who committed suicide in despair and in protest, and to the Tunisian working class in general, we extend our deepest condolences on the deaths of these martyrs for freedom! We regret losing them in such a way. What a heavy loss that some of the best, most educated and qualified youth of the region, are pushed to resort to suicide!

We understand the motives that drove these youth to this method of protest, and we place full responsibility for this on the system of oppression, the dictatorship of the capitalist system. However, we do not think this is the correct method for protest and struggle. We oppose these forms of protest because we consider them not conducive to the goal of overthrowing the capitalist system and eliminating hunger and unemployment.

The struggle against unemployment, poverty and oppression requires of us, the workers and youth, to organize our ranks in revolutionary workers' parties. To organize our struggles through democratically elected workers' councils and popular councils. And to organize in the trade unions to fight a revolutionary class struggle through general strikes and armed uprising and other forms of popular revolutionary struggle in order to bring down the capitalist system which is responsible for all the suffering from exploitation, unemployment and oppression.

The position of imperialism

The imperialist powers considered the Tunisian dictatorial regime to be their star pupil, and this is why they never stopped praising it as "a model for the region and beyond" as David Walsh, Assistant U.S. Secretary of State for Near Eastern Affairs in the Bush administration, put it (*Al-Horria*). And it wasn't so long ago –*Tribune Mediatique*, September 24, 2010 – that the current American ambassador noted the excellent relations between Tunisia and the United States of America. And in the same vein, Newsweek issued a study which ranked Tunisia first place on the continent of Africa as a part of its list of the "100 best countries in the world"!

This is why the imperialists have never stopped giving support and everything required for the suppression of the Tunisian people and the perpetuation of its slavery to domestic and foreign capital. Even when the popular mass uprising broke out beginning from the area of Sidi Bouzid and it was met with fierce repression by the dictatorial regime, resulting so far in the killing of two martyrs and an unknown number of wounded and arrested, the imperialist powers preferred to cynically stand by for more than two weeks in the hope that the dictator would be able to crush his people. The French foreign ministry, in its regular press conference on Friday, used the phrase "we are watching the situation closely" when referring to developments in Algeria, whereas no comment was forthcoming on the situation in Tunisia. And when two bloggers and activists were arrested on Thursday, France refrained from asking publicly for their release[2].

But the intifada continued despite the repression, if it wasn't even further enflamed by that very repression. And so imperialism changed its stance in the same way that a snake changes its skin. And so American imperialism manoeuvred yet again: "The US State Department summoned the Tunisian ambassador in Washington and expressed *concern* about the handling of the protests by the Tunisian authorities... and the *restrictions on freedoms*"[3].

But the workers and youth of Tunis must be sceptical of these hypocritical pronouncements. Imperialism is the main ally of all the dictatorships in the region. It provides them with the weapons they kill us with, and it encourages them to remain perched on us. It is our enemy, not our friend, it is the primary enemy for the peoples of the whole world: in Iraq, Palestine, Venezuela and everywhere, and so we must not place any confidence in these lies, we must not be fooled by these reactionary manoeuvres. We must fight the attempts to sow illusions amongst our ranks, especially the illusion that we can rely on imperialist powers and their international institutions to stop the repression. An end to the repression can only come from our revolutionary struggle, the workers, the poor, and the youth, to bring down the regimes of oppression and exploitation, the agents of imperialism.

On the other hand it is our duty to orient towards the working class across the whole world, by issuing a call, for all those who share with us the reality of oppression and an interest in a better tomorrow, to stand with us and come out in solidarity with our struggle. Already signs are appearing and growing of a workers' solidarity movement supporting our struggle, and it will gradually gain strength. No reliance on imperialism – yes to internationalist workers' solidarity!

The task of revolutionary worker activists

In order that these heroic struggles and heavy sacrifices are not to be in vain, the militant activists, workers and revolutionaries need to organize themselves. The trade unionists and revolutionary working class activists need to put forward

2 *Now Lebanon*, January 7, 2011.
3 Al Jazeera, January 8, 2011.

within the movement a transitional program springing from the most burning demands of the masses and expanding their horizons continuously by connecting them to the goal of elimination the root of injustice and oppression: the dictatorship of capital.

Recently, comrade Hamma Hammami, the spokesman for the Tunisian Communist Workers' Party, in a speech that was published online, said the following about the movement, its demands and perspectives:

> The masses want freedom, they do not want the shuffling around of ministers, they want freedom, freedom of association, freedom to protest, freedom of assembly, freedom of expression; they want to put an end to injustice, they want respect and dignity... The unemployed want action against unemployment, they want unemployment compensation, they want free medical treatment, and they want free public transportation. People want concrete action against the high cost of living. They want to improve wages and income.

And this is correct! These demands and other democratic demands, "participation in the planning of the economy and the struggle against corruption, etc..." are what should be condensed, developed, and brought together in a program of struggle.

Of course we must raise the banner of a people's trial for all those responsible for the killings and repression against the revolutionary masses, and all those responsible for plundering the wealth of the country, beginning with the criminal Ben Ali and the Mafia gang that surrounds him.

We must propose a program of struggle for the right to a job for all (women and men), work which is decent, stable and appropriate to the skills and training of the worker. No more casual and limited contract labour, yes to permanent, stable and appropriate job contracts. Reduction of the working week to 35 hours without loss of pay. And faced with the layoffs and corporate restructuring, working hours should be divided amongst all the workers without loss of pay! The demand should be raised for unemployment pay which is equal to the minimum wage, until a job appropriate to their qualifications and skills is provided. With social security and free public transportation provided for unemployed workers.

We must put forward the demand of raising the minimum wage, at the national level and in all sectors, without exception, with the imposition of the sliding scale of wages whereby wages rise in proportion to any increase in prices. And the elimination of wage discrimination on the basis of sex or age: equal pay for equal work! And limit the wages of state officials so that any official – anyone – is paid no more than the average workers' wage.

We must raise the demand for the overthrow of the dictatorial capitalist system and its replacement with a system of workers' democracy, based on the nationalization of the most important companies, placing them under the control and management of the democratically elected workers' and popular councils. Expropriate the expropriators!

This is how the mass intifada can be given a clear way forward, and we can ensure that the sacrifices were not in vain. This is how the Tunisian working class can avenge its martyrs and build its own system, where all the unemployment, exploitation, oppression, hunger and other nightmares will be things of the past!

January 8th, 2011

TUNISIAN REVOLT GOES ON UNABATED: 'WE DO NOT FEAR YOU ANYMORE!'

In Defence of Marxism, Middle East correspondent

Fear has changed sides in Tunisia. For years the Tunisian population, its youth, its workers, its mothers were paralysed by fear of repression. Political lethargy was the rule, revolt the odd exception. Now things have turned upside down. Defiance of the brutal regime, its state, its spies, its media, its ruling party, its police and its army has become the rule during the three weeks of the uprising which has shaken Tunisia. This represents a seismic change in the consciousness of the youth and the general psyche of the masses, the poor as well as the middle class. This has had an impact not only in Tunisia but in the whole Arab world.

The movement has not been subdued by persecution, imprisonment, torture and killings. Nevertheless the regime continues to kill, maim and torture the best of its youth. This weekend alone, the orgy of repression reached a new climax as 20 protesters were killed by the forces of repression. The police fired live ammunition into the crowds in Thala, Kasserine and Regueb. "Legitimate self defence" is the explanation coming from the police headquarters. This is how the General-President responds to the advice of restraint coming from Washington. The young hearts beating for freedom and justice can only expect bullets and empty promises from this regime.

How can they imagine that they will be able to terrorise the youth into submission when that same youth is ready to immolate itself in protest against poverty?

The movement that started in the Central and Western rural areas of Tunisia has by now reached almost all corners of the country. Unemployment, poverty and a suffocating police state are pushing the masses into action. In the last weeks many others villages and cities witnessed one form or another of protest. In some cities the demonstrators attacked and destroyed government buildings, banks, police headquarters and the offices of the ruling party, the RCD. In others, trade union activists demonstrated in front of the headquarters of the union, the Union Général des Travailleurs de Tunisie (UGTT). In an about-turn, the domesticated leadership of the UGTT has been forced by the pressure from below to condemn the actions of the government. Demonstrations have been organised in the industrial suburbs of Tunis, in Ben Assour or in the workers bastion of Gafsa in the mining area. Local branches of the UGTT especially in the regions most affected by the revolt have been calling for strikes.

The UGTT leadership instead called for "a one minute silence" of hundreds activists in front of its headquarters in the capital, Tunis. School students and university students are also joining the uprising. Pitched battles between police and the students have taken place on campuses and in front of high schools. A lawyer's demonstration in Tunis was also brutally baton charged by the police. The police have also cracked down on cyber activists and a famous rapper who made a song criticising the President. The song is called "President, your people are dead"[4]. In response to this, an international group of hackers ("Anonymous") have attacked and brought down many government websites. "His majesty's" opposition parties, the Progressive Democratic Party and the Movement for Renewal (Ettajdid, the former Communist Party) also called for an "end to violence".

Cracks are appearing in the regime. Indeed, all this repression is not a sign of strength but a sign of weakness, even of panic on the part of the dictatorship. Now the government has said that it will "respond" to the aspirations expressed by the three weeks of unrest. "The message has been received by the government and all political channels" declared Samir al-Obaidy, the country's communications minister. More promises of reform and investment will be made. But very few people trust those promises. They represent nothing compared with the needs of the population and compared with the wealth robbed over the years by the ruling clan. For instance the 15 billion Dinar plan of development of the central region promised last week represents only one fifth of the value of the villa of one of the sons in law of the President!

This uprising is to a large extent the result of spontaneous combustion. There is no central democratic organisation of the uprising and no clear program. But a layer of activists is reaching new conclusions and is starting to increase the level of organisation and consciousness at local and regional level. Within the UGTT union the tensions are rising between the rank and file and the dictatorship-friendly leaders. The student union, UGET, which has a tremendous tradition of struggle but was also hijacked by elements of the regime, is going through turbulent times. Militant students are trying to reclaim the union. Whatever the immediate result of this movement, Tunisia will not be the same again. Clearly, the regime has started its decline. The speed of this process will depend on the action of the masses.

The Tunisian uprising is also spreading to neighbouring Algeria. Protests broke out last week in the suburbs and working class areas of Algiers. Youth and families reacted angrily to the latest price hikes of sugar and salad oil. But those price increases are just a trigger of the new chain reaction of social revolt in the

---

4   http://www.facebook.com/video/video.php?v=132175546843487

country. Deeper causes are spurring the wave of riots and clashes with the state. Algeria is an oil rich country. The obscene profits of the oligarchy are in stark contrast to the despairing situation of Algeria's youth. Seventy five per cent of Algerians below 30 years of age have no job. Then you have the terrible housing crisis which forces people to live in slums.

The Tunisian uprising and the revolts in Algeria are amplifying a new cycle of struggle in the Arab world started in Egypt a few years ago. This is class struggle, against capitalism, its local dictators and its imperialist puppet masters in Europe and the United States.

Monday, 10 January 2011

FROM THE UPRISING OF SIDI BOUZID TO THE REVOLUTION! – BEN ALI AND HIS CLIQUE MUST GO NOW!

In Defence of Marxism, Middle East correspondent

The marvellous uprising of the Tunisian people has taken on revolutionary proportions. The coldblooded murder of more than 20 demonstrators by the police over the weekend did not have the effect the dictatorship hoped it would have. The result was not fewer demonstrations but more, with even more people taking part who were more determined than ever not to be intimidated any longer. One thing is sure now: this tug of war with the dictatorship will be waged until the very end by the masses.

Regional strikes have paralysed many cities in the central and eastern parts of the country. Violent clashes with the police, just like the scenes from the Intifada in Gaza, have continued without interruption in the neighbourhoods of many cities. In the space of a few days the movement has grown to unprecedented levels in recent Tunisian history. The volleys of bullets fired by the police continue to kill, but do not to scare the masses anymore. In total more than 60 youth and workers have been murdered in the attempt to break the new spirit of struggle. This will all be in vain. More importantly, the workers have started to move through their union, the UGTT, whose docile leadership has been forced to enter into opposition to the regime. Local and regional branches of the UGTT have taken the initiative to call strikes. The mass rallies have been like virtual occupations of whole cities.

Some sections of the union, like the teachers, the health workers and postal workers had already played an important role in pushing the UGTT into action. The journalists' union and the lawyers' associations have also been at the forefront of the struggle. But now the wider layers of the workers' movement have moved into action. Demonstrations like the ones in the rebellious workers' city of Sfax[5] or in Kasserine, mark the active entry of the workers onto the scene. The images of those demonstrations reveal an attitude of open defiance towards the regime, a mood of confidence and a feeling that victory is within reach.

---

5 Video here http://24sur24.posterous.com/2nd-video-tens-of-thousands-marching-in-sfax

Already last Sunday, January 9, the UGTT local affiliate in Sfax issued a call for a regional general strike. With only a few exceptions (hospitals and many bakeries that stayed open to help the people in struggle), the strike saw a 100 per cent turnout. In Sfax 30,000 workers and youths demonstrated on the streets. In Jendouba on January 12, there were 12,000 people demonstrating in a city of 30,000 inhabitants.

The local branches of the UGTT have become the centre of gravity of the resistance against the dictatorship. Mass meetings are held there, and the offices are used to organise many activities. This is no accident. It can only be explained by the specific weight this union has in the collective political memory of the Tunisian workers. The union played a decisive role in the anti-colonial struggle against the French occupation. Now it has become, despite the role of its leaders, the cornerstone of the resistance built up in the last few weeks.

In the last days this movement reached the suburbs of the capital, prompting the regime to impose a curfew. Military vehicles and soldiers were posted at strategic points around Tunis. Even tourist destinations such as Hammamet could not escape the sweep of the movement. Under terrible pressure from its ranks, the UGTT leaders have called for a 2-hour general strike in the country for today, Friday 14th January.

Realising that repression alone could not stave off the movement, the President General, Ben Ali, made promises of reform and concessions on three occasions this week. Napoleon Bonaparte a long time ago understood that you can do a lot of things with bayonets except sit on them.

The divisions within the regime are now opening up more and more. The head of the Army is said to have been sacked by Ben Ali for his refusal to shoot on the demonstrators. Anecdotes often reveal the real situation in the army, like the one of the young army officer on the streets of Sidi Bouzid saluting the angry funeral march of one of the demonstrators that were killed.

The most important "concessions" were announced yesterday evening when Ben Ali declared he would lift the censorship on the media, introduce more freedoms, investigate the killings of protesters during demonstrations, ask the police not to shoot on demonstrators with live ammunition and that he would not seek re-election as president of Tunisia in ... 2014.

This is a typical example of "everything changes so that nothing changes". Yesterday evening's stage managed demonstrations of supposed jubilant Ben Ali supporters in the centre of the capital were aimed at confusing the Tunisian people and the international media. But an awakened people cannot be fooled easily. Too many promises have been made in the past and too many have been broken.

The movement has also evolved from a localised social protest into a nationwide political movement confronting the mighty force of the state. The concessions now are "too little too late". No-one trusts Ben Ali and his clique any longer, no-one, that is, among the masses. There are still a few who trust this hated man. The main so-called opposition parties, including the former communist party, on hearing the concessions being made, have reacted with cautious optimism and called on Ben Ali to form a coalition government. But from the masses Ben Ali is getting a completely different response, not the kind of reaction he expected to the concessions he announced yesterday evening.

The Tunisian street, educated by years of oppression, lies and treachery by the representatives of the regime has replied with its feet. This morning the masses poured onto the streets all over Tunisia. More importantly, in the capital, tens of thousands have gathered in front of the once feared building of the Ministry of Interior. A demonstration in front of the "Minister of Terror" would have been unimaginable even 24 hours ago. One slogan unites the demonstration: Ben Ali out! Not tomorrow, not in 2014, but now! Others say: "We prefer to live on dry bread and water than to continue to live with Ben Ali".

Scenes of fraternisation between the army and the demonstrators have been shown on French television and broadcast around the world. The police who were out on the streets this morning did not dare to intervene. Later on in the day fresh police forces were sent in who tried to disperse the demonstrators with tear gas and baton charges, but to no avail.

Other demonstrators decided to go the Presidential Palace in Carthage to stage a sit-in. Prominent figures within the regime are abandoning the boat, like rats jumping from a sinking ship. The regime is losing its grip on whole sections of its state apparatus. Some reports indicate that sections of the army have come out in defence of the demonstrators. Journalists of the Tunisian state television are reported to have revolted today, as they took over the TV studios and decided to start reporting the truth of what has been going on in the country.

These are all signs of the death agony of the regime. Nobody can doubt any longer that a revolution is going on in Tunisia. This is the moment of truth in Tunisia. Friday 14th of January 2011 will be remembered as an historic day. It will be remembered as the day when the whole of the Tunisian people rose up against its dictator. Again it has been proven that it is the masses that make history.

Yesterday a blogger summarised very well the feeling of many Tunisians:

> Ben Ali has proposed we should work 'hand in hand' to build an illusory future, but his hands are covered in blood! We cannot tolerate that he should go in complete impunity.

> Having sacrificed our compatriots for some reduction of the price of bread, for opening access to YouTube and the illusion of democracy in 2014 would be unforgivable while freedom is within our grasp, in the grasp of the people that is capable of bringing a regime to its knees.

> Yesterday I saw a stressed and terrorised president... a president trembling, stammering, sometimes shouting and out of control. His speech was a confession of weakness, a cry for help. The man of 'Bikolli hazm' ['with a strong hand'] is on his knees. Let's finish him off.

The regime is manoeuvring in order to save its very skin, making all kinds of last minute desperate concessions. Ben Ali has dismissed his entire government in an attempt to save his own position. The legal reformist parties of the "opposition" are preparing to lend him a hand. Most likely they will try to form a government of national unity with some of Ben Ali's ministers together with representatives of so-called "civil society" and legal opposition figures. Most probably, however, Ben Ali will have to go. Such a government would be very unstable and govern with the shadow of the awakened masses on its back. This is how they will try to rob the masses of their victory.

The masses should have no illusion in any of these politicians. The struggle must be waged until the very end. The masses have learned in the space of a mere four weeks that they can only count on their own strength. Instead of conceding power to a government of national unity, the UGTT and all the other rank and file groups of youth, peasants, neighbourhood activists, should set up democratically elected committees at local, regional and national level. These could then form the democratic and political backbone of a new government with the aim of the eradication of poverty, unemployment, corruption and abuse. Within the confines of capitalism and imperialist domination, however, these aims are impossible to attain. Real democracy means also that the wealth, the economy, is owned collectively and run democratically. This is what socialism means.

The Tunisian people, its youth and its workers, are writing history now, this very minute. They have become the symbol of the struggle against oppression and exploitation in the whole of the Arab world. They are showing to the whole world the real face of the Arab working class, a class that is prepared to struggle to the very end. In this struggle we do not see Islamic fundamentalism coming to the fore, but the working class and its organisations. The Tunisian workers are showing the way to their Algerian and Moroccan brothers and sisters and to the peoples of the whole of North Africa and the Middle East and beyond.

There is not a stable regime in the whole of the Arab world. The same conditions that have ignited the movement in Tunisia exist in Jordan, Syria, Saudi Arabia, Egypt, etc. The same conditions will lead to similar developments. What we are witnessing is the unfolding of the Arab revolution, which will eventually spread from one country to another. The conditions exist for an international struggle that can only lead to one conclusion: the need for an all-Arab Socialist Federation.

- Down with Ben Ali and his mafia clique!
- Down with the Tunisian and foreign oppressors and exploiters!
- Forward to a socialist Tunisia!
- Long live the Tunisian revolution!

Friday, 14 January 2011

THE DICTATOR HAS FALLEN. NOW IT IS TIME FOR THE REGIME TO FALL!

Editorial Board of *Marxy.com*

E vents have been moving at an incredible speed in Tunisia. Yesterday, the old dictator gave his last speech where he made a series of promises and a series of veiled threats. After this, reports rolled in affirming that the masses had no confidence in these promises and were continuing the protests even more fiercely. This morning Reuters received reports of shots being fired near the headquarters of the Interior Ministry. Tear gas grenades were also fired at demonstrators in the capital Tunis. Despite the dictator's statement yesterday that he was putting a stop to shooting at demonstrators, the killing did not stop throughout the night and this morning, causing the death of thirteen martyrs last night in Tunis and its suburbs, as confirmed by Al Jazeera from hospital reports.

But neither promises nor repression could suppress the popular revolution. The dictator decided to play his last cards when he announced the dismissal of the government and the calling of early elections (in six months). But the masses continued their struggle and this provoked a military coup when the army's forces spread everywhere and announced a state of emergency in all corners of Tunisia. They took control of the airport and closed Tunisian airspace after helping the dictator and some of his family to escape the revenge of the people.

This was when Mohamed Ghannouchi named himself President of Tunisia and announced that he would meet with representatives of political parties to form a new government. The trade union bureaucracy and the leaders of the reformist parties are even more terrified than their bourgeois masters so instead of adopting independent class tactics, with independent class slogans and an independent banner, here they were jumping onto the bourgeois train, singing with one voice the song of the "national unity government", i.e. the government of the bourgeoisie and its murderers.

Meanwhile, the forces of the secret police and the fascist militias continue to wreak havoc in the country as they attack the masses and loot the homes of the workers, in order to create a picture whereby the alternative to dictatorship is chaos. These desperate attempts have not frightened the masses but have only served to accelerate the formation of neighbourhood committees of defence. The secretary general of the General Union of Tunisian Students (UGET), Shaker Al-Awadi, told Al Jazeera that there are popular committees being formed in every neighbourhood. Did Marx not say that the revolution needs the whip of the counterrevolution to move forward?

From the moment of the overthrow of the dictator Ben Ali, imperialism abandoned him like a rabid dog and let him fall. The United States announced that "the Tunisian people have the right to choose their leaders"! Obama announced that he "praises the bravery and the dignity of the Tunisian people", and France refused entry to his plane! The forces of the Tunisian police arrested some of the members of the Trabelsi family before they could leave from Tunis airport!

There is no doubt that the speed at which events are unfolding will make the heads of some dizzy and this is natural because during revolutionary periods, events which normally wouldn't happen for decades and decades are concentrated into very short periods of time. Hence, the bourgeois analysts have all proven that they are unable to foresee anything, whether in politics or economics, as it wasn't too long ago that they were claiming that Tunisia was the calmest and most stable country in North Africa.

In comparison, the Marxists were able to foresee these events much in advance, and understand and identify the perspectives for their development. We predicted in our article "The Tunisian Spring" that:

> This movement signals, from our point of view, the end of an era characterised by an apparent stagnation of the class struggle and is an expression of the accumulation of many explosive factors. It is the beginning of another stage of mass movements that sooner or later will overthrow the regime of tyranny and exploitation in Tunisia once and for all.

And this is not, of course, because we have a crystal ball. It is because we have a scientific world view, whose validity in interpreting developments and its ability to present an alternative to change them has been proven by more than 150 years of experience.

The reformists, as usual, at the service of the regime

The moment the old dictator Ben Ali fell, the reformists, prostituting themselves as could be expected, immediately got into bed with the new regime, in the same way they used to lie with the old one. They rushed to offer their services to the ruling class to help it save its system in return for some crumbs from the cake of the regime and some privileges. Of these reformist parties, the Movement of Social Democrats is perhaps the most willing of all to prostitute itself.

Not so long ago, this party was greeting "the celebration of the Tunisian people with honour and pride of the twenty-third anniversary of the transformation of the 7th of November which was led by the president, [Zine El Abidine Ben Ali]"! And on their website they declared that on this "national occasion the 'Electronic Future' published special files highlighting the importance of the great steps taken by our country thanks to the strategic decisions of the leadership at all levels of development which have made Tunisia surge amongst the developing economies and which have opened up big prospects for the future, filled with optimism under the shadow of the wise leadership of the president [Zine El Abidine Ben Ali]"![6]

It was not so long ago that they were urging "the parents of the youth to call for calm and dialogue". And this is what they had to say about President Ben Ali's speech, in which he described the protests as criminal and described the masses as terrorists and explicitly called for them to be killed:

> This situation has provoked feelings of sensitivity, sympathy, responsibility, at the very tops of the pyramid of the regime, which is consumed with the issues of the country's citizens and youth of this country, and with the questions of employment and the pressing societal issues, and which has all the facts and is keeping a watchful eye.

And they added that: "The president of the country spoke the language of honesty, realism and truth and his speech formed a break in the middle of these events which pulls the carpet out from under those people who rush to hooliganism and chaos and tears from them their veil of cheap 'solidarity' and reveals their real hidden intentions, to throw the country into a crisis created by them... but this crazy scenario will not pass... because the country has established laws which protect it within the confines of its democratic pluralistic path, and its social development policies, which the president is keen to give a fresh push forward to, are a priority."

And they urgently called on the masses to: "... understand President Ben Ali's developmental approach on the other hand, which is to ensure that the country does not become reliant on others, and does not sink into mounting debt..."

They then make an about-turn in a statement of the Emergency National Council which met on Friday 13 January, when they declare: "With all respect towards the spirit of the innocent victims... a decision to pursue all those involved in corruption, bribery and theft of the national funds".

And they demanded the formation: "...of a national unity coalition government which would work to create the necessary climate to meet international standards for carrying out early elections before the end of this coming year."

And if we're quoting these long passages, it is to keep a historical record of the positions of these criminals who are now trying to rob the revolution of its fruits, to turn it into a means to win positions and privileges for themselves within the regime.

We find the same thing with *Ettajdid* ("Movement for Renewal") which was not known for any serious opposition to the dictatorial regime. But the moment they saw the dictator flee from the country they released a statement on Friday, January 14th, demanding their rightful role in the regime and a share of the

---

6   http://www.mds.org.tn

crumbs from the cake. Despite the fact that the Prime Minister, Mohamed Ghannouchi, is one of the old cabal, and despite the mass popular protests demanding his removal, *Ettajdid* gives him legitimacy and demands from him: "...consultations with the factions of the serious opposition and the General Union of Tunisian Workers and the components of independent civil society in order to arrive at a consensus for the formation of an executive body that includes all factions to manage the process for political reform and democratic transition."

And in earlier times the "Progressive Democratic Party" opened what it called "a window for the beginning of a political solution" through "a collection of thoughts which create a roadmap out of the crisis" which called for a government of national emergency which can implement a plan to find 300,000 jobs for the unemployed by working with the different layers of society, particularly the youth.

"The secretary general of the Progressive Democratic Party, Maya Jribi, said in a statement that Tunisia needs more than ever before comprehensive reform and the formation of a government of national unity, noting that the new government will fight against corruption and guarantee the independence of the judiciary and prepare the road for holding early legislative elections, overseen by an independent electoral body. And she also called for constitutional amendments to guarantee the peaceful transition of power and the restoration of order to avoid anarchy."

Workers, these are your enemies, because all of them want their share of the booty! Workers, these are your enemies, because all of them want to extinguish the revolution and retreat behind closed doors to divide up the power and privileges!

The bankruptcy of reformism is clear, not only because they have become so used to bowing that they have forgotten how to do otherwise – for when there was a dictator they put themselves at his service and they were always in the service of the capitalist system – but also because they spent decades preaching social peace and negotiations and speaking out against the revolutionary struggle of the masses. And because they achieved nothing serious at all: for they achieved neither democracy nor bread. They achieved nothing whereas one month of the revolutionary mass movement was enough for the downfall of the dictator and the achievement of gains not just in Tunisia, but outside its borders as well!

And now after the dictator has fled, here they are falling over each other in a scramble for the gains so they can take them for themselves and give a new opportunity to the existing system and its executioners.

Working class of Tunisia, revolutionaries, we must not allow our enemies to steal our revolution from us! We must not allow them to cash it into their bank accounts! We have given tens of martyrs and all the other victims; we must continue the revolution until the destruction of the system of exploitation and murder, so that the nation and its wealth can belong to all!

No trust in the agents of the old order! No trust in its state or its courts or its laws! It was and remains an apparatus for repressing us and killing us and taking our freedom; it can never be in our service. We must establish our own state, our own courts, our own laws! From amongst the advanced revolutionary elements who distinguished themselves during the course of the revolution we must elect our own representatives to democratic workers' and people's councils in the poor neighbourhoods, the factories, the unions, the colleges and the villages.

The role of the army

As we predicted in a previous article, the army organized a coup to save the regime from being overthrown. And the country is now under the absolute control of the jack boot. This was the objective consequence of the lack of consciousness and organization amongst the ranks of the working class. The army is a critical element in the fate of every revolution and it has a critical role in the current revolution as well, which makes the discussion of its position now of utmost importance to develop the perspectives of the revolution and the position that we as workers must take.

When the ex-dictator ordered the army to intervene to crush the people, the leadership of the army refused and this is what pushed him to dismiss the army Chief of Staff General Rashid Ammar. There were also confirmed reports of the army fraternizing with the protesters and even protecting them from the assaults of the police forces. And this is what enabled this institution to gain an important authority amongst the ranks of the demonstrators.

But we must never forget that the institution of the army is not above the classes. We must not forget that it was always a tool in the hands of the ruling class for the repression of the protests of the workers and poor. Ben Ali himself is a legitimate son of this repressive institution. And the highest leadership in this institution belongs to the ruling class.

Therefore, no trust at all in the army as it is now, with the same old hierarchy and with the same old leadership and structures! No trust except in our own power! We must not allow the military clique to abort our revolution and replace one general with another general (clear or veiled).

But on the other hand, we have within this institution our brothers and our sons, the regular soldiers who come from our ranks and share with us the reality of persecution and poverty. And to them we must turn with fraternal appeals which ask that they too elect their officers and purge the army of all the fascists and enemies of the people, so that they can join the ranks of the revolution and aid in the formation of militias of the armed people, overseen and controlled by the trade unions and the popular councils.

We need now to complete the revolution, to the very end! For half a revolution is a complete mistake! We must not accept anything less than the expropriation of the property of the expropriators and at their head are the families of

Ben Ali and Trabelsi and the gang around them. We must not accept anything less than the expropriation of the property of imperialism which propped up the dictatorship and cooperated with it in keeping down the revolutions of the nation and this property must be placed under the control of the working people.

Friday, 14 January 2011

THE INSURRECTION IN TUNISIA AND THE FUTURE OF THE ARAB REVOLUTION
Alan Woods

The marvellous revolutionary movement of the Tunisian workers and youth is an inspiration and an example to the whole world. For more than one week Tunisia has been living through a revolution of epic dimensions. The mass uprising in Tunisia has ended in the overthrow of the hated dictator Zine El Abidine Ben Ali after 23 years in power.

The uprising took almost everyone by surprise, including the government. On January 6, *The Economist* said confidently: "Tunisia's troubles are unlikely to unseat the 74-year-old president or even to jolt his model of autocracy". The North African nation had been seen as a haven of stability and relative prosperity, albeit one ruled with an iron fist. For foreign investors, Tunisia has been a safe place to invest and a source of cheap labour. For the tourists, it was a place to lie in the sun and enjoy life.

But what looked like a thunderbolt from a clear blue sky had in reality been prepared for decades. It reflected in part the worsening of the economic situation, which has its most severe impact on people from the lower social strata. But it also reflected something else, less visible but more important. Revolution cannot be explained by poverty alone, since the masses have always suffered poverty. It is a dialectical process in which a thousand small injustices add up until the accumulation reaches a critical point at which an explosion is inevitable. When society reaches this point, any accident can provoke the explosion.

In this case it was the self-immolation of a fruit vendor in the town of Sidi Bouzid that was the spark that caused a general conflagration. Mohamed Bouazizi, the young man who set himself on fire was, in reality, a university graduate who, like so many others, was unable to find suitable work. He tried to scrape a living selling fruit and vegetables, but even that proved impossible when the police stopped him from selling without a permit. In desperation he decided to end his life in a dramatic gesture. He died a few weeks later. This incident provoked a massive wave of demonstrations and rioting.

The rise in the prices of food and other basic goods, rampant unemployment and the lack of freedom caused the riots to spread and become nation-wide. In addition to the poor people who started the agitation, thousands of students and workers came onto the streets to demonstrate their hatred of the regime. A new element in the equation is the emergence of a large layer of educated youth who have no job prospects. In a period when millions have access to television and the internet, when people are aware of the luxurious lifestyle of the rich, the lack of escape from grinding poverty and unemployment becomes increasingly unbearable.

Ben Ali and the Trabelsi clan were synonymous with corruption, huge inequality and political repression. Their corruption was so bad that it provoked the indignation of the US ambassador, as we know from the WikiLeaks revelations. Starting as a protest against intolerable living conditions, unemployment and the high cost of living, the mass movement rapidly acquired a political character. It can be summed up in a single slogan: Ben Ali must go!

Once the fire was lit there was no way of extinguishing it. A wave of unrest has swept the country, with continuous mass demonstrations against unemployment, food price rises and corruption. Large numbers of unemployed graduates, frustration with lack of freedoms, the excesses of the ruling class and anger at police brutality seem to have come together to spark an unstoppable wave of public anger.

From repression to concession

The clashes became much more deadly on the weekend of 8-9th January, and then spread to the capital Tunis. Shaken by the revolt on the streets, the regime attempted to save itself by a combination of repression and concessions. As always, the first recourse was the use of bullets, tear gas and batons. The ferocity of the police repression shocked even hardened western journalists. It is impossible to say how many lost their lives in these bloody clashes, but according to human rights organizations at least 60 people were killed.

But after a week it became evident that these methods were not working. On the contrary, they only served to pour more petrol on the flames. Once an entire people stands up and says "no", no state, army or police force in the world can stop them.

Once the masses begin to lose their fear, a dictatorial regime cannot save itself by repression alone.

At first, the President denied that the police over-reacted, saying they were protecting public property against a small number of "terrorists". This did nothing to pacify the protesters. All universities and schools were closed in a bid to keep young people at home and off the streets. This also failed. Little by little, as his regime crumbled before his eyes, reality began to penetrate even the thick skull of the president.

On 12 January, he sacked his interior minister and ordered the release of all those detained during the riots. He also created a special committee to "investigate corruption". This is like Satan investigating Beelzebub. He also promised to tackle the root cause of the problem by creating an extra 300,000 jobs. But the unrest continued and reached the centre of the capital on 13 January, despite a night-time curfew.

Ben Ali then promised to tackling rising food prices, allow freedom of the press and the internet, and to "deepen democracy and to revitalise pluralism". He also said he would not amend the constitution to enable him to stand for office again in 2014. In a last desperate move to save himself, Ben Ali appeared on television promising that the police would no longer be allowed to fire on demonstrators and announcing a series of reforms and concessions. It is easy to concede that which is no longer within one's power to preserve.

The President only ordered a halt to the shooting when it was clear that any further massacres by the police would provoke a mutiny in the army even at the top level. A French-language website reports the existence of growing unrest in the armed forces and an open split between the police and the army: "One of the new and important developments early this week was the distancing of part of the army from the regime. On Monday, a dozen soldiers stood guard in the courthouse of Kasserine, both to prevent possible unrest inside and to protect the lawyers, as reported by several witnesses."

There were many reports of fraternisation between the Army and the people and in some cases of the Army protecting the demonstrations against the police forces. This was the reason why the army was withdrawn from the streets of the capital and replaced by the police. When the mass demonstration reached the presidential palace the people and the soldiers embraced.

The protests came to a head on Friday as thousands of people gathered outside the Interior Ministry, a symbol of the regime. Many climbed onto its roof. Police responded with volleys of tear-gas grenades, but to no avail. The masses on the streets had acquired a sense of their power, and correctly interpreted the President's speech as a sign of weakness. Everywhere the slogan was raised: Ben Ali must go! Ben Ali had already promised to step down – in 2014. But this calculation proved to be somewhat optimistic. The people on the streets demanded – and got – his immediate resignation.

With indecent haste, the former president dissolved his government and the country's parliament, packed his bags and headed for the nearest airport. Mr Ben Ali and his family left Tunisia and are looking for a place of asylum. But this is easier said than done. It is a sad fact of life that when a man is successful and prosperous he has plenty of friends, but a failure finds all doors locked against him.

President Nicolas Sarkozy politely but firmly rejected a request for his old friend to land his plane in France. The latest reports say he ended up in Jeddah, in Saudi Arabia, where he will get a more sympathetic welcome from the members of the House of Saud, who must be beginning to worry that they may expect a similar fate sometime in the not too distant future.

The hasty departure of the President has prepared the ground for a manoeuvre at the top, with Washington's anxious hand pulling the strings from behind the scenes. As a first step, in a televised address on Friday afternoon, Prime

Minister Mohammed Ghannouchi announced that he would be taking over as interim president and a state of emergency has been declared.

Soldiers have already begun taking down the ubiquitous portraits of Mr Ben Ali from billboards and on the walls of public buildings around the country. The leaders hope that by removing the outward signs of authoritarian rule, the masses will be satisfied and go home. This would allow the same people that ruled before to retain all the levers of power, while allowing the people the illusion that something has changed.

To expect these people to introduce meaningful political reforms and free and fair elections would be the height of stupidity. Mohammed Ghannouchi is a leading member of the old regime. He is "Ben Ali's man". He was the architect of the very same economic policies which contributed to the present mess. He has been at the heart of the old regime from the beginning. He cannot be trusted to act in the interests of the people. While delivering fine speeches about democracy and constitutionalism, he bases himself on a state of emergency, enforced by the army and the security forces.

This is a stalling tactic by the army and the regime elite to suppress the protests and then restore their grip on power. The reality behind the "democratic" faÁade is the maintenance of the state of emergency decree which bans gatherings of more than three people and imposes a night-time curfew. Security forces have been authorised to open fire on anyone who defies these orders.

Hypocrisy of the imperialists

All this has set the alarm bells ringing in Washington, Paris and London. The imperialists have been shocked by events that they did not anticipate and are powerless to control. Revolutions are no respecters of frontiers and least of all the artificial frontiers established by imperialism in the past that divide the living body of the Maghreb.

North Africa and the Middle East are fundamental to the economic and strategic interests of the USA and the EU, especially France. A BBC Arab affairs analyst, Magdi Abdelhadi, was quoted as saying: "Mr Ben Ali's demise may rattle the entire post-colonial order in North Africa and the wider Arab world." This is very true, and it goes to the heart of the matter.

Now that the masses have overthrown the old tyrant by a heroic uprising, the western governments are falling over themselves in their haste to call for democracy. President Sarkozy said he stood side-by-side with the citizens of Tunisia, his country's former protectorate. Nicolas Sarkozy has raised cynicism to an art form. If there were a Nobel Prize for hypocrisy, he would undoubtedly win it.

On April 28, 2008, he declared during one of his trips to Tunisia: "Your country is engaged in the promotion of universal human rights and fundamental freedoms..." A few months later, the IMF Managing Director Dominique Strauss-

Kahn, said in Tunis that the Ben Ali regime was "the best model for many emerging countries".

These men cannot plead ignorance. For decades human rights organisations have denounced innumerable violations in Tunisia, but this did not prevent the French President from being the first Head of State (and one of the few) to congratulate Ben Ali after his rigged "re-election" in 2009. Now the same man can say without even blushing: "Only dialogue can bring a democratic and lasting solution to the current crisis".

These foxy words are intended as a trap for the unwary. The revolutionary masses are advised to stop fighting and instead enter a friendly dialogue – with whom? A dialogue with the same people who have robbed and oppressed them for decades, the same hangmen whose hands are stained red with the blood of the people? Who is the man who offers this friendly advice? He is the man who supported the hangmen right up to the very moment when Ben Ali was overthrown by the masses. Throughout the uprising of the people of Tunisia, Sarkozy was silent but his government was trying to save the dictatorship.

The army fired live ammunition at unarmed people but the spokesman of the French government, FranÁois Baroin, said that condemning the crackdown would "demonstrate interference". As if the permanent presence of the French army in many African countries that have nothing remotely to do with political democracies was not interference of the first order!

The Minister of Agriculture, Bruno Lemaire was quite open in his defence of the Tunisian dictator. Ben Ali "is someone who is often misjudged" but "did a lot of things", he said. We will not know what "things" he was referring to, whether they were good or bad. What we do know is that the French Foreign Minister, Alliot-Marie, went even further than her colleague, offering Ben Ali the "know-how of our security forces". Thus the "democrats" in Paris offered the dictatorship means to help suppress its own people in a country France had colonized for 73 years. Old ways die hard.

Three days after the shooting of unarmed crowds FranÁois Fillon said he was "worried" about the "disproportionate use of violence", thus placing victims and executioners on the same level. Following the usual trickery, he called on *all parties* to exercise restraint and to choose the path of dialogue. But nobody has ever explained how it is possible to "choose the path of dialogue" with police who shoot at anything that moves.

Now that the game is up, all these "democrats" are anxious to advise the Tunisian people. And not just in Paris. Barack Obama has graciously condemned violence against Tunisian citizens "peacefully voicing their opinion in Tunisia". But this same man, as we know from the WikiLeaks revelations, was in full possession of all the facts concerning the corrupt and repressive regime in Tunis *and did absolutely nothing about it.*

Now this same man says: "I applaud the courage and dignity of the Tunisian people." But he hastened to add: "I urge all parties to maintain calm and avoid violence, and call on the Tunisian government to respect human rights, and to hold free and fair elections in the near future that reflect the true will and aspirations of the Tunisian people."

The same song is being sung on all sides. It is a soothing lullaby and like all lullabies it is designed to send the masses back to sleep. They are asked to be calm, and to "avoid violence". All that is required of the masses is that they go home quietly, "stay calm" and above all "avoid violence". Is it not strange that it is always the masses who are asked to be calm, stay quiet and "avoid violence" when it is the rich and powerful who have a monopoly on violence, and use this monopoly to defend their power and privileges?

People have had to brave the bullets and truncheons of the police. They have seen their comrades, friends and relatives, brutally beaten, kicked, tear-gassed, arrested, tortured and murdered in cold blood. They were even refused access to the mangled corpses of their loved ones. Now they are advised to keep quiet, "avoid violence" and above all get off the streets, demobilize and go home in order to allow a gang of thieves to determine their fate. This is a joke in very bad taste.

The revolt spreads

The eruption of popular discontent in Tunisia and neighbouring Algeria is a nightmare for authoritarian leaders across North Africa and the wider Arab world. The corrupt and reactionary regimes in North Africa and the Middle East are shaking in their shoes. They fear that the example set by the masses in Tunisia will be followed tomorrow by the workers and peasants of other countries where the same problems exist. That is why within a few days the revolt had expanded to the neighbouring country of Algeria over price hikes in sugar, milk and flour, which resulted in the death of at least five people.

Al Jazeera reported that youths were heard chanting 'bring us sugar' and demonstrators broke into warehouses to steal sacks of flour in protest against food prices, which had risen between 20 and 30 per cent in the first week of January. In a bid to calm the protesters, the Algerian government imposed urgent cuts on import duties and taxes to help bring down food costs and states that it has now "turned the page" on the nationwide food riots.

Riots in several Algerian towns subsided only after the government promised to do whatever was necessary to protect citizens from the rising cost of living. Libya, Morocco and Jordan have also announced plans to ease prices of basic goods. But the situation in Algeria remains very unstable. Let us remember that during the whole year of 2001 the southern Berber region of Algeria (Kabilia) was the scene of a widespread insurrection. In Morocco too, the reactionary regime of King Mohammed VI is very unstable and has many similarities to the situation in Tunisia.

Just before Ben Ali was overthrown, columnist Abdelrahman al-Rashed wrote in the *Ash-Sharq al-Awsat* newspaper: "Much of what prevents protest and civil disobedience is simply the psychological barrier." The overthrow of Ben Ali, as well as efforts in Algeria to appease anger over price increases, will have had the effect of puncturing the fear that has long kept discontent in check across the region. Satellite news and social media can sidestep such autocratic tactics and can quickly fuse the frustrations of young people in isolated, deprived regions into a broad movement.

The flame of revolt is spreading to other Arab countries. The revolutionary movement in Tunisia has been closely followed on regional satellite television channels and the Internet across the Middle East where high unemployment, bulging young populations, rocketing inflation and a widening gap between rich and poor are adding fuel to the fire.

Algeria is just next door to Tunisia, but the Jordanian capital Amman is 1,500 miles (2,500km) from Tunis. Nevertheless, the reason for the protesters' anger was the same, and so too were the calls for the leader to resign. Feeling the ground quake under his feet, King Abdullah II ordered a reduction in prices and taxes on some foods and fuels. The government has already allocated £141m in the 2011 budget to subsidise bread, on which many poor in the country of 7 million people depend. The money will also be used to reduce the price of fuel as well as creating jobs, but it was a case of too little and too late.

According to a report by Al Jazeera, demonstrators were seen holding banners reading 'Jordan is not only for the rich. Bread is a red line. Beware of our starvation and fury'. More than 5,000 people staged protests across Jordan in "a day of rage" to protest against escalating food prices and unemployment on the same day as, in another part of the Arab world, Tunisia's president fled the north African state after weeks of violent demonstrations.

Jordanian University students and Ba'athist party supporters also held rallies in Irbid, Karak, Salt and Maan, demanding that the Prime Minister, Samir Rifai, step down. Official reports claim that police successfully contained the demonstrators by forming circles around them and no arrests were made. After seeing what happened in Tunisia, the Jordanian authorities realised that bloody clashes could turn the protests into an insurrection.

Jordanian blog *Ammon News* reported that at the protest, called "the day of rage", people chanted: "United class, united government has sucked your blood," and waved posters with bread attached. "We are protesting against the policies of the government, high prices and repeated taxation that made the Jordanian people revolt," Tawfiq al-Batoush, a former head of Karak municipality, told Reuters.

A report by Tom Pfeiffer, Reuters, Saturday, January 15, 2011 contained very interesting quotes: "This could happen anywhere," said Imane, a restaurant owner in Egypt who did not want to give her full name. "The satellite and Internet images we can see nowadays mean people who would normally be subdued can now see others getting what they want."

"We are not used to something like this in this part of the world," said Kamal Mohsen, a 23-year-old Lebanese student. "It is bigger than a dream in a region where people keep saying 'what can we do?'

"Young people across the Arab world should go to the streets and do the same. It is time that we claimed our rights," said Mohsen, the Lebanese student. "Arab leaders should be very scared because they do not have anything to offer their people but fear and when Tunisians win, the fear will be broken and what happens will be contagious. It is only a matter of time," he added.

Of all the Arab countries, the most important is Egypt, with its powerful working class. The concerns about its future were expressed in a recent article in the *Daily Star*, a Lebanese daily:

> Anyone expecting a region-wide revolution would do well to look at Egypt, which imports around half of the food eaten by its 79 million strong population and is struggling with inflation of more than 10 per cent.

> With a massive security apparatus quick to suppress large street protests and the main opposition Muslim Brotherhood excluded from formal politics, the state's biggest challenge comes from factory strikes in the Nile Delta industrial belt.

> Egypt's Internet based campaign for political change, the country's most critical voice, has failed to filter down from the chattering middle classes to the poor on the street.

> 'There has been such a division between economic struggles and political struggles in Egypt,' said Laleh Khalili, a Middle East expert at the University of London. 'Strikes have been going on, but not spilling into the public domain.'

> This could however change if rising discontent over food price inflation feeds into the wider malaise about political and economic stagnation and the lack of opportunities and freedom.

The International Monetary Fund said that with current unemployment rates already very high, the region needs to create close to 100 million new jobs by 2020. But in a situation where budgets are being strained by the soaring cost of imported food and fuel, this will be impossible, especially in those countries lacking big energy reserves.

"There is a danger in ... getting a bit too comfortable with the 'Arab state will muddle through' argument," said Stephen Cook of the U.S. Council on Foreign Relations in a blog this week. "It may not be the last days of ... [Egypt's President

Hosni] Mubarak or any other Middle Eastern strongman. But there is clearly something going on in the region."

The need for a revolutionary perspective

Bourgeois political experts console themselves with the idea that the Tunisia's example will not spread and unseat autocratic governments from Rabat to Riyadh because opposition movements are weak and demoralized. But that misses the point entirely.

The uprising in Tunisia was not organized by the opposition, which is also weak and demoralized. It was a spontaneous uprising of the masses, and was unstoppable precisely because there was no "responsible" reformist organization to lead it into safe channels. The weakness or absence of reformist mass organizations is not a reflection of the strength of autocratic regimes, but of weakness. Once the masses begin to move, it will be like a car going downhill with no brakes.

As we pointed out in relation to Iran, the spontaneous character of the movement is at the same time its strength and its weakness. In Tunisia the masses were strong enough to overthrow a corrupt and rotten regime. But the question is: what happens now?

"Our big problem is the lack of a political perspective," said Nizar Amami, one of the leaders of the PTT postal workers branch of the UGTT, speaking to Mediapart on noon on Monday in Tunis. "No party has emerged; the Democratic Progressive Party (PDP, the legal opposition party) is too weak. The UGTT has taken the place of the opposition to launch slogans, solidarity actions and so on, but as for the [political] project... Still, the regime has been really destabilized, and that is something really unprecedented."

Emma Murphy is a professor at the School of Government and International Affairs at Durham University and an expert on Tunisian affairs. She was asked by the BBC: "Can they [the legal opposition] deliver anything more for the Tunisian people?"

She answered as follows: "Probably not. But if democracy is going to come, the leadership council needs to make very early indications that there will be substantial reforms to the political party system, the election processes, freedom of association, civil rights and the freedom of the media well in advance of the elections.

"An early end to the state of emergency and some clear indication that the committee into corruption announced a few days ago will directly address the activities of the Ben Ali and Trabelsi clans would go a long way towards convincing Tunisians that, this time, the promises of constitutional rule will be fulfilled, that this time national reconciliation will really mean just that, and that the army, in defending stability, will not once more succumb to the defence of authoritarian rule."

We can confidently predict that in the next weeks and months an army of "friends of democracy" will descend on Tunis: representatives of "free" trade unions with suitcases full of dollars, men in suits from the USA and the EU, NGOs by the dozen, the "Socialist" International, the Friedrich Ebert Foundation, and other "respectable" fronts for the CIA, all anxious to provide advice and (for those willing to follow it) considerable material resources. The aim of these people can be summed up in one word: *the restoration of order*.

Order can be restored by different means. Counter-revolution can be carried out in a democratic as well as a dictatorial guise. What Ben Ali could not achieve by bullets and truncheons, his successors and their imperialist backers hope to achieve through smiles and kind words, aided by dollars and Euros. However, the objective remains the same: to get the people off the streets, to return the worker to his lathe, the peasant to his farm, the student to his studies. What they fervently desire is a speedy return to normality: *that is to say, a speedy return to the old slavery under a new name.*

Absolutely no trust can be placed in these hypocritical "democrats". These self-same governments backed the dictatorial regime of Zine El Abidine Ben Ali. Western big business made handsome profits there and had no reason to complain about the low wages, since that was the basis for their profits in the first place. These ladies and gentlemen maintained a polite silence for decades about the rotten and repressive regime in Tunis because that same regime was defending their profits. Now that that regime has been overthrown, they suddenly find a voice to plead for "calm".

Events are moving with lightening speed. Even as I write these lines, Ghannouchi has already been replaced by the speaker of the Parliament Foued Mebazaa, who is attempting to cobble together a national unity government to call new elections in 60 days. This shows that the regime is weak and riven with splits.

Workers and youth of Tunisia, be on your guard! What you have conquered is the result of your own heroic struggles and sacrifices. Do not allow what has been won with blood to be taken from you by fraud! Do not place your trust in fine speeches and hollow promises! Trust only your own strength, your own self-organization, your own determination!

The idea of a "national government", inclusive of the various legal political parties and perhaps one or two others whom the military do not consider a threat to the stability of the country and its relations with important allies such as the US and the EU, is yet another trap. The "legal opposition" is a pack of weak, cowardly opportunists, compromised by years of collusion with – or submission to – the Ben Ali regime.

The people of Tunisia are not fools or little children to be lulled to sleep by hypocritical words. They must not demobilize but, on the contrary, step up the mobilization and give it an organized and generalized expression. The remnants of the old regime must be given no respite. These gangsters must not be allowed to re-organize a new "democratic" version of the old regime. The time for talking is long past. No more intrigues! Down with the government! An immediate end to the state of emergency! For full freedom of assembly, organization and speech! For a revolutionary constituent assembly! For the immediate disbanding of all repressive bodies and a people's trial for the murderers and torturers!

In order to achieve these demands, a nationwide general strike must be organized. The working class is the only force that has the necessary weight to overthrow the old regime and to rebuild society from top to bottom. The proletariat must place itself at the head of society. This is the only way forward. The call for a general strike has already found an echo in sections of the UGTT. According to reports, regional general strikes took place in several regions last week (Kasserine, Sfax, Gabes, Kairouan and Jendouba).

In order to prepare a general strike action committees must be formed at all levels: local, regional and national. Life itself teaches us that the only way to get freedom and justice is through the direct action of the masses. In Tunisia the question of power is posed point blank. It is necessary to organize and mobilize the entire people to bring about the decisive overthrow of the old regime.

There have been reports of widespread looting all last night. This has been clearly organised by the police force and agent provocateurs loyal to Ben Ali. They want to create a situation of chaos which they hope would allow them to derail the revolution and make a comeback. There are also reports of neighbourhood committees being set up for self-defence.

The workers must fraternize with the soldiers who are on their side. There should be an appeal to the ranks of the army to form soldiers' committees to link up with the people. The workers and peasants must obtain arms for self-defence and set up a people's militia in every factory, district and village to keep order and defend themselves against bandits and counterrevolutionaries. This is crucial to the success of the revolution.

The revival of Arab Marxism

I have no doubt that there will be "clever" people who for some peculiar reason consider themselves to be Marxists who will say that what is happening in Tunisia is "not a revolution", although, truth to tell, they cannot say what it is. In his book *The Permanent Revolution*, Trotsky compares Mensheviks to an old school teacher who for many years has given lessons on the spring. Then one morning he opens the window and when he is greeted by radiant sunshine and birdsong, slams the window shut and declares these things to be a monstrous aberration of Nature.

Genuine Marxists proceed from living reality, not lifeless schemas. The revolution in Tunisia in many ways resembles the February revolution in Russia in 1917. The revolution has clearly begun, but it is not finished. It has succeeded in overthrowing the old regime, but has not yet been able to put anything in its place. Therefore, it is possible that the revolution may be defeated, particularly in the absence of a genuinely revolutionary leadership.

If it had not been for the presence of the Bolshevik Party, the February Revolution would have ended in defeat. Moreover, if it had not been for the presence of Lenin and Trotsky, the Bolshevik Party itself would have been incapable of playing the role that it did. The leadership would have remained with the reformist leaders of the soviets, and the revolution would have ended in shipwreck. If that had occurred, there can be no doubt that the same "clever" Marxists would be writing learned books explaining that, of course, there was no revolution in Russia, because of A, B, C, and D.

As I was preparing this article and reading different reports on the Internet, I happened to read a few anarchist blogs. I was interested to see that there are "clever" people, not only among the Marxists but also among the anarchists. The author of one of the blogs complained bitterly about the lack of support for the revolution in Tunisia because it does not fit in with anarchist prejudices. He at least has healthy revolutionary instincts, unlike the pedants who refuse to give the Tunisian revolution a birth certificate because it does not fit in with their stupid preconceptions.

For decades the idea has been carefully cultivated that there is no basis for socialism and Marxism among the masses of the Middle East and North Africa. Insofar as there is any opposition – so the argument goes – it is under the banner of Islamic fundamentalism. But this argument is false to the core and is disproved by events in Tunisia. The young women who went onto the streets to confront the police did not wear the *burka*. They are educated and intelligent people who speak good French and English. They are not demanding the introduction of *sharia* law but democratic rights and jobs.

Those so-called leftists who have been flirting with Islamic fundamentalism display contempt for the level of understanding of the Arab workers and youth. To paint the fundamentalists as a revolutionary tendency is a betrayal of the cause of socialism. The future Arab Revolution will take place not under the black flag of Islamic fundamentalism but under the red flag of socialism.

In the past there was a strong socialist and communist tradition in the Arab world. But the crimes of Stalinism had their most terrible effect in this part of the world. The mass Communist Parties in Iraq and Sudan were destroyed by the treacherous policy of "two stages", which handed power on a plate to so-called bourgeois progressives like Qasim and Nimeiri. This led to the annihilation of the Communist vanguard and the consolidation of dictatorial regimes like that of Saddam Hussein, with all that this implied for the peoples of the Middle East.

Nature abhors a vacuum. The same is true of politics. Into the vacuum left by the collapse of Stalinism stepped the Islamic fundamentalists, who pose as "anti-imperialists", despite the fact that they were supported and financed by US imperialism to combat "communism" and fight the Soviet forces in Afghanistan.

It is sufficient to recall that Osama bin Laden was an agent of the CIA until he quarrelled with his old friends in Washington.

On the demonstration in Brussels this afternoon (January 15), a comrade reported a conversation with an old Tunisian woman. She asked: "Have you seen men with long beards at our demonstrations in Tunisia? No! Because we do not need those people to liberate us." The fundamentalists have always been used as a means of diverting the masses from the socialist revolution. It is no accident that Rashid Ghannouchi, an Islamic leader, has been allowed to come back from exile and is now being played up in the Tunisian media. Many are saying: "We did not kick out Ben Ali to get the Islamists!"

It is very important to stress that this is the first time that an Arab dictator has been overthrown by the people themselves without outside intervention. This represents a decisive break with a fatalistic view that has unfortunately become widespread in the Arab world that says: "yes, there have been many struggles, but we were always defeated". It is significant that on the Brussels demonstration today the main slogan chanted was: "Yes, we can!"

Regarding the impact in other countries, an activist in the movement, writing in the *nawaat.org* website, one of the voices of the insurrection, had this to say: "The Tunisian people have given a lesson to the whole world, and to those oppressed in the Arab world in particular: expect nothing from anyone else and everything from yourself, and overcome the fear that paralyses your will and your energy."

The socialist traditions are still alive and are gathering strength. A new generation of Arab activists is growing up under conditions of capitalist crisis. In the course of struggle they are learning fast. What they are looking for is the ideas of Marxism. The magnificent work of *Marxy.com*, the Arab website of the IMT, is beginning to produce important results, not just in defending the ideas and principles of Marxism, but in organizing practical revolutionary work and solidarity, as their campaign in support of the Tunisian Revolution shows.

Yesterday evening during a program on the Tunisian-based television Nessma (the television of the Greater Maghreb) with intellectuals and journalists, the question was asked about how to get back the wealth the Ben Ali family had robbed from the people. One journalist said: "We should nationalise the banks and all assets of the Trabelsi clan". Then another one mentioned "The Tunisian Spring" article, the first article on *Marxy.com* on the Tunisian insurrection, and the other added, "Yes, we know about that Marxist article but we have not reached that spring yet".

This is a small anecdote, but it reveals the echo that the ideas of Marxism are getting amongst the left in Tunisia. What we have just witnessed in Tunisia is nothing less than the beginnings of the Arab Revolution, a colossal event that will change the course of world history. From one country to another the flames of revolt will spread from the Atlantic to the Euphrates. The revolutionary movement will develop and mature and raise itself to the level of the tasks demanded by history. Fighting shoulder to shoulder with the masses, the forces of Marxism will grow with them. The Arab Revolution will triumph as a socialist revolution or it will not triumph at all.

- Down with the Foued Mebazaa regime!
- Full democratic rights now!
- For a revolutionary constituent assembly!
- For the expropriation of all the ill-gotten goods of the Trabelsi clique!
- Victory to the Tunisian workers and youth!
- Long live the Arab Socialist Revolution!

Saturday, 15 January 2011

REJECT THE FARCE OF NATIONAL UNITY — CONTINUE THE REVOLUTION UNTIL VICTORY

Jorge Martín

As soon as Ben Ali was on the plane to Saudi Arabia on Friday, January 14, ousted by the mass revolutionary movement of the Tunisian workers and youth, the Tunisian ruling class and its imperialist puppet masters started manoeuvring to make sure that they remained in control of the situation.

They were intent on not allowing power to slip from the corridors of parliament and the presidential palace to the streets where the masses were celebrating the flight of the hated dictator. It was crucial for them above all to ensure the maintenance of "constitutional order". Articles 56 and 57 of the Constitution were invoked and different figures were put in charge with lightning speed, trying to form a new government as soon as possible. First it was Ben Ali's Prime Minister Mohamed Ghannouchi, quickly replaced by the speaker of the parliament, Foued Mebazaa, who then, in turn, proceeded to ask Ghannouchi to have talks with all political forces in order to form a national unity government charged with calling elections.

Talks were frantic during the whole weekend. From the point of view of the ruling class this government had to fulfil two aims: 1) to ensure the continuity of the old regime, 2) to do it by pretending that it was "new" in order to gain some legitimacy on the streets where the Tunisian people had carried out the revolutionary overthrow of Ben Ali. For this purpose a number of figures from the "loyal opposition" were included as a fig leaf.

Meanwhile, the remains of Ben Ali's hated police force and secret services were roaming the streets in unmarked cars, shooting at civilians, organizing looting and generally attempting to create a mood of chaos, violence and fear from which they hoped to benefit. An amazing 120,000 people were employed by the police in a country of just over 10 million inhabitants, controlling all aspects of everyday life and spying on the population on a massive scale. Many of those are still loyal to the dictator, armed and fighting for their own survival.

Starting on Friday night, the Tunisian people started to organise to fight back against them. In neighbourhoods around the country groups of men, women and children armed themselves with sticks, stones, knives and whatever else they could get their hands on and set up barricades and roadblocks to protect themselves, revealing a sharp revolutionary instinct.

One eyewitness described the situation: "Every single corner had a collection of men, young boys and even a few women brandishing all sorts of weapons (except guns). They had built barricades out of random trash to block traffic and were standing around them." These peoples' committees fought, and on many occasions defeated, the ministry of interior forces who were terrorizing the population: "These terrorists were armed with automatic weapons and driving around in cars, and we were all on foot armed only with axe handles, knives and badly constructed barricades," the same eyewitness explained.

Some of these committees also started to undertake tasks of ensuring the provisioning of food as well as maintaining public order. Elements of dual power started to emerge. In Bizerte, one of the epicentres of the revolution, the army went to the neighbourhood committees and told them that they were taking over, but the committees said they were staying and the army had no other alternative but to accept. The same was true throughout the country, as army soldiers collaborated with the committees to maintain order and fight the police and ministry of interior forces.

Last week during the revolutionary events that led to the ousting of Ben Ali, there were already many reports of fraternization between soldiers and lower ranking officers and the workers and youth on the streets. As a matter of fact, Ben Ali was forced to withdraw the Army from the streets of the capital and replace them with the police for fear of the soldiers joining with the people.

During every real revolutionary movement cracks appear within the state apparatus, and particularly the army which is a conscript army drawn from the people. Some generals at the top of the Tunisian Army probably realized that they could not use the soldiers against the people and therefore understood that Ben Ali was finished and decided to switch their allegiance. General Rachid Ammar is reported as having refused an order for the soldiers to fire on the demonstrators and was removed from his command by Ben Ali. This has added to the popularity of the Army amongst the population.

It is not unprecedented for Army officers to play a role in revolutions, particularly in the absence of a revolutionary party with strong roots amongst the working class. This was the case during the Portuguese revolution in 1974. For a brief period of time general Spinola took over control of the situation, pretending to be a friend of the revolution, only to be removed as the revolution moved further to the left. The same Spinola was to attempt a coup against the very same revolution he had pretended to be a part of.[7]

The workers and youth of Tunisia should be very wary of any such false friends of the revolution. These false friends are behaving as they are only because the balance of forces has swung massively in favour of the ordinary work-

---

7   See *The Portuguese Revolution*, by Alan Woods, June, 1974; *The Revolution in Portugal*, by Ted Grant, May 1975; and *Worker's History – Portuguese Revolution 1974*, by Phil Mitchinson, May 1994 for a detailed analysis of the 1974 Portuguese revolution and the role played by such figures.

ing people. They will lean towards the masses in order to win their confidence, only to betray them later.

In Tunisia as in any capitalist country, the army as an institution is a capitalist body, created in order to defend the interests of the ruling class, however much it attempts to present itself as defending the people and the nation. Workers and youth should have no trust in Army generals. However, the lower ranks are much closer to the masses in social composition and background. With these layers – ordinary soldiers and lower ranking officers – the masses should build and strengthen their links. Soldiers and revolutionary officers should form their own committees and these should be linked to the committees in the workplaces and the neighbourhoods. They should denounce those officers involved in corruption and repression under Ben Ali and remove them from the institution.

As news of the new "national unity" government started to emerge, workers and youth were back on the streets. In Bizerte, Sfax and other places there were demonstrations on Saturday, some of them marching on the headquarters of the hated RCD ruling party and setting them on fire. In Bizerte the people defeated the Ben Ali militias and set their motorbikes on fire. There was a growing feeling that the revolution was being stolen from them.

Even before the actual composition of the new government had been announced demonstrations were being called for in the capital and most regional capitals for Monday. In Tunis a militant crowd of thousands gathered outside the offices of the UGTT trade union and then marched towards the Ministry of the Interior. Similar demonstrations took place in Sfax, Kasserine, Monastir, Bizerte, Jendouba, etc. In many cases these demonstrations were organized by and rallied from the regional headquarters of the UGTT union. "The revolution continues, down with the RCD" was the common slogan. "They cannot steal the revolution from us," said Abdel Haq Kharshouni, one of the protesters quoted by the *Financial Times*, "we do not want to be ruled by tyrants anymore." In the capital, the demonstrators were met with riot police with water cannons and dispersed.

Finally, late on Monday 18, the composition of the new government was announced. Ministers from the old Ben Ali government kept all key positions including the Prime Minister and the ministries of Defence, Interior, Economy and Foreign Affairs. A few figures from the legal opposition were given token ministries: Moustapha Ben Jaafar, from the social democratic "Forum démocratique pour le travail et la liberté" (FDTL) getting the Health Ministry, Ahmed Ibrahim, from the former Communist Party *Ettajdid* was given Higher Education, and the head of the "centre-left" PDP Najib Chebbi was appointed as Minister for Regional Development.

As usual the former Stalinists and reformist leaders play the worst role of all. These are all parties which were legal under Ben Ali; some had representation in parliament and played no role during the insurrection. Significantly, when Ghannouchi announced the new government, he was flanked by Abdallah Kallel, former Minister of the Interior, well known for implementing brutal repression and directly responsible for the torture of thousands of political opponents. A number of figures from "civil society" were thrown in for good measure to try to increase the authority of the new government amongst the masses, including a blogger who had been arrested, a barrister, human rights figures, a cinema director, etc. Three representatives from the UGTT trade union were also included in the new government, in recognition of the need for the ruling class to get some support amongst the workers.

The Tunisian Communist Workers Party (PCOT), illegal up until now, has correctly denounced this government as a manoeuvre to maintain the Ben Ali regime without Ben Ali. The PCOT has also called for the spreading of the committees and for the convening of a Constituent Assembly.

The only other party not to have been invited to this "new" government is the Islamist En Nahda, also illegal under Ben Ali. However, its leaders have declared they would be ready to join such a government. At the same time, it has been reported that one of the leaders of En Nahda, just released from prison, was present at the anti-government demonstration in Tunis this morning. The Islamists, who play no role in the actual revolution, are now attempting to win support by presenting themselves as more consistent democrats. These are not friends of the revolution, but just cynically trying to take advantage of it to promote their own reactionary views.

This new government does not have the support of the revolutionary masses. They quite rightly see that they made the revolution and now a government is being formed which is mainly made up of those they fought against, people who were part of the Ben Ali government right until the end, who are co-responsible for the 80 people who were killed by the regime during the insurrection. The fact that a few "oppositionists" who did not play any significant role during the movement are being included does not change anything. The promises of freedom for all political prisoners, freedom of expression and democratic elections do not change anything. The people fear that their victory on Friday is being stolen in front of their own eyes. A young unemployed worker summarized the feelings of the people: "It is as if Ben Ali was still here. The people from this government never had the courage to say 'enough' to Ben Ali. They want to steal our revolution. They did nothing to remove him. They should go!"

A new and powerful wave of anger is building up from below. This morning (Tuesday January 18), new demonstrations took place, including a few thousand in the capital, 10,000 in Sfax (where a general strike has been called for tomorrow)[8], thousands in Sidi Bouzid, 1000 in Regueb (population 7,000), thousands in Kairouan[9], 3,000 in Kelibia and also 500 in Kasserine. In Tataouine the

---

8   See video: http://www.youtube.com/watch?v=_JPY524ANL0
9   video: http://24sur24.posterous.com/sidibouzid-video-today-anti-rcd-prosts-in-kai

demonstrators ransacked the headquarters of the RCD. There were also demonstrations, numbering thousands, in Béja[10], in Gabes[11], in Mahdia, Hamma, Gafsa, Feriana, Kairouan, Zarzis, Kelibia, etc. Many of these demonstrations were organised by or rallied at the headquarters of the regional and local unions of the UGTT. One observer put it this way: "The Tunisian population feels that the Revolution is being driven away from its ideals. The main view of the opposition is that the people who made the revolution are not represented and that by keeping the RCD on board, and even at the steering wheel, the former regime is perpetuating itself." This forced the UGTT national leadership today to announce that it does not recognize the new government and that it is withdrawing from it, this less than 24 hours from its formation!

The national leadership of the UGTT is not known for its radicalism. Last week it met with Ben Ali and welcomed the promises he made in a last desperate attempt to save his skin. On Sunday they went on national TV to distance themselves from appeals for demonstrations on Monday and called on all workers to report back for work and "re-establish normality". If they have now been forced to make such a statement it means that the pressure coming from the rank and file of the trade unions and from the regional unions must be very strong and they fear losing their positions. Even the former communist party Ettajdid, which has joined the new government, issued a statement saying that their participation in it was conditional on a number of demands, including the removal of all RCD ministers!

As part of the unfulfilled tasks of the revolution, workers and ordinary trade union members should organise the democratization of the trade union movement and the cleansing of the UGTT of all those who collaborated with the Ben Ali regime. Workers require unions that are genuine expressions of their interests. This means elections in the workplaces must take place, and a new leadership must be prepared to take over.

The next few hours and days will be crucial. The workers and youth of Tunisia have shown great courage and revolutionary determination. They must not allow the revolution to be taken away from them. They should rely only on their own forces, the forces that brought down Ben Ali. The Committees which exist in the neighbourhoods should be maintained and should link up through elected representatives at a local, regional and national level. Similar committees should be set up in the work places, within the ranks of the Army, amongst the students, etc. These are the only bodies that are legitimate representatives of the revolutionary people and which should be tasked with convening the Constituent Assembly. None of the politicians from the old regime can be trusted as the masses correctly understand.

---

10 video: http://www.facebook.com/video/video.php?v=119637294774827
11 http://www.facebook.com/video/video.php?v=194981193849966

The slogans of the day should be: Down with the national unity government! For a revolutionary constituent assembly based on the committees! Fraternisation with the army ranks and setting up of soldiers' committees! The UGTT should call a general strike to enforce the will of the people! Trial and punishment of those responsible for repression under the Ben Ali regime! Expropriation of the wealth of the Trabelsi clan! The revolution continues; the workers and youth should remain vigilant!

The Ben Ali regime was not only a dictatorship, but a *capitalist* dictatorship. This is the reason why France, Italy, the US and the rest of the imperialist powers supported Ben Ali right until the very last minute. We also note that the Socialist International has decided to remove the RCD from its ranks, an embarrassing decision which shows that when it comes to imperialism the social democratic leaders always play the same imperialist tune.

If the revolution is to be taken to its logical conclusions, and the demands for work and dignity are to be fulfilled, the wealth of the Tunisian capitalist class, the banks, industries and companies which supported, backed, financed and benefited from the dictatorship, must be expropriated. Only in this way, can the wealth of the country created by working people be put under the control of this same working people in order to fulfil the needs of the population. The aspirations of the Tunisian masses can only be genuinely satisfied through a social, as well as a political revolution: a socialist revolution.

Tuesday, 18 January 2011

AS THE RULING CLASS MANOEUVRES AT THE TOP
ELEMENTS OF DUAL POWER DEVELOP FROM BELOW

Jorge Martín

Wednesday 19 and Thursday 20 saw the continuation of mass demonstrations all over Tunisia against the "new" national unity government and demanding an end to the RCD ruling party. Tens of thousands marched throughout the country under the slogan "RCD degagé" (Out with the RCD), clearly identifying the national unity government as a continuation of the old regime.

The seven key ministries (including the prime minister, finances, foreign affairs, interior and defence) are held by the same people who held these ministries under the hated dictator Ben Ali. The people feel that their revolution, which forced Ben Ali to flee the country on Friday 14, will not be finished until the old regime is completely destroyed. "Ben Ali has gone to Saudi Arabia! The government should go there too," was one of the slogans. The rallying cry of these demonstrations was: "We want a new parliament, a new constitution, a new republic! People rise up against the Ben Ali loyalists!"

It is worth watching some of the videos of these demonstrations in order to get a feel for the real mood of the Tunisian workers and youth: Bizerte, January 19[12]; Tunis, January 19[13]; Gabes, January 19[14]; Bizerte, Jan 19[15]; occupation of the RCD offices in Sousse (now renamed Bouazizi Peoples' House), January 19[16]; Sfax, Jan 19[17]; Bizerte, January 20[18]; Touzer, January 20[19]; Almzop, January 20[20]; Kairouan, January 20[21].

These angry and militant marches are not just *demanding* the disbanding of the RCD and the old regime at all levels, but they are taking direct action to

12 http://www.facebook.com/video/video.php?v=1276997781504
13 http://www.facebook.com/video/video.php?v=145800948810331
14 http://www.facebook.com/video/video.php?v=195330310481721
15 http://www.facebook.com/video/video.php?v=1677754075999
16 http://www.facebook.com/video/video.php?v=498037449613
17 http://www.facebook.com/video/video.php?v=129234237143031
18 http://www.facebook.com/video/video.php?v=1679208152350
19 http://www.facebook.com/video/video.php?v=196011427081238
20 http://www.facebook.com/video/video.php?v=1689246405492
21 http://www.facebook.com/video/video.php?v=1538172893535

implement their demands. In more than 30 towns and cities in the provinces massive demonstrations, mainly gathering outside the offices of the UGTT trade union, have marched on the RCD headquarters and occupied them. As a matter of fact, as the RCD controlled not only the national, regional and municipal governments, but also controlled all aspects of public life (professional associations, the police, the judiciary, etc), the destruction of the power of the RCD means that power is passing from the old regime to the masses on the streets and to the neighbourhood committees which have sprung up over the last week. These committees are tasked with maintaining public order and defending the population against the remains of the old regime (police officers, secret services, the presidential guard), which are still desperately trying to protect what is left of the old dictatorship.

The most advanced example of these emerging elements of dual power that we know of is in the town of Sidi Bou Ali, in Sousse, with a population of just over 10,000 people. There, on Sunday 16, the masses gathered in the town square and after deliberating about the "new" national unity government, decided to take power into their own hands. This is the statement that was passed which we reproduce in full:

> Following the decision to entrust 'Mohamed Ghannouchi' with forming a new government tasked with overseeing the new presidential elections for the country; following the administrative vacuum and in the city of Sidi Bou Ali, Sousse Governorate; we, citizens of the town of Sidi Bou Ali meeting in the 'People's Square' in the city resolve the following:
>
> • We reject this decision which is based on an undemocratic constitution, not a peoples' one, which has been violated many times and does not guarantee the rights of all national opinions in the country;
>
> • Our rejection of the domination of the ruling party over the political life of the country, represented by all symbols in the current government and its lackeys;
>
> • The public election of a provisional local council in order to manage all city affairs and to work at a local level, and in coordination at regional and national level, to maintain the normal functioning of civilian life, economic, cultural and political life in the country until the drafting of a new constitution of a democratic and popular character, which will pave the way for elections to ensure the peaceful transfer of power and without a monopoly over it, and ensures that all the national parties are represented.
>
> The functions of this Council will be:
>
> • The formation of committees to protect the neighbourhoods and their coordination;
>
> • To work to restore economic life and to secure the necessities of daily life for the citizens;
>
> • To work to re-establish working civilian institutions (banks, hospitals, municipalities, schools, institutes, post offices, the tax office ...);

- To protect public property;
- Coordination with local and regional councils formed;
- Communication and contact with the national army as the only existing force in the country.

We have decided on the distribution of tasks amongst the following commissions:

- The commission on Publicity and Media;
- Commission on contacts with the National Army;
- Defence Committee for the Protection of the Neighbourhoods;
- Commission on protection of municipal property;
- Commission of supply of essential goods;
- Awareness, leadership and culture Committee"

This statement is most extraordinary, and we have no doubt that similar action has been taken in many other towns and cities. Faced with the vacuum of power left by the destruction of the old institutions the youth, the workers, the people in general, have taken it upon themselves to start building a new "institutionality", based on democratic committees "publicly elected" in mass meetings.

In Sidi Bou Ali, the "provisional council" which has been set up is not just a committee of struggle, but has taken over the running of all affairs (public order, provisioning, the economy, the post office, education, etc). They have de facto taken power in the town.

These are in fact, in embryonic form, soviets (i.e. workers' councils), the emergence of which is a true sign of a genuine revolution taking place. It is clear that in some cities it has been the local executives of the UGTT trade unions which have taken the initiative in creating such committees.

These are the first steps in the right direction. These committees must now be generalized in every factory, in every workplace, in every neighbourhood. The committees should be coordinated at a local, regional and national level through representatives elected democratically and subject to the right of recall, as the resolution from Sidi Bou Ali clearly points out.

We would like to make two comments on this statement which are relevant for the whole of the revolutionary movement in Tunisia. The first is in relation to the question of the Army. The statement talks of liaising and communicating with the Army. It is clear that the Army at this point commands a lot of respect amongst the people. As we have reported before, there were many instances of fraternization between the Army and the demonstrators during the uprising last week and it was the police and the presidential guard, rather than the Army, which played the key role in the brutal repression of the people which took between 100 and 200 lives. In the last few days, the Army has fought running battles with the remains of the Ben Ali loyalist police forces. This explains the attitude of the people.

However, we must warn that the rank and file soldiers and even some lower ranking officers who can be won over to the side of the revolution are one thing, but the Army as an institution and particularly its top command is a completely different matter. The Army is part of the capitalist state apparatus of the Ben Ali dictatorship and if the revolutionary movement of the people presents a decisive challenge to the capitalist system, it will either split down the middle along class lines or side with the ruling class.

In the last few days we have already seen incidents in which the Army has been used to "maintain order" as against the anti-RCD demonstrators. In the capital marchers were allowed to demonstrate but prevented by the Army from reaching the Ministry of Interior. The reason is probably that inside the Ministry of the Interior, the Ben Ali henchmen are busy destroying any proof of their brutal repression, torturing and spying on the Tunisian people.

On the evening of January 19, a small group of a few hundred youth decided to challenge the curfew (starting at 8pm every night) declared by the "new" government. A detachment of the Army went to try and disperse them. A tense situation developed. The army officer in charge, a Colonel, was received with shouts of "long live the Army". He argued that "the army is with the people", that they had a "legitimate right" to demonstrate, and that the "Army would not fire on the people", but that they had "to respect the curfew", that "a palace of gold cannot be built overnight", that they should be "patient" and "return the day after". In the end the standoff ended in a draw and the protesters stayed, therefore breaking the curfew. The day after, January 20, when thousands marched on the RCD offices in Mohammed V Avenue, the Army fired warning shots in the air to try to disperse them. In the end the building was taken over by the protesters.

These are early days regarding the Army. The top generals know full well that they cannot use the conscript soldiers, infected by the virus of revolution during the last few weeks, against the people and it would be foolish to try to do so. However, step by step, they will work to reclaim the streets and if the revolutionary people lower their guard and withdraw from the streets, then the Army will be back in power as the armed wing of the ruling class and its state apparatus and it will be used to defend the interests of the capitalists, not those of the people.

For this reason, it is necessary to build and strengthen the links with the army ranks, with the soldiers and lower ranking officers who are closer to the people. They should be encouraged to set up their own committees and send representatives to the local revolutionary councils. The soldier's committees must take it upon themselves to denounce the reactionary officers, all those who were directly involved in repression, those who had personal, economic and other ties to the ruling class and the Ben Ali regime and publicly expose them, arrest them and put them on trial.

Soldiers committees linked closely to the revolutionary committees of workers and youth would be a guarantee that no-one has either the power or the strength to make a move against the will of the people.

The second observation we would make on the statement of the revolutionary people of Sidi Bou Ali is that it talks about a new constitution, democratic elections and the representation of all parties (it is understood that the RCD would be excluded). We would say that this can be achieved through a constituent assembly, but who would convene such an assembly? As of yet there is no power which has the legitimacy to do so. The "new" national unity government is nothing but the continuation of the old regime. But if the revolutionary councils were to be linked at a regional and national level, they would have the legitimacy to convene such a constituent assembly to decide over the profound reorganization of the country's life.

Manoeuvres at the top

While the workers and youth continue the struggle on the streets, the ruling class continue their manoeuvres at the top to try to create a "new" government with some legitimacy. The resignation of the three UGTT trade union members from the government (less than 24 hours from its announcement and even before its first meeting), was followed by the resignation of the minister representing the social democratic FDLT. The former Communist Party, *Ettajdid*, issued a strongly worded communiqué demanding the removal of all RCD ministers from the government and conditioning its participation on their withdrawal... but stayed in the government nevertheless.

In a surreal twist to the story, all RCD ministers in the "new" government then proceeded to resign from the RCD, as if this changed their character. The RCD in turn expelled Ben Ali, trying to distance itself from the dictatorship, and disbanded its Central Committee from which most of its members had already resigned. Now, one of the RCD ministers has also resigned from the government. This is a bit like all the world's Archbishops resigning from the Catholic Church and then the Church deciding to expel the Pope from its ranks. These are clearly desperate manoeuvres which will not fool the Tunisian people.

The different imperialist powers, having been caught by surprise by the revolutionary uprising, are now busy behind the scenes, attempting to make sure that "order" (i.e. normal capitalist exploitation) is restored as soon as possible. The Tunisian people should reject any foreign imperialist interference. The US and particularly the French imperialists (of both right-wing and social-democratic varieties) have their hands soaked in the blood of the Tunisian people. They fully backed Ben Ali right until the end. They have no right to pretend now that they are friends of the Tunisian revolution and that they can help "supervise" democratic elections. On the contrary, the Tunisian workers and youth must launch an internationalist appeal to their class brothers and sisters in the whole of the

Maghreb and the Middle East to follow their example, and to the workers of Europe to join them in the struggle against their imperialist masters.

A situation is developing in which a rift has opened between the power of the streets and the official power of the new government. Elements of dual power are clearly present, but these cannot last indefinitely. The workers and youth must take the initiative and push forward, otherwise the initiative will return to the official institutions of power... and this will mean the restoration of the old regime with some new faces.

Mass demonstrations in the streets and the setting up and linking up of the revolutionary committees must be continued and strengthened. That, however, will not be enough. The UGTT national leadership, under immense pressure from below has been forced to abandon the so-called national unity government. It should now organise and call a general strike to render the government powerless. The regional and local bodies of the UGTT should take the initiative for this in close coordination with the revolutionary committees.

Political and social revolution

A thorough purge is required at all levels of society. All the agents of the old regime in all public and private institutions should be removed and put on trial. The revolutionary people have already started the job by occupying the RCD headquarters. This should be extended to the forces of repression (the secret police, the presidential guard, etc) which should be disbanded and their officials put on trial.

But this revolution was not only about overthrowing a dictatorship. The slogans of the people were demanding "Jobs, bread – out with Ben Ali", clearly linking political with social demands. The achievement of democracy, in itself, without a change in the socio-economic system, will not fundamentally change anything.

The question of the property of the means of production should be posed by the movement. To start with, the property of the Ben Ali family and his Trabelsi clan should be expropriated and put under the democratic control of the working people. That in itself would mean a serious blow to capitalism in Tunisia, as the Trabelsi clan controlled large parts of the economy (banking, construction, housing, car dealerships, telecommunications, media, tourism, airlines, import-export, agriculture, oil, cement, etc. there is almost no sector in which the clan did not have decisive business participation.) It is said that "half of the Tunisian business world is linked to Ben Ali in one way or another". The Tunisian revolution, in order to be genuinely democratic, must also become a social revolution against the capitalist system.

Down with the "unity government"– RCD Out! Disband the forces of repression! Arrest and trial of all those officials linked to the old regime at all levels! Strengthen the people's committees at a local, regional and national level! A democratic Constituent Assembly to decide the country's future! Soldiers' committees! Expropriation of the property of the Trabelsi clan under the control of the working people! No to imperialist intervention!

Thursday, 20 January 2011

THE REVOLUTIONARY INITIATIVE OF THE MASSES CONTINUES

Jorge Martín

While the "new" Tunisian government of "national unity" (in fact, stacked with Ben Ali ministers) had its first meeting on Thursday, January 20, and attempted to rush through a series of measures which would gain it some legitimacy, the revolution continues on the streets and in the workplaces with workers taking on anyone in authority who had links to the old Ben Ali regime.

The "new" president Ghannouchi was forced to announce the legalisation of all political parties, a general amnesty (though this was just a project, to be discussed in parliament) and the nationalisation of all buildings of the hated RCD ruling party. The government also declared three days of national mourning for the martyrs of the revolution. What utter hypocrisy considering that the key ministers in this government were part of the government that killed these martyrs! There can be no mourning until those responsible for the killings are removed from the government and other official positions and put on trial.

Yesterday, we reported that there had been demonstrations throughout the country of tens of thousands in every town and city, even the most remote. The growing anger against the government of Ghannouchi (Ben Ali's prime minister) has developed into a national movement of protest which is spreading to all sections of society. Today, there were even reports of a strike and demonstrations by police officers in Monastir, Bizerte and even parts of Tunis. Some were at work directing traffic, but wearing red arm bands in protest.

The demonstrations continue and today, Friday 21st, general strikes have already been called for in many different regions, with demands for the dismissal of the government of Ghannouchi. "You stole the country's wealth, but you will not steal the revolution – Resignation of the government – we will always be loyal to the blood of our martyrs," were amongst the slogans.

Yesterday, we reported how a Provisional Council had taken over the running of all affairs in Sidi Bou Ali. We have now received a report that a similar development has taken place in the city of Siliana, in the North west, where "the citizens have set up a local council for the protection of the revolution and the management of public affairs". Their founding statement says that, "faced with the vacuum of power created by the flight of officials linked to the RCD", they have decided to create a local and a regional council "to protect the revolution and to manage the running of the city and the governorate."

In a very significant development the Army seemed to be testing the ground as to how far they can go in restoring "order", i.e. the old authorities, in the towns and cities which have been taken over by the peoples' revolutionary committees. In the town of Sidi Bou Rouis, also in the Siliana governorate, the "Council for the Protection of the People's Revolution" has issued the following statement:

> The Army Commander has called the Bou Rouis local committees and told them that within the framework of things being brought back to normal functioning, the return of council members and mayors has been approved.

> As a result of this dangerous development 'the Bou Rouis Council for the Protection of the People's Revolution' has called an emergency meeting this evening to discuss the new situation and how to deal with it, and calls for the mobilisation of the whole people today and tomorrow in mass rallies and agrees the following urgent demands:

> 1) The formation of a national transitional government consisting of national figures known for their integrity and who were not involved with the former regime to run state affairs and draft a new constitution and new electoral rules.

> 2) The dissolution of the House of Representatives and the Council of Advisers which lost all semblance of legitimacy during the people's revolution for freedom and dignity.

> 3) The issuing of a ban to prevent elements of the former regime from exercising any political activity on the grounds of complicity with the former ruling party which plunged the country into a dark period dominated by injustice and tyranny, corruption and unemployment and the wastage of an unprecedented amount of wealth of the country at the expense of the public who are subject to all forms of repression and deprivation.

> Long live the People... Long live the Revolution

> Glory to the people... Glory to the martyrs... Glory to the revolution of Tunisia for dignity and freedom.

> Time: 15:40, Bou Rouis, 20 January.

This is, again, an extraordinary state of affairs in which the people have not only taken power in the whole of the Siliana governorate, but are standing strong in the face of the attempt of the Army to restore the old mayors back in power. We see how, as in the statement from the Provisional Council of Sidi Bou Ali, they call for a provisional government to be formed, composed of nationally recognized figures not linked to the old regime. We think that it should be the revolutionary committees and councils themselves who should organise such a transitional body, which should be charged with convening a genuinely democratic national assembly.

Meanwhile, the masses continue their direct action, deepening the scope of the revolution also into the workplaces. There are many reports of journalists in state owned newspapers, radio stations, TV channels, etc., which used to be nothing but disgusting mouthpieces of Ben Ali's propaganda, getting organized and taking over the editorial line.

This is the case at the state-owned *La Presse*. El-Heni, a journalist at the foreign desk explains: "We had an important meeting and decided to create two elected editorial committees to supervise the editorial line, and we told the boss that he would no longer have any editorial control... He is only here for finance and administration. He was clever enough to understand that."

One of the *La Presse* journalists, who had been sacked for political reasons, has been reinstated as the head of the journalists' union at the paper.

In state owned companies, ministries and private companies, owned or linked to the Trabelsi family, workers' assemblies and strikes have been organised to drive out the hated RCD managers, CEOs and high ranking officials.

On Tuesday, January 18, UGTT workers at STAR, one of the country's main insurance companies, went on strike and expelled the company's CEO, Abdelkarim Merdassi, in protest at his links with the Trabelsi clan. The extraordinary scenes in which the workers physically expelled him from his office while singing the national anthem were captured on video[22].

Similar movements developed at the oil distribution company SNDP, where the CEO Rafaa Dkhul was also kicked out by the workers who criticized his close links with the Trabelsi family. Dkhul had given the Trabelsi clan concessions in a number of petrol stations worth millions of euros. At the Banque de Tunisie, its general director Alia Abdallah and all high ranking officers have been barred by the workers, organized by the UGTT, from entering their offices in order to prevent the destruction of potentially incriminating documents. The workers have seized all sensitive documents and computers.

Also expelled from their positions by the action of the workers and their trade unions are Moncef Bouden, from the Tax Office, Moncef Dakhli, CEO of the National Agricultural Bank and Montassar Ouaïli, CEO of Tunisie Telecom. The outgoing Minister of Sports, Abdelhamid Slama, was prevented by the workers from entering his old ministry to pick up his things. The list of companies where the workers have taken action is very long. Today, the workers of the Tunis public transport went on strike also demanding the dismissal of the CEO of their company.

The Tunisian business press is full of articles complaining about the "lack of respect for the law" and asking "what is the Ministry of the Interior doing" about these actions on the part of the workers. An opinion article on the business website *Web Manager Centre* implored, "Let's not put businessmen on their knees". Another was entitled "Discipline – 'comrades'."

---

22 Available here http://www.youtube.com/watch?v=5T7wHHHaITo

The workers feel confident and are moving forward, not just against the bosses, but also against their own bureaucratic trade union leaders who until very recently were supporting the dictatorship of Ben Ali. An appeal is circulating for an extraordinary national congress of the UGTT to be convened in order to remove the current leadership.

Workers, however, should not stop at removing the old managers, directors and officials, but they should replace them with their own elected representatives, establishing workers' control over production and the economy.

Clearly, the Tunisian revolution has shaken society from top to bottom. The workers and youth are on the streets and in a confident mood. The government commands no authority and the initiative is still firmly on the streets. Mass demonstrations are expected tomorrow.

The revolutionary movement of the Tunisian masses urgently needs to give itself a more organized character and a national coordination. The revolutionary committees and democratic trade unions need to be spread and strengthened at all levels. A national meeting of delegates from local, neighbourhood, regional and workplace committees and trade unions should be called at the earliest possible opportunity. Only such a body would have the legitimacy to convene a democratic constituent assembly. Workers and youth should continue and deepen their revolutionary activities in sweeping away all the institutions and representatives of the old regime. This is the only real homage that can be paid to the martyrs that died for freedom, dignity, bread and jobs.

The next few days will be crucial. If the revolutionary movement does not advance in a bold manner and clearly pose the question of taking power, then slowly, but surely, the forces of the ruling class will reclaim the authority they have lost. A situation of dual power cannot last indefinitely. The Tunisian people have a rich revolutionary history, but every uprising and general strike has been followed by a period of concessions and trickery, and then the ruling class reasserting its power again, through brutal repression. This is the time to put an end to this cycle and throw the Tunisian ruling class into the dustbin of history.

- Long live the People!
- Long live the Workers and Youth!
- Long live the Revolution!

Friday, 21 January 2011

"WE ARE HERE TO OVERTHROW THE GOVERNMENT"

Jorge Martín

Events over the weekend have shown the strength of the revolutionary movement in Tunisia and revealed the weakness of the national unity government. The organisation of a "Liberation Caravan" marching to the capital has the potential, if combined with a mass movement of demonstrations and strikes, to bring down the government.

Saturday, 22 January, saw extraordinary scenes in the capital when thousands marched on the prime minister's office demanding the resignation of the government. Mass demonstrations took place on Sunday in most regional capitals and cities, including Gabes, Monastir, Sfax, etc. Following on from Friday, when police officers throughout the country went on strike and demonstrated, hundreds of police officers joined the demonstration in the capital, many in uniform, others wearing red armbands. In many of the cities where they have demonstrated they have contacted the local UGTT union and asked for help to set up their own trade union organisation.

"Several dozen police officers, some in civilian clothes and some in uniform and wearing red armbands, arrived today [Friday 21] at the Regional Workers' Union in Ben Guerdane [on the border with Libya], to demand the formation of a trade union in order to defend their moral and material rights," reported Hssine Betaïeb, a UGTT trade unionist to AFP. "They have told us that whatever the regime might be, they will never in the future use violence against the population again."

This is very significant. It is clear that in a police force composed of 120,000 people there are many different layers, from the brutal torturer to the callous anti-riot police to the traffic police and so on. Some of them wish to disassociate themselves from the Ben Ali regime in order to protect themselves. Others have been infected by the prevailing revolutionary mood and are bringing out their accumulated grievances. What is true is that the state apparatus in Tunisia, the armed bodies of men in defence of private property of which Engels spoke, has been extremely weakened by the revolutionary events, though not yet completely destroyed.

This was graphically demonstrated on Saturday when the demonstration arrived at the office of the Prime Minister, which was protected by barbed wire and the presence of anti-riot police. Faced with thousands of angry demonstrators carrying Tunisian banners and a Che Guevara flag, the police could only *plead* with the protestors: "Do whatever you want to do but *please* don't storm the office of the prime minister." Had there been a clear leadership, they could have taken over the Prime Minister's office. The government is truly suspended in mid-air in the face of the developing revolutionary movement.

On Friday 21, Ghannouchi made a speech on live TV *begging* the people to allow him to rule. Further to all the promises he had already made, he added that the victims of repression would be compensated and that he would quit politics altogether after fresh elections take place. "My role is to bring my country out of this temporary phase and even if I am nominated, I will refuse it and leave politics," he said. He added that he had "lived and suffered" like ordinary Tunisians under the dictatorship. What utter hypocrisy from someone who was a minister of Ben Ali for more than 20 years!

These incidents reflect the real balance of forces in the country: the government on the defensive, *asking* the people for trust, the masses on the streets *taking power into their own hands*, but still lacking the national coordination and clear leadership which would allow them to take power once and for all.

The Trade Union Movement

On Friday, there was a further meeting of the Central Committee of the UGTT. There is a clear split within the trade union body between those who were loyal to Ben Ali until the last minute but who have been forced into opposition by the mass movement and a growing number of union federations (including postal workers and teachers) and regional union bodies which are further to the left and playing an important role in the movement. It was a meeting of the CC last week, which forced the Executive Bureau to go back on its decision of joining Ghannouchi's government of "national unity". There were rumours that the Executive was moving again in the direction of rejoining the government, but they were soundly defeated at the CC meeting on Friday.

The union issued a statement calling "for the dissolution of the government and the setting up of a national coalition government which responds to the demands of the demonstrators, the political parties, the NGOs and the population as a whole." The statement further declared that the UGTT is "committed to continuing the legitimate struggle, be that through strikes or peaceful demonstrations, until the reestablishment of the government according to the conditions set by the UGTT". In reality, the UGTT national leadership is trailing behind events as the regional bodies of the union are already calling regional general strikes and demanding that talk be followed up with action.

The way to bring down the government would be to call a national general strike and paralyse the country's economy. In Jendouba, for instance, the regional UGTT has called for a regional general strike on Wednesday 26. The teachers' union has called for a national indefinite strike "until the fall of the government" starting today, Monday 24, which is the day schools and universities are resuming activities. According to Nabil Haouachi, from the national leadership of the primary school teachers' union, the strike is already "an unprecedented success". He confirmed a very high participation throughout the country with "rates of 100% participation in the strike in Médenine (South East), Sidi Bouzid, Kasserine (Centre West), Béja, Jendouba (North West) and Kairouan (Centre)... and 90% in Zaghouan (near Tunis) where there is no trade union tradition and also a very solid strike in Tunis."

The national executive of the UGTT, as a matter of fact, is more concerned about establishing a "restoration of normality" than actually bringing down the farcical government of national unity. In a separate statement the union's general secretary calls "upon all workers to respond to all attempts to stop the activity of our economic order and to maintain the normal mode of activity and vigilance to ensure the smooth running and management of the companies, and renews the call upon all progressive and democratic forces to maintain what has been achieved by the uprising of our people, to avert all risks to circumvent them and their objectives."

Reports coming in at the end of last week referred to the resumption of production at the country's main industrial centres by Friday, meaning that they had been paralyzed, either by strike action or the general chaos caused by the revolutionary events, for nearly a week.

As we reported on Friday, workers in state owned companies and in others that have been privatized have been taking all sorts of direct action (strikes, occupations, sit-ins, petitions) to demand their rights and particularly to remove the most corrupt managers and those with links to the Ben Ali-Trabelsi clan.

As well as the examples we already reported (STAR insurance, National Agricultural Bank, Tunisie Telecom, national tax office, etc), there were also strike movements and occupations at the National Water Company where workers occupied the company's buildings demanding the removal of managers and directors linked to the old regime. In Béja, workers and doctors at the local hospital demonstrated demanding the removal of RCD symbols from the premises. Also in the Béja region there were reports of peasants occupying land which they said had been confiscated from them by Ben Ali's nephew.

Air stewards of Tunisair marched to the central headquarters of the company in the Charguia industrial area, demanding the removal of the company's CEOs but also the regularization of their contracts. Civil Aviation Office workers also demanded the removal of their director who, they said, had been involved in handing over public property and airport concessions to Ben Ali's relatives. In Monastir, airport workers have announced the occupation of the installations today (Monday 24th). Political demands against corruption, for the removal of managers, etc, have been become united with social demands, for better wages and conditions, etc.

The movement is not only affecting traditional sectors of the working class, but also "liberal" professionals, middle ranking layers, etc. In Tunis, scientists and other personnel at the City of Sciences also decided to occupy the installations until the director is removed. Thousands of workers in culture and the arts (artists, theatre workers, cinema technicians, writers, etc) gathered on Saturday night outside the National Theatre to demand the resignation of the government and pay tribute to the martyrs of the revolution.

Meanwhile, in Siliana, where the revolutionary people have created local and regional councils and decided to take power, a mass demonstration on Saturday marched on the regional governor's office. The governor had to be whisked away under the protection of the Army and the masses proceeded to occupy the governorate building. With their actions they proved that their statements were serious and that they meant business. Siliana is now under the control of the revolutionary people. We recommend all our readers watch the video footage of this glorious episode of the Tunisian revolution[23].

"Liberation Caravan"

After a week of regional strikes and mass demonstrations against the government, a growing feeling of anger and frustration was developing among sections of the movement. They could feel that Ghannouchi's government was stealing the revolution from the workers and youth and that something was needed to put an end to it.

The initiative came from the revolutionary youth in Sidi Bouzid, which quickly spread throughout the country. They have organised a "Liberation Caravan" that has marched on the capital with the aim of "overthrowing the government". At first the march was supposed to walk all the way to Tunis, but the youth got impatient and they decided to drive, in order to get there faster. By Sunday afternoon, some 1000 youth from Sidi Bouzid, Regueb and other towns and cities from the interior had arrived in the capital and camped in the yard outside the Kasbah, the site of the Prime Minister's office. "The Kasbah is the Bastille of Tunis, and we will bring it down as the French sans-culottes destroyed the Bastille in 1789," said one of the demonstrators. Another added: "We have overthrown Ben Ali, but we have not yet overthrown his system."

The sit-in was in clear violation of the curfew imposed by the government, but there was not much the police or the army could do at that point. There were reports of similar caravans coming from other towns and cities in the country, but also of movements by the Army to stop them, even leading to clashes. On Sunday evening, protesters from Borj Cedra and Soliman, South of Tunis, were blocked by the Army when they were on their way to the capital, but it seems that after some wrangling they were allowed through. On the same day, the army

---

23 Available online here: http://www.facebook.com/video/video.php?v=148782311842966

attempted to stop three buses and a number of cars leaving the mining city of Gafsa for the capital. After the youth threatened to go back to Gafsa and declare a general strike, the army allowed them through. A similar situation developed in Kasserine, when the army also blocked the caravan leaving for the capital and even fired warning shots against the crowd. After some struggle the youth fought their way through.

Early this morning (Monday 24th), there were clashes between the police and the protesters outside the Prime Minister's building. The army and the police had cordoned off the Kasbah. According to some reports, the Army put itself between the protesters and the police and broke up the skirmishes with warning shots in the air.

We can see in these skirmishes how the government is already testing the ground, trying to reassert its authority and seeing how strong the movement is and how much they can use the forces of repression against it. So far, all the reports of mostly minor clashes between the Army and the police and the revolutionary people have ended up with the masses imposing their will.

It is crucial that the revolutionary committees, which have already sprung up in the neighbourhoods, cities and regions, should establish close links with the rank and file soldiers, encourage them to set up their own committees for revolutionary vigilance. The same should be done with police officers setting up trade unions.

This situation of dual power between the government and the streets cannot last indefinitely. What is lacking is a clear leadership of the movement. A nationwide general strike, the coordination of the revolutionary committees and the formation of soldiers' committees could very rapidly lead to the overthrow of the government of Ghannouchi and its replacement by a genuine revolutionary government to convene a constituent assembly. It is not ruled out that the UGTT, under enormous pressure from below, might be forced to call such a general strike.

Mass demonstrations have taken place again today, Monday, in most cities. In Regueb and Sidi Bouzid it was a women's march this time, while in the mining city of Gafsa students and teachers marched together against the government. A massive demonstration took place in Kef as well.

But the question still remains: who is to replace the current government? A national assembly of elected representatives from the revolutionary committees and from the workplace and local unions could elect a government trusted by the revolutionary people. Failing that there are different options opening up.

There have already been intense rumours of a new government being set up on the initiative of "trusted" political figures from the past who might still command certain legitimacy and who are not directly tainted by association with Ben Ali. There has been talk of a "Committee for the Channelling of the Revolution" being set up by people from the Bourguiba era, such as Ahmed Mestiri, Ahmed

Bensalah and Mostafa El Filali, who are already holding talks with "NGOs, civil society organizations and the UGTT".

A political analyst who defends the current government has "warned" that the alternative to this is the Army stepping in: "With the continuation of the people's marches, organized by the left wing of the UGTT, we will end up with an '18 Brumaire à la Tunisienne' with calls for the army to take power." This cannot be ruled out, and it is probably one of the reasons why the Army high command has, so far, kept a low profile and cultivated an image of itself as an institution that is on the side of the people.

At the moment, however, the balance of forces is extremely favourable to the revolution. Real power is in the hands of the masses "on the streets". The state has been enormously weakened, with the rank and file soldiers and police sympathising with the mass movement. The government pleads with the masses, begs the masses to allow it to govern. But the movement marches on relentlessly. Everywhere, in the offices, the factories, on the TV, radio and in newspaper offices, the workers have taken control.

In these conditions there is no force that could stop the Tunisian workers and youth from taking power. It is there for the taking. What is missing is a party of the working class that is prepared to lead all the oppressed layers of society in completing the revolution. A general strike of all workers with the taking over of all factories and offices, a strike of the university and school students with the occupation of all schools and universities, combined with an appeal to the rank and file soldiers and police, would sweep aside all the remnants of the old Ben Ali regime.

Unless this is done, the Tunisian ruling elite will reorganise behind other, less tainted, figures. They will even push to one side the present farcical government if that is what it takes to appease the masses. They will bring on board opposition figures, even people who have been in exile, as long as these new politicians accept the continued existence of capitalism in Tunisia. For as long as this rotten, corrupt elite manages to hold on to the key economic levers in the country, they will be able to play for time and prepare a comeback in more favourable conditions in the future.

What is required is a clean break. Democracy yes, but with it must come the expropriation of this elite. That is the only way of making sure they never come back. What is lacking is a clear leadership which would raise such a perspective and settle the matter decisively in favour of the revolutionary masses, brushing to one side this government and with it the remains of the old regime.

Monday, 24 January 2011

FOR A NATIONAL GENERAL STRIKE AGAINST THE GHANNOUCHI GOVERNMENT!

Jorge Martín

Wednesday, January 26 was marked by yet more massive demonstrations throughout Tunisia against the "national unity" government, whose key ministers come from the government of the hated dictator Ben Ali. The masses forced him to flee two weeks ago, but his ministers are still in power.

The regional structures of the UGTT had called for general strikes in Sfax, El Kef, Sidi Bouzid, Jendouba, Kairouan, Siliana, Gabés, Nabeul and others. The strikes and mobilizations had a common slogan and a united aim: to bring down the government, which the masses correctly consider simply a continuation of the hated RCD regime of Ben Ali.

A government suspended in mid-air

Meanwhile, in the capital, thousands of youth, arrived from all corners of the country as part of the Caravan for Liberation, were still camped outside the government buildings. Attempts by the riot police on Monday and Tuesday to remove them had failed. General Rachid Ammar, the Chief of Staff of the Tunisian Army, who was removed by Ben Ali for refusing to use the army against the revolutionary movement, also attempted to get the demonstrators to clear the way and allow the government to work. Using the enormous authority that the Army and he have gained by appearing to be on the side of the people against Ben Ali, he addressed the crowd.

He told them that their demands were justified and gave them guarantees that the Army would defend their revolution. He also gave them assurances that the Army "would respect the constitution" (though he did not say which one) and asked them, politely, to leave: "I would love it if this place was to be emptied, so that the government can work". Without appearing to be too close to the current government of Ghannouchi (the former Prime Minister under Ben Ali), he also added that inside the government compound that the demonstrators have been surrounding since Sunday "there are not only Ministers, but also functionaries who are attempting to make the country work".

And then he added an ominous warning: "your movement can be manipulated by other elements, to create a vacuum of power, and when there is a vacuum of power, the Army would have to intervene". Neither nice polite words, nor veiled threats worked. The crowd applauded, ecstatically; sang the national anthem, praised the army general whom they see as having sided with the revolution... but remained solidly in the Kasbah esplanade, blocking the government building. The revolutionary youth who have marched to the capital have a very clear idea of why they are there: "The battle will be decided in Tunis. This is the reason why we have come. The government must be overthrown. They are like a cancer, which needs to be cleaned out, not a shred can be left behind."

This really shows the enormous power of the revolutionary movement at the present time and the extremely favourable balance of forces. The Chief of Staff of the Army is forced to go and speak to the people directly and asks them to please go away and allow the government to work, and when they refuse there is nothing he can do. Who has power in Tunisia? The streets or the government and the state?

Inside, having entered through some back door, the council of ministers met and announced that there was going to be an "imminent government reshuffle". But the announcement never came. And 48 hours later, it still has not arrived. There were also rumours of a "Committee of the Wise" being formed, but nothing has yet come out of it. This really shows the enormous difficulties of the Tunisian ruling class (and their imperialist puppet masters) are encountering in finding a government which is acceptable to the masses and has some legitimacy. The revolutionary movement of the workers and youth prevents them from regaining full control of the situation.

On Tuesday we saw the first attempts of the counter-revolution to regroup. Gangs of thugs and militias from the RCD attacked union offices in Gafsa, Kasserine (West) Béja (North), Monastir and Mahdia (Centre). In the mining region of Gafsa a gang of men armed with sticks, knives and chains, attacked the offices of the regional union and injured a number of trade unionists present. The Army intervened, firing warning shots in the air and evicted them from the premises. Also in the capital Tunis, a demonstration had been called *in favour* of the national unity government. This was part of a growing media campaign "against strikes", "against chaos", against "disrupting the economy", and generally against "extremist elements within the UGTT". Showing the real balance of forces, the demonstration gathered about 200 people and was quickly dispersed by protesters against the government despite having heavy police protection. If the situation is not decisively resolved in favour of the workers and youth, then such demonstrations might grow and reaction can gain support in the streets. But at the present time, they are extremely weak.

Regional general strikes and mass demonstrations

It is in this context that the regional strikes are taking place today, Wednesday 26, and they could be crucial to force the downfall of the government. In the statement calling for the strike, the regional UGTT in Sfax made clear what were the aims of the movement: "After examining the general situation in the country and the latest political and social developments on light of our people's revolution, and what is being plotted against it by internal and external conspiracies aimed to circumvent its objectives and gains, we decided to start a general strike on Wednesday, January 26, 2011 in defence of the demands of our people *to overthrow the government of the former regime and to dissolve the Constitutional Democratic Rally."*

The Sfax strike, and the other regional strikes, are quite clearly *political general strikes for the overthrow of the government*, showing the revolutionary character of the movement of the Tunisian workers and the extremely advanced character of their demands.

Also very significant is the fact that the regional trade union structures and the revolutionary committees are increasingly taking over tasks of the administration of public and economic life. As well as the examples we have already mentioned in Siliana (where the regional revolutionary council has expelled the governor and effectively taken power) and Sidi Bou Ali, the Sfax UGTT also started to make decisions over the economy. The statement says: "from the keenness of the Regional Executive Bureau to provide basic and vital services to the citizens, we decide to exclude from the general strike the workers in the vital sectors especially hospitals and clinics, water and electricity, gas and bakeries, and municipalities graves, we also decided to secure trips from and to the Kerkennah islands."

So, not only the unions are calling a political strike to overthrow the existing government, but also they decided which sectors of the workers will continue to work under their authority in order to guarantee basic essential services. This is an answer to all those who cry and shout about "chaos" and "disruption". As a matter of fact it is precisely workers' power, workers' control, which can guarantee order, but revolutionary order, not capitalist order. This was already demonstrated by the setting up of neighbourhood self-defence committees to maintain order against the RCD and police gangs.

The demonstration in Sfax, the country's second largest city and the most important industrial centre was huge, of historic proportions. Some reports talked of 100,000 demonstrators, and even the bourgeois media put the figure at "over 50,000". The mood was extremely radical and angry as can be seen in these videos.

Amongst the slogans which the demonstrators chanted were: "the people want to bring down the government", "Tunisia is free – RCD Out!", "Tunisia is Free – Down with the government!" and showing a great awareness of the international repercussion of the Tunisian revolution: "Thawra hatta'l nasr (revolution until victory) – from Tunis to Cairo". Another slogan that was heard on the demo was "Tunisia is Arabic – No foreign tutelage" and "Tunisia is Arabic – no American tutelage," in opposition to the visit of US Assistant Secretary of State for Near East Affairs, Jeffrey D. Feltman, who is currently in Tunisia. Many suspect that the US had a hand in the way in which Ben Ali was replaced by a government packed with his own ministers and there is a deep felt anti-imperialist anger at the continuing US behind the scenes meddling to abort the revolution. The demonstration ended with an appeal by the regional UGTT for the demonstrators to march on Tunis on Thursday 27, to join the Caravan of Liberation for the overthrow of the government. That is also the day fixed by the secondary teachers' union for their national strike.

Similar mass demonstrations took place in towns and cities around the country, including Nabeul, Kairouan, Djerba, Kelibia, as well as in Tunis, where there were clashes with the police and the presence of provocateurs from the RCD.

The situation, as we have been stressing for some time, is one where the workers and youth could take power relatively easily. The government is suspended in mid-air, forced to enter its own meeting rooms through the back door, not able to use either the Army or the police to crush the movement and looking desperately for a way forward. One final push on the part of the revolutionary movement would bring it down. A nation-wide general strike combined with workplace occupations and a march on the capital could topple the current weak government. An appeal to the Army ranks and to the police officers wanting to set up a union would paralyse the effective force of the capitalist state.

Down with the government! But what is the alternative?

However, in order to bring down the government an answer needs to be provided to the question: what to put in its place. Here is where there is more confusion and this confusion and lack of leadership has prevented the movement from taking power so far.

The legal opposition parties are part of the current government and they have no authority amongst the masses, as they played no role whatsoever in the revolution and stayed with Ben Ali right until the end. The former Communist Party (Ettijdad) is probably the worst of all. Having conditioned its participation in the government on there not being any RCD linked ministers, then stayed in the government anyway and went on to organise rallies and campaign in favour of it! They must subscribe to the Groucho Marx version of Marxism, based on the motto: "Those are my principles, and if you don't like them... well, I have others"!

The leadership of the UGTT, the Executive Bureau, was also in favour of participating in the government and was forced by the more radical forces in the Central Administration Council (the Central Committee) to withdraw its ministers and later on to call for action to overthrow the government. As I write, the EB of the UGTT is conducting frantic negotiations at the UGTT national headquarters with all sorts of liberal figures, human rights advocates, lawyers, etc, to put together a proposal for a new government which they will then present to the interim president Foued Mebazaa for his approval! This is parliamentary cretinism of the worst sort. The executive of the UGTT is under enormous pressure from below, from the revolutionary workers and youth to lead the struggle for the overthrow of the current government. However, instead of bringing it down through action, the UGTT leadership wants to ask the current government, politely, to appoint a new one!

But even amongst the most advanced elements of the revolutionary left in the UGTT and also in the smaller left wing political parties which were illegal until very recently, there seems to be no clear idea of what or how to replace the Ghannouchi government.

The general strike call of the Sfax UGTT talks of "replacing it with a national salvation government in which enemies of our people are excluded." This is a very good slogan, and one that is similar to that of the recently formed *14th of January Front*, which talks of "an interim government which enjoys the confidence of the people, of the militant progressive political, social, and trade-union forces, and of the youth." The 14th of January Front has been formed mainly by the Party of Tunisian Communist Workers (PCOT), the Tunisian Patriotic and Democratic Labour Party, and some smaller left wing, Nasserite and left Arab nationalist currents.

The declaration of the 14th of January Front correctly talks about the need to widen the scope of the committees: "The Front hails all the committees, associations, and forms of popular self-organization and invites them to widen their sphere of intervention to all that concerns the conduct of public affairs and various aspects of everyday life."

Basically it is calling the revolutionary committees to take power, to become real soviets. What is missing is the crucial aspect of the need to link them up at a local, regional and national level, thus becoming the basis for dual power *nationally*, not only at a local or regional level as it is already the case in some places.

Amongst the organizations in the Front is the recently created Left Workers League, which on January 24 issued a statement calling for "achieving a Constituent and a people's democratic workers government, with a social and economic programme which puts an end to the neo-liberal approach imposed by world capital." This is clearly a more advanced demand, as it defines that the new government should be a workers' government, a democratic government and a people's government. The formulation is a bit confused, but if what is meant is that there should be a government that responds to the interests of the revolutionary masses of the working people who have made this revolution, then, there is no objection.

But, how is such a government to be formed? In our opinion a revolutionary government cannot be based on any of the institutions of the old regime, but should be set up on the basis of the existing revolutionary committees and councils, the regional trade union structures and workers' committees in the workplaces. A national assembly of delegates from these bodies should be convened in the capital, taking advantage of the presence of the revolutionary youth from all provinces. They should elect, amongst themselves, a provisional revolutionary government of national salvation to convene a constituent assembly within the shortest space of time possible.

In the same way that the revolutionary left within the UGTT has imposed its withdrawal from the Ghannouchi government and the call for its overthrow, they should force the CC of the UGTT to adopt such a program for a national salvation government based on the revolutionary committees.

Down with the dictatorship and the capitalist system it served

The 14th of January Front also calls for the expropriation of "the former ruling family, their close relations and associates, and all the civil servants who used their positions to grow rich at the expense of the people," as well as "to renationalise those institutions which have been privatized". These demands are absolutely correct, and as a matter of fact, the expropriation of the properties of the Trabelsi clan and all those associated to it would go a long way in giving such a government control over the key levers of the economy. If you added to that the properties of all imperialist powers which supported and benefited from the Ben Ali regime, then you would have abolished capitalism in Tunisia. However the Front does not go all the way in calling for a break with capitalism and instead talks of the need "to formulate an economic and social policy which breaks with the liberal capitalist approach", as if there was another approach to capitalism which would be nicer to the workers and the people.

It has to be said clearly that the ruling class is already extremely worried about the revolutionary movement of the workers encroaching on the sacred right of private property. This is how a business magazine described the situation: "The Tunisian revolution has entered like a storm in the companies and public institutions. Directors are being chased away in parking lots and workers collectives are moving into self-management mode".

The article continues: "Tunisian workers, in companies and public institutions have brought the revolution to their workplaces" and "directors and managers of public companies have had to run seeking refuge, followed by a crowd of vindictive workers". It concludes: "the hope of the government and the businessmen is that the movement will limit itself to those corrupt functionaries linked to the Ben Ali-Trabelsi clan. But it is not certain that this will be the case."

If there was a serious appeal on the part of the trade union left, for workers to occupy the workplaces and implement workers' control, such a movement would spread like wildfire. There are already instances where the workers have demanded the opening of the books of their companies in order to investigate the corrupt dealings of the Trabelsi clan. The workers at the tax office have kicked out their directors and taken over the dossiers which shed light into some of those. The potential is there for a movement which not only sweeps away the whole of the undemocratic state apparatus of the dictatorship, but also does away with the capitalist economic system it served.

Down with the national unity government!
- For a national general strike!
- For a revolutionary government based on the committees and the trade unions!
- For a revolutionary constituent assembly! For a revolutionary socialist Tunisia!
- For a Socialist Federation of the Arab World, with full democratic rights to all ethnic, national and religious minorities!

Wednesday, 26 January 2011

REJECT THE GOVERNMENT RESHUFFLE, THE REVOLUTIONARY PEOPLE MUST TAKE POWER

Jorge Martín

Finally, after a long wait, Prime Minister Ghannouchi announced changes in the government of national unity which was formed in Tunisia after the overthrow of Ben Ali. The masses of workers and youth, for two weeks, have been demanding the overthrow of this government, which they consider as a continuation of the old regime. They have staged massive regional strikes and demonstrations and a sit-in outside the government's office. This new government of Ghannouchi must also be rejected and the people take power into their own hands.

The reason why it took so long for the composition of the new government to be announced was the extreme weakness of the ruling class when faced with the mass revolutionary movement of the people. They needed to find a government which would be accepted by the masses, and above all, which the UGTT national leadership would be able to sell to its ranks.

The composition of the new government is designed to *appear* as fundamental change, by removing the majority of ministers who were part of Ben Ali's last government, but in reality to change nothing fundamentally. The ministers of Foreign Affairs (who resigned during the discussions), Interior, Finances and Defence are removed and the new cabinet is stacked with "technocratic" figures and "independent businessmen". In total, the number of ministers from the last Ben Ali government is down, from 7 to 3. However, three of Ben Ali's ministers remain; the "new" minister of Defence had already been a minister of Ben Ali in the early 2000s, and above all, the hated Ghannouchi remains as Prime Minister.

What legitimacy do these people have to carry out any "transition to democracy"? What role did any of them play in revolution which overthrew Ben Ali? None. This is a transparent attempt of the ruling class (and the US and French imperialists behind the scenes) to present a "clean" government which can clear the masses from the streets and send them back to their homes and off the political arena. Ghannouchi himself was clear, as he announced the government reshuffle, when he appealed for Tunisians "to go back to work". The message was repeated by the bosses' organisation UTICA, which showed its full support for the government and appealed "to all economic forces to go back to work".

Significantly, the Central Committee of the UGTT trade union met in the evening, after the announcement to discuss what position to take regarding this new government. The body voted in favour of accepting this government and Ghannouchi as a prime minister, though the union itself would take no ministerial positions in it. The vote was 72 in favour, 11 against and 4 abstentions. Amongst those who voted against were 4 out of the 12 members of the Executive Bureau, as well as the representatives of primary and secondary teachers, health sector workers, postal and telecommunication workers, and also the regional structures of Sfax and Jendouba.

It is clear that the pressure on the trade union bureaucracy on the part of bourgeois public opinion was very strong. As we have reported before, the majority of the EB, headed by the general secretary Abdessalem Jerad, had in fact been loyal to Ben Ali right until the end. In the last few days all sorts of EU and US delegations have been in Tunis, and surely, part of their brief was to bring the UGTT leadership into line. Jerad has also announced that Ghannouchi is "prepared to meet with the demonstrators" who have been blocking his offices for the last week.

In the last couple of weeks there have already been strong voices calling for a cleansing of the UGTT of pro-RCD elements. Now these will grow even stronger. It is very unlikely that the UGTT leadership will be able to sell a government headed by Ghannouchi to the masses.

On Thursday, January 27, mass demonstrations and regional strikes took place again, demanding the overthrow of Ghannouchi's government of national unity. The focus was on Sidi Bouzid, where the regional UGTT had called a general strike. Like the day before in Sfax, the following was almost total and the demonstration was unprecedented both in size and militancy, with 20,000 participating.

Some of the slogans were: "Our march will continue, down with the RCD", "Neither French nor American (interference), Tunisians will not be underestimated or insulted" and "We mean it, we will kick the RCD gang out". Significantly, the crowd specifically attacked the so-called opposition parties which have been part of Ghannouchi's government from day one: "The PDP and Ettajdid betrayed the martyrs". The PDP started as a "Marxist-Leninist" party and Ettajdid (Renewal) is the former Communist Party, both members of Ben Ali's loyal "opposition". One of the banners clearly stated the aims of the masses: "The peoples' revolution has these demands: suspension of the Constitution, a Constituent Assembly, dissolution of Parliament and the RCD because they are not democratic and the formation of a government of national salvation".

As well as Sidi Bouzid, there were also marches in Bizerte, Tunisia, Kelibia, Mahdia (where teachers and students marched together), Monastir, Sousse, Sfax, where a regional strike had taken a day earlier, Kasserine, Tozeur, Gabes, El Kef, Siliana, where there was also a regional strike, Tataouine, Zarzis and many other cities and towns, including a large march in Tunis itself. Secondary education teachers also observed a national strike which had overwhelming support.

The 14th of January Front opposes the government reshuffle

Meanwhile, the recently formed January 14 Front issued a statement on January 28, rejecting the government reshuffle and calling for a National Conference for the Defence of the Revolution. Such a Conference would be composed of: "a) all the political parties, associations and trade union organizations and human rights, youth and cultural organizations and independent personalities, that sponsor the demands of the people's revolution and the struggle to achieve them; b) representatives of the forces created by the revolution in all parts of the country through the councils or committees or associations formed at the initiative of the masses; c) representatives of associations and organizations of the Tunisian immigration, which have resisted the dictatorship and supported the revolution in Tunisia."

The Conference would elect an "interim government" which would be task with "dissolving parliament and other bodies, dissolving the ruling party and its militia, expropriating its property and bringing to account those involved in economic and political crimes, dissolving the political police..." and above all "the preparation of elections for a Constituent Assembly" which would draft "a new constitution for the Republic of Tunisia civil, democratic and modern aspirations of the Tunisian people to liberty, equality and social justice and dignity."

This is clearly a step in the right direction, though, we would argue that the Conference should be composed of elected representatives from the revolutionary committees and trade unions, and any "independent personalities" should only be present if they are elected as delegates. This would ensure that the revolutionary workers and youth are properly represented, as opposed to the middle class liberals who played a little role in the revolution. It should also be pointed out that the revolution, in order to be carried out until the end, should not only create a "civil, democratic and modern" Tunisia, but also one that is free from exploitation, a socialist Tunisia.

The statements of the Front, probably inspired by its stronger component, the Tunisian Communist Workers Party (PCOT), still show a strong tendency to postpone the social tasks of the revolution to the future and concentrate merely on the democratic tasks. At the same time, they show illusions in all sorts of "independent personalities" and petty bourgeois elements.

In reality, the revolutionary workers and youth of Tunisia should trust no other forces than their own. They alone carried out the revolution, provided the martyrs, organized the regional strikes and mass demonstrations which brought Ben Ali down. They should now take power into their own hands, not only at a local and regional level as has already happened in some regions, but nationally.

The "new technocratic" government shows its real face

Today, Friday 28, there were repeated attempts to convince the revolutionary youth outside the Prime Minister's office to end the sit-in. According to reports we have received, delegations from the UGTT bureaucracy and the Lawyers' Association tried in vain to convince them to leave. They failed and the youth remained firm in their struggle *to clear out the old regime completely* and were not satisfied by cosmetic changes.

In the last few days, the state has used all the methods at its disposal to try to remove the revolutionary youth from the regions. They were offered money, drugs, agent provocateurs were sent, the Army generals, trade union bureaucrats and lawyers tried to convince them. But they all failed. So finally, the capitalist state showed again its ugly face. Today in the afternoon, as we write these lines, reports are coming in of the Army withdrawing and the anti-riot police brutally attacking the sit-in and dispersing the youth with batons and tear-gas canisters. They are now regrouping and are being joined by the local population in a big and angry demonstration. Appeals have been issued to the population of Tunis poor and working class neighbourhoods to come in the aid of the revolutionary youth.

The next few hours will be crucial. The response of the masses in the streets today and tomorrow will show whether the government change has worked in temporarily defusing the mass movement. Even if that is the case, the deep rooted social, economic and political grievances that this revolution has raised will not go away easily. The only way they can be solved is if the revolutionary people (the workers, the youth, the women, the poor peasants and the professionals who joined them in the streets) take power into their hands and completely uproot the old regime and all its institutions.

Friday, 28 January 2011

ONE MONTH SINCE THE OVERTHROW OF BEN ALI

Jorge Martín

Today marks one month since the revolutionary overthrow of the hated dictator Ben Ali in Tunisia on January 14. The last month has been a constant struggle between the ruling class which wants to return to bourgeois normality and workers and youth who carried out the revolution and who are struggling to stop the old regime from trying to make a comeback.

For nearly two weeks after January 14 the country saw a series of regional general strikes and mass demonstrations against the new Government of National Unity (GNU) of Ghannouchi. All the key ministers (Defence, Foreign Affairs, Prime Minister, President, Finances, Home Affairs, etc) of the GNU had been ministers under Ben Ali, many occupying the same positions.

The pressure from below forced the national leadership of the UGTT to withdraw from this government and its local structures played a key role in mobilising against it. The revolutionary youth from the regions marched on the capital Tunis on January 23 with the aim of speeding up the overthrow of the government of Ghannouchi. Once in the capital there was a march on the Prime Minister's office in the Kasbah where they set up camp, effectively preventing the GNU from working from its offices.

The wave of regional strikes reached its peak with the historic strike of Sfax, on January 26, when 100,000 marched through the streets of this industrial city, and also the unprecedented march of 20,000 in Sidi Bouzid on January 27. On the same day, a long awaited ministerial reshuffle was announced which removed from the GNU most of the ministers who had been members of Ben Ali's RCD, but left untouched the Prime Minister Ghannouchi and the President, both part of the Ben Ali regime.

However, this "new" government had to be ratified by the Administrative Council of the UGTT trade union, or it would have not even lasted 24 hours. Even though a majority of members voted in favour, federations and regional unions which represent a majority of the UGTT membership voted against and refused to recognise the government. These were the Union of Secondary School Educators, the Postal Workers Federation, the Public Heath Care Workers Union, the Union of Youth and Infant Care Workers, the Regional Federation of Sfax, the Regional Federation of Bizerte and the Regional Federation of Jendouba.

However, since no clear lead was given by anyone, the formal acceptance on the part of the UGTT leadership of the Ghannouchi government gave a certain room for manoeuvre, a degree of legitimacy which it did not possess before. It quickly used it, on January 28, by unleashing a brutal repression against the youth camped at the Kasbah esplanade, who were dispersed and sent back to their regions of origin.

Revolution is a war between the classes and as in a war between nations, leadership is crucial. Once the momentum is lost, it is difficult to regain it again. For two weeks, between January 14 and January 27, the GNU was suspended in mid-air. The revolutionary workers and youth could have taken power. This was graphically demonstrated on January 22 and 23 when the people marched on the Prime Minister's office and all that the officer in charge of the Army guarding the building could do was to ask them politely not to enter the premises. Police officers were demonstrating all over the country demanding their right to form a union. There would have been no force capable of stopping the revolutionary masses from taking power.

At that moment in time, in the context of regional general strikes and mass demonstrations, a new alternative Revolutionary Council, based on the local and regional councils and the local and regional structures of the trade unions, could have taken power, but there was no-one to actually carry it out.

It is true that the 14th of January Front, a coalition dominated by the formerly banned Tunisian Party of Communist Workers (PCOT), was firm in its opposition to the GNU and called for the committees to be strengthened at all levels. In a communiqué on January 28, after the government reshuffle and the vote at the UGTT Administrative Council, it even called for a National Conference for the Defence of the Revolution to elect a provisional government. But it never went as far as actually *convening* such a national congress of the committees, something that could have been done taking advantage of the presence in Tunis of the revolutionary youth from the provinces. This would have been possible *before* January 27, but more difficult *after* the GNU had gained legitimacy from the UGTT.

Even though many opportunities were missed, this is not to say that the revolutionary initiative of the masses has ebbed completely and that the Ghannouchi government is in control of the situation. On the contrary, the overthrow of Ben Ali has unleashed all the pent up frustrations of all sections of society. The revolution has changed their outlook with the mood being expressed by, "We are not afraid anymore." In addition, groups of workers and youth all over the country are taking direct action, with no respect for any established authority (which are after all just a leftover of the old regime). There was even talk of the Imams of the mosques wanting to set up a trade union!

In state owned companies, ministries and departments, workers organising through committees or through the union, have kicked out the old managers and in some cases have refused to accept the new ones appointed by the government which has then been forced to change them again. The civil servants at the Ministry of Foreign Affairs went on strike and organised sit-ins until they got the removal of the Minister Ahmed Ounaies, on February 13. It is clearly not a normal situation for the ruling class when the government appoints a minister and the workers at the ministry kick him out!

In many official media outlets, newspapers, TV and radio, the workers have organised and forced the removal of the managers and in varying degrees taken control over the editorial line. In one case, they even rejected the newly appointed manager as they had not been consulted.

On February 3, the government decided to appoint new regional governors. This was another important step towards bourgeois normalisation. The overthrow of Ben Ali had meant the complete collapse of state power in many towns and even some regions. Revolutionary committees and councils had taken over the running of public affairs. From the point of view of the ruling elite it was important to reassert the power of the capitalist state over them.

Revealing its true colours, 19 out of the 24 "new" governors were connected with the RCD and the old regime. This was too much of a provocation and it provoked a new wave of demonstrations and strikes in the regions, in some cases leading to the expulsion of the "new" governors (as in Gabès, Kebili, Zaghouan, Nabeul and Béja), often protected by the Army. In Redeyef (in the Gafsa mining basin) a general strike for a combination of political and economic demands paralysed the town. In Kasserine, El Kef and Kebili the clashes with the police and in some cases the army led to several demonstrators being killed – the first victims killed by the Ghannouchi government. In Zaghouan the revolutionary people expelled the local council. In all of these towns it is the committees for the defence of the revolution that have effective control over public order.

Once again, the government has been forced to withdraw its decision and on February 8 announced that a new set of governors would be appointed "in consultation with the UGTT"! This is unprecedented and it shows the real balance of forces, even today. The official government appoints governors, who are then rejected and expelled by the people, and the government has to go and negotiate with the trade unions the appointment of new acceptable governors. Who rules the country? The government of Ghannouchi or the revolutionary people? There are clearly elements of dual power still present in the situation in Tunisia.

The government was also forced to decree the dissolution of the RCD on February 7, another of the demands of the people, in a further attempt to appease the masses. At the same time, in order to deal with the question of its own legitimacy, Ghannouchi had to ask Parliament for powers to rule by decree. This is yet another provocation, as it means that the Parliament which gives Ghannouchi his powers is Ben Ali's Parliament, composed overwhelmingly of RCD deputies (the party which has just been disbanded!).

Clearly, while the government of Ghannouchi has taken some steps towards asserting its power, the situation is still very much in flux. All the economic and social grievances that gave rise to the revolutionary movement are still present, and they cannot really be solved under capitalism. A foreign diplomat warned that, "The people have shown great maturity, but they could descend onto the streets again".

An article in AFP aptly summarises the situation of revolutionary ferment which is still present in Tunisia: "From north to south, the country has become for the last two weeks a permanent demonstration: sudden strikes, wildcat stoppages, daily demonstrations by employees and the unemployed who yell demands silenced for more than a quarter of a century. Every day the national TV brings from the provinces images of the angry cries of misery and distress."

The government can only rule by relying on the UGTT leadership. It has just announced "national negotiations on a wide range of social issues". UGTT leader Abid Briki warned that these negotiations were in the interest of the government because otherwise it risked "a social explosion". What the government really needs is for the UGTT to police the growing wave of strikes. The UGTT leaders, headed by Abdesselem Jerad (who was a loyal supporter of Ben Ali until the very last minute) would be quite happy to fulfil that role, if they could. Jerad was on national TV asking his members to be patient, to "delay" their demands and above all, to "coordinate all their actions with the national leadership". As a matter of fact, the UGTT national leaders do not lead this movement, they never have. Briki admits that they do not "coordinate or organise all of these strikes ... the UGTT has been overtaken by these social movements".

The leadership of the UGTT itself is contested, with regular demonstrations outside its central headquarters in Tunis demanding the democratisation of the union and the removal of Jerad and his accomplices because of his collaboration with Ben Ali. In one of these demonstrations Jilali Hammami, general secretary of the postal workers explains: "All those involved in class collaboration with the old regime, who have sold out the blood of the martyrs, must go. We demand a genuine trade union democracy and a militant trade union at the service of the working class. We will not allow counter-revolutionary forces to steal the revolution."

A commentator in a business newspaper compared the situation to the French Popular Front and the wave of strikes of 1936 in France. "Who is at the helm?" he asked. His conclusion was that Tunisia needed her own Maurice Thorez, the French Stalinist leader of the PCF who "had the courage to bring the strikes to a halt". The problem for the ruling class is that the Tunisian Thorez's of the former communist party Ettajdid have been widely discredited for their collaboration with Ben Ali. They are actually part of the Ghannouchi government and were from the very beginning. The Thorezs of this world are only useful to the ruling class if they are actually able to keep the working masses under control. This is clearly not the case in Tunisia.

One month after the revolutionary overthrow of Ben Ali, the Tunisian revolution has only started. The only thing missing is a revolutionary leadership with a clear understanding of the tasks ahead. The workers and youth have shown enormous courage and given nearly 300 of its finest representatives to the cause of the radical social and political transformation of the county. All these sacrifice must not be in vain. The process will have its ebbs and flows, but the fundamental contradictions which brought about this revolution cannot be solved within the limits of capitalism. The most advanced elements need to understand that and stand firmly on a programme of workers' power and international socialism, the only way to complete the Tunisian revolution which has started.

The words of the mother of one of the martyrs in Kasserine sums it up: "We're watching events, but if nothing real changes in people's lives here – no equality, no opportunities, no chance to work, the stranglehold of the RCD party – we'll stage a new revolution."

Monday, 14 February 2011

THE SECOND WAVE OF THE TUNISIAN REVOLUTION: DOWN WITH GHANNOUCHI — ALL POWER TO THE REVOLUTIONARY PEOPLE

Jorge Martín

Hundreds of thousands marched today in the streets of the main cities and towns of Tunisia against the Ghannouchi government and demanding a Constituent Assembly. According to the revolutionary youth which has taken the initiative of these demonstrations, 250,000 marched in the capital Tunis alone, and another 100,000 in other cities[24]. A police source in Tunis gave the figure for demonstrators in the capital at "over 100,000". The Red Crescent said that this was "the largest demonstration since the fall of Ben Ali".

The demonstrators marched through Bourghiba Avenue and to the Kasbah Esplanade, outside the offices of the Prime Minister. As a matter of fact, Ghannouchi has had to move to the presidential Palace of Carthage, chased by the constant demonstrations of the revolutionary youth, the workers, the unemployed and so on. A massive banner headed the rally with the following slogan: "Sit-in until the dissolution of the government". The main slogans shouted by the masses were; "Ghannouchi, dégage" (Ghannouchi out), "RCD dégage", "Enough farces", "Shame on this Government". Revealing the internationalist character of the movement there were also shouts of "Thawra Tunis, Thawra Masr, thawra thawra hatta'l nasr" ("Revolution in Tunis, Revolution in Egypt, Revolution until Victory") and in support of the Libyan revolution against Gaddafi.

This is an extraordinary resurgence of the movement which shows that the enormous revolutionary upsurge, which overthrew the hated Ben Ali on January 14, has not dissipated. Immediately after the revolutionary people had achieved that first victory, which cost the lives of many martyrs, the ruling class and the politicians of the old regime started to plot behind the scenes in order to make sure that although the dictator had gone the regime would remain untouched.

In reality, the problem that the ruling class in Tunisia faced with — and still faces — is that Ben Ali was not just a dictator, but his family clan completely dominated all aspects of life and particularly large parts of the economy. A thorough democratic cleansing of the old regime represents a threat to the whole of the capitalist system.

---

24 See video of demonstration in Sfax http://www.facebook.com/video/video.php?v=10150147 617422174&oid=147972581925535

First of all they created a "new" government of national unity where all the key ministers were Ben Ali ministers, adding a few official "left" opposition parties, one blogger and a few trade union figures to give it some legitimacy. Showing a sharp revolutionary instinct the masses did not fall for this. Within 24 hours, pressure from below forced the UGTT trade union to withdraw from this farce of a government. A series of massive regional general strikes forced Ghannouchi to remove the majority of RCD ministers from the government on January 27 and then announce the dissolution of the RCD itself.

The UGTT bureaucracy then accepted this government. Again, the masses did not fall for that. Ghannouchi was still the Prime Minister but he was also a prominent representative of the old regime. To add insult to injury, his government appointed new regional governors in order to wrest power away from the different revolutionary committees which had emerged during the revolution and which had, in effect, taken power in the regions. Of these 24 "new" governors 19 had links to the old regime! Mass demonstrations against them forced them to flee under Army protection.

These mobilisations were combined with a wave of strikes, wildcat walkouts, the physical removal of managers and directors linked to Ben Ali in state owned companies and ministries. The removal of Ben Ali opened up the lid for all the pent up frustration which had been accumulating for decades. The UGTT bureaucracy was unable to stop this wave of strikes, despite repeated public appeals by its general secretary Abdessalem Jerad, who had been a Ben Ali loyalist right until the end. He even went as far as to say that those calling the strikes were "agents of the RCD, intent on causing chaos" and threatened to take action against those trade union federations who did not follow the back-to-work instructions!

The Tunisian revolution started with a combination of democratic, social and economic slogans. The revolutionary youth, who sparked the movement, were fighting for jobs, bread, against repression and for dignity. The removal of Ben Ali was a first victory of the movement, but they now want solutions to their demands. Empty talk about a new constitution drafted by a panel of experts, rebuilding the country all together and so-called Committees for the Protection of the Revolution will not give them jobs or bread. What makes them particularly angry is that all the symbols of the old regime are still in place, starting with the president Ghannouchi who on February 20 declared that all demonstrations would be banned.

On February 20 there was a massive demonstration by tens of thousands who again marched to the Kasbah where a large number of youth decided to organise a new sit-in. Their demands are clear: a clean break with the old regime, the dismissal of the Ghannouchi government and a Constituent Assembly elected by the people to decide the future of the country.

In order to once again try to divert the attention of the masses, the UGTT corrupt leaders, together with "left" legal parties and "civil society" associations, were putting pressure on for the formation of a "Council for the Protection of the Revolution". Despite its grand sounding name, which was designed to attempt to fool the masses, the aim of such a committee was clear: to "give the new government its legitimacy", according to the leader of the Democratic Forum for Labour and Liberties (FDTL – legal opposition under Ben Ali) Khalil Zaouia. The question that arises is this: Who is going to make up such a committee and who is going to elect its members? The idea of the UGTT and FDTL leaders was to exercise some sort of supervision over the Ghannouchi government in order to make the masses think that their interests were being protected. Incredibly, the leaders of the 14th of January Front went along with this idea despite the fact that these Councils included organisations which accept the Ghannouchi government and even accepted the inclusion of the Islamist right wing party Ennahdha in it.

Immediately, all government parties rejected such an idea. There is already a government, they argued, so why should there be another body above it or next to it to supervise its work. The main problem remains unsolved from the point of view of the ruling class: neither the government nor the Committee or Council have any legitimacy amongst the masses, particularly because they are completely unable to solve any of the urgent demands of the masses who carried out the revolution.

The 14th of January Front, a coalition of left wing and left nationalist organisations, the main component of which is the Tunisian Communist Workers 'Party (PCOT), has been unable to channel the growing anger against the Ghannouchi government. Although the Front has an advanced programme, which demands the downfall of the government, a constituent assembly, the expropriation of the representatives of the old regime and a national revolutionary convention, it has failed to take any initiative to actually organise a movement to fight for these demands. The Front even had a massive rally on February 12, with 8,000 in attendance – a very impressive and enthusiastic meeting – but it was just a rally where nothing was decided, nothing was proposed.

The 14th of January Front has threatened to call a national convention in defence of the revolution. Such a body, if made up of elected representatives from the revolutionary committees in the different towns, regions, workplaces and schools, could lay the basis for a revolutionary government representing the real will of the people. However, the Front, and the PCOT as its strongest force, has just *talked* about it, rather than actually *convening* such a meeting. Alma Allende, who has been sending regular chronicles from the revolution, related the following incident. On February 20, when tens of thousands filled the Kasbah and started the new sit-in, two members of the Front arrived "to find out who had organised the occupation." "Reality moves faster than us," admitted Front members. This is a sorry state of affairs. A genuine communist party must prove it is worthy of its name by providing *leadership* for the masses. Having the right slogans is an important part of leadership, but in a revolutionary situation a communist organisation must also give practical leadership.

What is most amazing is that in this situation, faced with the attempts of all legal political parties to fool the masses through different tricks, and the failure of the anti-government left to offer any practical alternative, the revolutionary people have maintained such a level of mobilisation. This shows an extremely high level of consciousness on the part of the Tunisian workers and revolutionary youth.

Starting with the reoccupation of the Kasbah on February 20, a new wave of demonstrations has swept Tunisia. The participation of the youth has been key, especially high school students who day after day have come out in their tens of thousands, providing the backbone of the movement. All this work of leafleting, fly-posting, word of mouth, coordination over Facebook and Twitter (with groups like Takriz playing a key role) has culminated in the massive demonstration today. The demonstrations have affected the whole country and during the week there have been almost daily protests in Gabés, Ben Guerden, Monastir, Sfax, Redeyef, Kairouan, Sousse, Djerba and many other places.

The mood against Ghannouchi as a representative of the old regime is widespread and deep-rooted. An opinion poll on February 24 showed that 50.6 per cent of the population were dissatisfied with the government (and only 33 per cent had a favourable opinion). The same poll showed that 62 per cent of the people put unemployment at the top of their list of worries. Even more revealing was the fact that more than 83 per cent do not identify with any of the existing parties! This shows the extent of the discrediting of all the parties that were legal under Ben Ali, as people quite rightly identify them as part of his regime.

It is interesting to note that the Islamic party Ennahdha was only supported by 3.1 per cent of the people in this poll, demolishing the idea promoted by bourgeois commentators that in these countries it was a case of supporting pro-Western dictators in order to prevent the rise of Islamic fundamentalism to power. On Saturday, February 19th, there was also a large demonstration with a strong presence of women defending the secular character of Tunisian society.

The mobilisation today was impressive, but the question arises: what next? The overthrow of Ben Ali was not carried out just by mass demonstrations, but with massive strikes in every region. The same was the case when the revolutionary movement forced the removal of many of the RCD ministers. Mass demonstrations will probably not be enough to bring down Ghannouchi. They need to be linked to regional strikes, culminating in a national strike, which brings to the fore the question: "Who rules the country: the illegitimate government or the revolutionary people?"

The fact that the UGTT leadership accepted the second Ghannouchi government should not fool us. Regional federations and national unions which represent a majority of the UGTT voted against the decision. It is the task of revolutionary trade union militants at all levels of the union to force a reversal of that decision and also to start the task of cleansing the UGTT itself of agents of the old regime, starting with Jerad himself.

Another important question that needs to be answered is: if the government falls what is going to replace it? The revolutionary committees which already exist need to be strengthened, spread to every neighbourhood, workplace, school and university, give themselves fully democratic structures and functioning, and link up at local, regional and national level through elected and recallable representatives. In the current conditions, the convening of a national assembly of delegates from the revolutionary committees could be the basis for a provisional revolutionary council which could be tasked with convening a democratic and revolutionary Constituent Assembly. Such an assembly would be able to decide the future of the country in a fully democratic way, sweeping aside all the structures of the old regime.

These revolutionary committees, as is already the case in many places, should be in charge of running everyday life and all public affairs (service delivery, public order, mobilisation, information, etc.). In other words, the committees, as the only legitimate representatives of the Tunisian people, need to take power and remove the illegitimate government of Ghannouchi.

The task of the revolutionary reorganisation of Tunisian society should start with the confiscation of the wealth and property of the Trabelsi clan and the re-nationalisation of all the companies privatised by the Ben Ali regime. This wealth should be put under democratic workers' control and could provide the basis for a massive plan of public works, the building of hospitals, schools, roads and infrastructure, which would start to address the problems of unemployment and poverty.

The Tunisian revolution has already served as an inspiration for the revolutionary wave which is sweeping the whole of the Arab world. If it manages to remove not only the dictator but also the whole edifice of the capitalist system he served, then its example would be followed by the millions of workers and youth who are finally removing the chains of exploitation and oppression which have shackled them for decades and centuries.

- Down with Ghannouchi!
- Down with the old regime!
- Revolutionary cleansing of the UGTT!
- General strike and mass demonstrations!
- For a national convention of the revolutionary committees to elect a provisional revolutionary council!
- A Revolutionary Constituent Assembly!
- All power to the revolutionary people!

The latest news from Tunisia is that after the massive demonstrations today, the Ghannouchi government has announced that there will be elections "at the latest in mid-July". This is yet another attempt to defuse the movement of the revolutionary workers and youth. The current government has no legitimacy to call elections. Before there can be any genuine democratic elections all the institutions of the old regime must be brushed aside. The Tunisian workers and youth have the right to decide what kind of regime they want to give themselves, through a democratically elected revolutionary constituent assembly. While waving the elections carrot in one hand, in the other hand the Ghannouchi government has also used the stick, sending in the police (the same police force of Ben Ali) to fire tear gas canisters against the demonstrators outside the Ministry of Interior and the army to fire warning shots.

Friday, 25 February 2011

THE NEW GOVERNMENT OF EL SEBSI FORCED TO MAKE CONCESSIONS

Jorge Martín

On Monday, March 7, Tunisia's new Prime Minister Beji Caid el Sebsi announced the composition of his government, the third since the overthrow of Ben Ali by the revolutionary uprising of the people on January 14. El Sebsi himself only came to power on February 27, after the resignation of Mohamed Ghannouchi, who had been Ben Ali's prime minister and continued in the same role after his overthrow.

Ghannouchi's resignation came as a result of the pressure of mass demonstrations throughout the country which culminated in huge rallies in Tunis on February 25, 26 and 27, the largest since the fall of the Ben Ali. When demonstrators attempted to enter the building of the hated Ministry of the Interior they were met with brutal repression on the part of the police leading to at least five protesters being killed and hundreds arrested.

The resignation of Ghannouchi was followed by the resignation of a number of his ministers, including representatives of Ben Ali's legal opposition parties Ahmed Ibrahim (from Ettajdid, the former Communist Party) and Ahmed Néjib Chebbi (from the PDP), who had been providing the national unity government with a left cover. These parties are widely despised by the masses that see them as having collaborated with Ben Ali until the last minute only to then join a "unity" government dominated by Ben Ali's ministers. Under pressure from the masses other ministers also resigned, including most of those in charge of the economic portfolios, businessman Elyes Jouini, Ben Ali's minister for privatization Mohamed Nouri Jouini, and Mohamed Afif Chelbi who had also been involved in Ben Ali's economic policy.

There is an open struggle in Tunisia between the revolutionary masses, who are pushing forward, and the ruling class which is trying to contain the movement within the safe limits of bourgeois democracy. So far, the balance of forces remains favourable to the masses, which have been forcing concession after concession. First it was the removal of all ministers from the old ruling party from Ghannouchi's government. Then it was the dissolution of the RCD itself. The masses also threw out the regional governors appointed by the government. The workers expelled managers linked to the old regime from companies and government institutions. Finally, the revolutionary workers and youth brought down Ghannouchi himself and many of his ministers.

The bringing in of el Sebsi is a ploy to put a more acceptable figure at the head of the attempt to restore bourgeois normality and put an end to the revolutionary fervour of the masses. El Sebsi, a lawyer, was a minister under Bourguiba and is presented as having had little to do with the Ben Ali regime.

In the current conditions in Tunisia, he can only rule by appearing to be making concessions to the masses. His first decision after announcing the composition of his government was that of the dissolution of the hated political police and the directorate of state security, the two bodies most responsible for repression under the old regime. At the same time, he announced that instead of presidential elections, as originally planned, there would be elections to a Constituent Assembly on July 24. Mr. Caid el Sebsi asserted that all those responsible for crimes under the old regime would be brought to justice, starting with Ben Ali himself, who had committed the crime of "high treason," not to mention all the key figures of the old system. He added that he "understood" the feelings of those youth who had organized the sit-in at the Kasbah.

Sebsi is forced to tread carefully, insisting his is also a "government of continuity", and, in fact, the crucial defence, interior, justice and foreign-affairs ministers remain in their posts. He insisted that what was needed was to "re-establish security, which is the key to solve all of our other problems", since, he said, "without security there will be no development". The main priority of his government, he said, would be "work conditions, productivity, efficiency and the continuity of the state". In other words, he wants the restoration of normal capitalist order in the field of the economy, putting an end to the "nuisance" of constant strikes, wildcat walk-outs, workers demanding the resignation of managers, etc., and also the restoration of the normal capitalist order within the state, putting an end to these constant sit-ins, demonstrations, demands, the rule of revolutionary committees and trade unions, etc.

If one looks more closely at the composition of this "technocratic" government, we can see clearly whose interests it represents: those of the capitalist class and imperialism. The government is full of ministers who have received training in French universities and have worked in international institutions (the OECD, the World Bank, etc). Abdelhamid Triki, Minister of planning and international cooperation, was part of Ben Ali's economic team (as secretary of state for international cooperation and foreign investment), and was also an alternate director at the World Bank.

No wonder that the employers' organization UTICA welcomed the new government: "we have the feeling that Tunisia will go back to a normal life and the measures taken reassure this feeling," said Hammadi Ben Sedrine, the bosses' boss.

It is clear that the concessions wrested by the revolutionary masses are important, and there is a certain feeling of having won yet another battle. The Constituent Assembly was one of the key demands of the masses and for them it represented a clean break with the old system. However, those who are now calling for it are the representatives of the ruling class. None of them played any role in the revolution but they are now attempting to claim a legitimacy which they do not have.

The war is far from over. The youth who sparked off this movement, the workers who mobilized massively to overthrow the old regime, were fighting for bread, jobs and dignity. For them democracy does not *only* mean the right to form political parties, the right to say what you want without fear, the right to vote every so often, but also, and above all, the right to have a job, a decent wage, to be able to buy food.

As we have explained in previous articles, the balance of forces in Tunisia is extremely favourable for the workers. However, one thing is lacking: a revolutionary leadership able to provide a way out. Amongst the organizations of the left in Tunisia there seems to be a disease of issuing statements but not taking any concrete measures to implement them. The newly formed Council for the Protection of the Revolution, which includes revolutionary organizations, but also others, including the Islamist party Ennahda which played no role in the revolution, is awaiting legal recognition from the government.

What these organisations should have done is to call and organise a national assembly of delegates from the revolutionary committees (which still exist in towns, cities and neighbourhoods throughout the country), which would be the only body with legitimacy to speak in the name of the revolution.

The road to bourgeois normality which the ruling class is pursuing, however, will be a difficult one. On the one hand, it cannot guarantee the demands of the people. On the other, there is in Tunisia a people which has awoken to political life, has achieved a whole series of victories through mass mobilization and direct action, and feels confidence in its own strength.

The key question is that it requires a revolutionary leadership armed with a clear programme of socialist transformation, the only one that can fulfil the aspirations of the masses for a better life.

Wednesday, 09 March 2011

EGYPT

EGYPT

THE GATHERING STORM

Hamid Alizadeh and Frederik Ohsten

The tensions in Egypt are reaching boiling point. The crisis of the regime is reflected in a number of splits and growing opposition. The emergence of Mohamed ElBaradei on the political scene signifies an important change in the struggle against the regime. Until now, the masses have lacked a national point of reference to connect up the different struggles, but this is now changing. Revolution is developing just beneath the surface.

In the Middle East, Egypt is a key country. Not only is it the most populated Arab country and a strategic pillar of support for imperialism, it also has a strong working class with militant traditions. Over the last few years, the Mubarak dictatorship has been shaken by strikes and protests, but it has become increasingly clear that all factors are pointing in the direction of revolution.

Economic war against the masses

The economic situation in Egypt is becoming more acute and unbearable as each day passes. Booming inflation eats into the living standard of the masses, while a small elite of wealthy bankers, industrialists and state bureaucrats continue to enrich themselves. The gap between rich and poor is as big as ever.

The minimum wage has been 35 Egyptian pounds (US$6.30) per month since 1984. When bonuses, incentives and annual increases are included, the minimum monthly salary of government employees and public sector workers reaches 289 Egyptian pounds (US$53). Some private sector employees earn much less. But while wages have been stagnating, prices have soared.

A study from the Egyptian Centre for Economic Studies issued in 2009 showed that when the minimum wage is related to per capita GNP (gross national product), it appears that this rate has decreased from nearly 60 per cent in 1984 to 19.4 per cent in 1991/92 and to 13 per cent in 2007. When the ratio of the minimum wage to per capita GNP is compared to other countries, Egypt appears amongst the lowest. By comparison, the rate is 26 per cent in Spain, 51 per cent in France and 78 per cent in Turkey. The rotten ruling class has waged a one-sided economic war against the masses.

Middle East Report writes: "Between 2005 and 2010, the Egyptian economy has weathered two major blows to the state's staple revenues: the global food crisis in 2007 and the world recession in 2008. As international trade diminished, according to *The Economist* Intelligence Unit data, receipts from transit of the Suez Canal also declined. Following the Dubai debt crisis, many Egyptians working in the Gulf returned home, reducing remittances; meanwhile, the global downturn depressed foreign direct investment, which fell from US$9.5 billion in 2008 to $6.7 billion in 2009. The value of Egypt's exports dropped by 11.8 per cent in 2009. The official unemployment rate went up from 8.7 per cent in 2008 to 9.4 per cent in 2009, but as is well known, official rates are unreliable; the real figure is believed to be in the double digits. Inflation peaked in 2008 at 11.8 per cent, triggered by the spike in commodity prices, and stood at 10.5 per cent in May." [25]

The misery suffered by the masses is becoming unbearable and a critical point is being reached. The regime is very well aware of this, which is shown by the fact that they are desperately trying to avoid food riots as in 2007-08 and a situation like the 1977 "bread intifada" by securing the food supply. Minister of Trade Rashid Muhammad Rashid has signed a free trade agreement with the South American bloc Mercosur to ensure the flow of grain and meat imports to feed the population. He said similar agreements with Russia and South Africa would be signed before the end of 2010. However, it is unclear whether such deals can be made as Russia's ban on grain exports (scheduled to run until December 31) may not be lifted if the results of the harvest in that country are not better than anticipated.

The regime shaken by the workers

The most remarkable development in recent years in Egypt has been the awakening of the working class. In December 2006, the Egyptian proletariat entered the stage with the strike and factory occupation of the Mahalla textile workers. Led by the 3,000 low-paid female workers in the spinning department, 27,000 workers laid down tools and staged a sit-down strike on December 7. When a representative of the regime came to negotiate, he was almost beaten to death by female workers.

The militancy and steadfastness showed by the Mahalla workers led to a wave of strikes and factory occupations all over Egypt in the period 2007-08. The cement workers of Helwan and Tora had already come out on strike in December 2006. In January 2007, the workers on the Cairo-Alexandria Railway struck. This was followed by strikes and actions by the Cairo Metro workers, bus drivers, poultry workers, refuse collectors, sewage workers and gardeners. More importantly, the workers in the key textile industry followed the example of Mahalla. In February 2007, 21,000 textile workers struck in the Nile Delta region and

---

25 *The Dynamics of Egypt's Elections*, Mona El-Ghobashy, September 29, 2010.

12,000 workers at Kafr al-Dawa occupied their factory with the slogan "Strike until death! Strike until pay!"

In April 2007, 5,000 workers at three flour-producing plants in Cairo and Giza occupied the factories. During the occupation, the workers continued producing flour for the community under their own control.

In September 2007, the 27,000 textile workers at the Misr Spinning and Weaving textile factory in Mahalla once again occupied their factory. At night 10-15,000 workers slept in the factory premises. During the day, more than 20,000 workers were present at the factory for demonstrations and the celebration of Ramadan. The Grain Mill Workers staged a demonstration in solidarity with the Mahalla workers, and all over Egypt workers raised money for the strikers. Such collections took place in Mahalla, Tanta, Helwan, Shoubra, Tenth of Ramadan City, Suez, Beheira, Mansoura and Port Said.

In this period, the workers have not suffered any serious defeats as a class. In most cases, the regime had to give in to the workers' demands. However, the regime had some success in repressing a would-be general strike on April 6, 2008. This highlighted the need for national organisation of the working class. But the entire movement of the workers has been the most dangerous for the regime for decades, and it clearly demonstrated the all-important role of the working class. Only the Egyptian proletariat has the social weight to bring down the dictatorship.

After accelerating privatisation of public sector companies from 2005 to 2008, in May the government announced an indefinite postponement of the programme in an attempt to stem the tide of protests triggered by unemployment and high inflation. At the same time, the Ministry of Economic Development announced an increase in the monthly minimum wage to 280 Egyptian pounds (about US$49) after a series of protests and a court ruling that certified workers' hardship claims, but no start date was specified. Finally, in early 2010, the government delayed implementation of the Property Tax Law originally passed in 2008, in response to public opposition.

Even though the protests and strikes have not assumed a truly national character, the regime has not felt confident enough to carry through all the dictates of the IMF and keep the wages as catastrophically low as before. They can feel the hot breath of the workers on their necks.

The unstable situation is also reflected within the regime itself. This has become even clearer in the last few years. And the clearest expression of this is the debacle over who is going to succeed the current president, Hosni Mubarak.

Splits in the regime

An Egyptian joke goes something like this: "Gamal Abdel Nasser gave us industrialisation. Anwar Sadat gave us the market economy. What did Hosni Mubarak give to the Egyptians? Answer: a son!"

Next year, there are going to be presidential elections in Egypt. These will of course not bear any resemblance to genuine democratic elections, but the elections are nevertheless very important. It will be a test of strength between the various factions of the regime – and of the mass movement confronting the regime. The beginning of this process is developing around the parliamentary elections in November (the exact date is yet to be announced) this year.

Hosni Mubarak's son, Gamal Mubarak has emerged as the most likely candidate of the ruling elite. However, there are large factions within the regime who are not very satisfied with this succession from father to son. Gamal Mubarak represents an important layer of the capitalist class in Egypt. But there are other forces – especially in the army and the state bureaucracy – that might prefer other candidates to represent them.

The New York Times reports: "Military officials have expressed reservations in interviews and in the Egyptian news media about Gamal Mubarak, one of the most frequently mentioned potential successors of the president. Retired officers and other analysts said the military would not support his candidacy without ironclad guarantees that it would retain its pre-eminent position in the nation's affairs. Retired officers circulated an open letter criticizing Gamal Mubarak's candidacy last month, and several retired Egyptian officers said in interviews that they were sceptical of hereditary succession."

"Many in the military chafe at the idea of a Gamal Mubarak presidency, especially as he ascends to the office through the kind of heavily manipulated ballots to which Egypt has grown accustomed. If he wants to succeed his father, said Mohamed Kadry Said, a retired general, he must win in 'clean elections'."

"Much of the military's distrust of Gamal Mubarak stems from his ties to a younger generation of ruling party cadres who have made fortunes in the business world. The military is tied to the National Democratic Party's 'old guard', a substantially less wealthy elite who made their careers as ministers, officers and apparatchiks. Military officers said they feared that Gamal Mubarak might erode the military's institutional powers." [26]

The splits in the regime are opening up room for the masses, drawing them in to the arena. As the pressure from below increases this self-perpetuating process will magnify all the internal contradictions of the regime and force its different factions into opposing camps.

Regime loses its social basis

The cohesion of the regime is constantly being undermined by centrifugal forces. The sky-rocketing inflation, pressure from the masses, military conflicts with the

---

26 *Succession Gives Army a Stiff Test in Egypt*, NYT, September 11, 2010.

Sinai Bedouins, pressure from US Imperialism and the IMF all add to this process. A significant development in the process is the alienation of the very social basis of the regime – the lower ranking state bureaucracy.

In the wake of the massive wave of strikes and factory occupations of 2007-08, other layers of society have entered the scene of struggle against the regime. For instance, 55,000 tax collectors waged a bitter struggle for better conditions. The national strike was run by an independent committee, with elected representatives from the provinces. The state-backed General Union of Bank, Insurance and Finance Employees was hostile to the strikers. In the course of struggle, the tax collectors formed the first independent union in Egypt since 1957.

Middle East Report writes: "In the past, election campaigns have witnessed an increased flow of petition and complaint upward, and the distribution of goods and services downward. The 2010 elections roll around at a time when citizens have not been idly waiting to vote, but have been airing their economic and political demands in daily demonstrations. The last election cycle in 2005 had energized pro-democracy protests by the Kifaya movement, as well as a series of post-election protests in the spring of 2006 to support independent judges targeted by the government for overly competent election supervision. *The new dimension today is the diffusion of protests among new categories of citizens, especially the street-level bureaucrats who, as scions of the lower middle class embodied by Gamal Abdel Nasser, have constituted the social base of the Egyptian state since 1952.* The great majority of protests are not the work of labour unions or political parties. Every day, newspapers report on self-organized street actions by an aggrieved sector of the population, be it downwardly mobile civil servants, North Sinai residents, auto mechanics, nurses, Copts, laid-off industrial workers, stricken rice farmers or technologically savvy young people. These small-scale rallies constitute a new language of popular politics now routinely used by citizens demanding responsiveness from negligent government officials." [27]

The movement of the Egyptian proletariat – especially the Mahalla textile workers – gave an enormous impetus to other sectors of society. It struck fear into the hearts of the regime which is reflected by the concessions given on the industrial front, but it also paved the way for the middle classes to come out against the regime. This is a very significant fact that spells even bigger convulsions in the period ahead.

---

27 *The Dynamics of Egypt's Elections*. Our emphasis.

The Muslim Brotherhood

The biggest so-called opposition to the regime is the *Ikhwan al-Muslimeen*, the Muslim Brotherhood. In reality, this party plays the strategic role as the second line of defence for capitalism in Egypt.

Throughout the upsurge of workers' struggles, the Muslim Brotherhood has played a despicable role. At best, they have distanced themselves from strikers and criticized their actions. In reality, they play the role of "loyal opposition" to the regime. This has become clear on several occasions – notably the nationwide strike on April 6, 2008 (when they issued a statement of non-participation) and during the demonstrations against the Israeli massacre in Gaza in December 2008-January 2009. During these demonstrations, the Muslim Brotherhood acted as policemen of the regime, cracking down on protestors who were chanting slogans against the Mubarak dictatorship and its alliance with Israel and America.

The Brotherhood has very little support in the factories where it is a marginal force. The Muslim Brotherhood has gained support thanks to its extensive network of charity, its social demagogy and its "opposition" to President Mubarak. It is widely acknowledged that the Muslim Brotherhood has made secret deals with the very regime it pretends to combat, and of course also with the USA who sees in it a 'safe' alternative solution in case of a revolutionary explosion. In the event of a revolutionary overthrow of the regime, the ruling class will try to install the Brotherhood in government to save capitalism.

Many pessimistic elements in the cosy corridors of the universities and "research" institutions are often blinded by the ideological "hegemony" of, especially, Muslim movements. Marxists agree that religion does play a role in holding back the masses for long periods, especially the most backward layers. But in the final analysis, and especially in times of revolution it is the material conditions that play the main role. This is now also being seen within the Muslim Brotherhood that is showing signs of splits on a class basis.

It is especially the question of boycott that has divided the waters within the organisation. The so-called conservative wing of the Muslim Brotherhood (that won the party's internal elections this January and is headed by Muhammad Badie) have maintained a conciliatory attitude towards the regime and accepts the elections, while other sectors of the Muslim Brotherhood – the so-called reformist wing – can sense the pressure from the masses and are advocating for a boycott, even a boycott for 20 years.

The divisions inside the Muslim Brotherhood have already reached unheard-of levels. The official leadership of the Muslim Brotherhood have maintained a position of participating in the elections, although they continue to utter support for the seven demands of the National Association for Change.

The Muslim Brotherhood's European spokesman and former chairman Kamal al-Helbawy has called on the Brotherhood to boycott the upcoming elections. Al-Helbawy told *Al-Masry Al-Youm* that "the Muslim Brotherhood needs to convince the various political parties to boycott these elections and to stand behind ElBaradei in his call for a boycott as a prelude to civil disobedience."

The divisions have now reached a level where proponents of a boycott have challenged the legitimacy of the membership of some members of the Guidance Bureau, saying they were appointed, not elected. Those advocating participation in the election, on the other hand, claim that those who want a boycott are currently not connected to the organisation.

These are the first signs of a split in the Muslim Brotherhood, and we can state with absolute certainty that these divisions will continue to grow in scope and depth under pressure from the masses. The leading Muslim Brotherhood figures will try to save the regime, but they also have to be careful not to lose all support. This last concern will especially affect the lower ranking leaders who are more directly dependent on popular support from the middle classes.

Revolutionary dynamic

Perhaps the most significant development in the Egyptian situation this year is the rise of Mohamed ElBaradei and his "National Association for Change". In the absence of a national mass organisation to express themselves through, the masses are increasingly rallying behind this figure as a focal point for struggle against the regime.

Mohamed ElBaradei, former head of the UN's International Atomic Energy Agency, is an outsider in the corridors of the power struggle in Egypt. The regime has tried to block his candidacy for the presidential elections in 2011 on the grounds that he does not represent a party and does not fulfil the conditions of Article 76 of the constitution – an article designed to block opposition candidates (as well as unruly figures from the ruling National Democratic Party) from standing.

The reaction of the regime – in effect an attempt to squash the campaign of ElBaradei – reflects the fact that it has no room for such an outsider without organic connections to the ruling elite. The military, the state bureaucracy and private capital do not want to share their power with ElBaradei, who they look upon with contempt. This has forced him to lean on the support of the masses to protect him from the blows of the regime, thus creating a situation with its own revolutionary dynamics.

The programme of ElBaradei's campaign is centred on democratic demands, which is a natural first step under a dictatorship like Egypt. So far, ElBaradei has launched a campaign for the right to stand in the presidential elections next year. The demands of the campaign are:

1. An end to the state of emergency that has existed since 1981.
2. Empowerment of the Egyptian judiciary to supervise the electoral process.
3. The elections must be checked by national and international NGOs.
4. Equal access to the media for all candidates, especially in the presidential elections.
5. Egyptians living abroad must be able to exercise their right to vote in embassies and consulates.
6. Ensure the right to stand in the presidential elections without arbitrary restrictions and limiting the right to run for president to two terms.
7. Elections by national number.

The boycott campaign

ElBaradei has called for boycotting the parliamentary elections in November. At an *iftar* meal to celebrate the end of Ramadan, ElBaradei told 200 activists that: "Anyone who participates in the vote, either as a candidate or as a voter, goes against the national will." He urged "civil disobedience" to force the regime to grant political reforms. "If the whole people boycott the elections totally, it will be, in my view, the end of the regime," he said, adding that he will not stand for President if democratic reforms are not introduced.

For the masses, this is seen as a call for mobilisation. They sense that ElBaradei's campaign can be a vehicle for protest and a force to carry through their demands by uniting against the regime in a national campaign. The masses' instinctive striving for unity is at present the most powerful force.

The boycott campaign can only be carried out in an efficient manner if the masses sense a clear purpose to fight for – a plan of action for the downfall of the regime. At this moment, the boycott campaign is seen as a natural rallying point that serves this end. This is affecting all classes and social strata in Egypt. Around a million signatures have been collected in support of the campaign.

In general, for Marxists participation in parliamentary elections is not a question of principle – even when, as in the case of Egypt, it is a bogus parliament without any real power. The Bolsheviks conducted excellent work in the rotten tsarist Duma by using it as a platform to reach the masses. But the question of boycott is not a question which can be seen in isolation from the rest of the class struggle. In Egypt, all that is vibrant in society is gathering around ElBaradei and his boycott campaign.

On this basis we are fully in support of the campaign, but we must also emphasise that a boycott is not enough in itself. It must be connected to an alternative and with concrete action. In a country like Egypt where there are as yet no other organs of mass struggle to take power, the democratic programme must be linked with the demand for a revolutionary constituent assembly which can be put forward when the time is ripe. Also there must be organised a thorough and consistent campaign to set up action committees in all neighbourhoods, factories and schools to coordinate the campaign.

ElBaradei has been forced to lean on the most radical and revolutionary elements in order to protect himself from the blows of the regime. He even went to Mahalla, known as "Egypt's Petrograd", to have a meeting with the workers. At the meeting he said that change in Egypt must be obtained in "unconventional ways". He also said that "The people's representatives in parliament will not do the job (...) I hope Egypt doesn't face a violent, hunger-driven revolution against the regime."

The meaning of ElBaradei

The real meaning of ElBaradei and his campaign is this: for the first time, the militant workers, youth and poor masses have a national point of reference for the struggle against the regime. The impressive struggles over the last years reached a certain limit exactly because of the lack of national organisation. Now, this is beginning to change.

In order to take control of the situation, carry out an efficient struggle against the regime and a mass boycott, there is urgent need for organisation. Committees in the factories, in the neighbourhoods and universities must be set up and take charge of the campaign, organise discussions and common action.

It is hard to say whether the campaign will be successful or not. This will be determined by many factors: the regional and national situation in terms of economy and war (Israel and Iran); the ability of the regime and their agents (including the Muslim Brotherhood) to weaken and split the movement and to keep their social forces intact; the quality and development of leaders among the masses, and of the actions taken by ElBaradei himself. At some stage, the more intelligent parts of the regime may try to buy him. The regime will split even more into different factions. Some sections will try to stem the revolutionary tide by loosening up and conceding some reforms. Some sections will try to crush the movement by force, relying solely on the well-known measures of torture, police-roundups and mass arrests. Both of these factions will fail in their objectives. They will not be able to obtain their goal.

If the campaign develops into a true mass movement, the role of ElBaradei will be quite minimal. The masses will carry him forward in a confrontation with the regime, but he will not be able to control the very movement that is pushing him forward. The natural focal point for such a movement will be the presidential elections in 2012. The masses will aim to overthrow the hated regime. This, in turn will pave the way for revolutionary explosions. This is the true meaning of ElBaradei: an accidental figure, acting as a catalyst for the revolutionary process.

The meaning of democratic demands

In many countries of the so-called Third World, the development of mass organisations has taken a peculiar form. In the same way that these countries' economic development does not follow the same pattern as Europe, the political development of mass parties is taking a combined and uneven course. The lack of any real mass organisations creates a situation where individual leaders – under the right conditions – can suddenly emerge as "leaders" of the masses. This is the case to some degree or other with Mousavi in Iran, who is an accidental figure thrown up by the impasse in the regime, to Zelaya in Honduras, and to Chavez in Venezuela who embodies the very revolution itself.

In the case of Mousavi, we are dealing with a man who comes from within the Islamic regime itself, and is more interested in holding back the movement than giving it genuine expression. Zelaya was pushed much further, starting off as a bourgeois democrat and then being pushed by the mass movement into opposition against the local oligarchy. Chavez, however, is not a man that comes from within the old regime of the oligarchy; he is a man who started off wanting to achieve basic democratic reforms, but because of the opposition of the bourgeoisie has moved much further to the left, even declaring himself a Marxist and raising the need for socialist transformation of society.

There are some parallels that can be made between Zelaya and ElBaradei. ElBaradei's political ambitions have been met with resistance on the part of the regime. This is due to the fact that he has no direct organic links to the ruling elite. This situation – under circumstances where the masses are rallying behind him as a means of struggle against the regime – can unleash a process, where ElBaradei could be pushed to take a much more radical stance than he intends to at the present moment.

ElBaradei is not a socialist, much less a Marxist. Furthermore, it is not at all certain that he can be trusted to carry out the struggle against the regime in any consistent manner. This will be clear through the course of events. ElBaradei is a moderate reformist, and his demands are most modest. There should be no illusions in ElBaradei, but at the same time, we should keep an eye on the political developments. ElBaradei can be forced to go a lot further than intended, but it is far from certain that he will pass the tests of the revolutionary dynamics of his "own" movement.

At this moment, the movement's official slogans are made up of democratic demands. The demands for an end to the State of Emergency, the right to organise unions, fair elections and so on are demands that are supported wholeheartedly by the Marxists. At the same time, it must be made clear that in order to fight against the dictatorship; one must fight against the material forces upholding it: the capitalist class, the top bureaucracy in the state and the army, as well as foreign capital and the interests of imperialism.

What would be the consequences if the democratic demands were won? It would signify an explosion of the class struggle. The winning of basic democratic demands on the part of the Egyptian masses would enormously boost the confidence and organisation of the working class. Mass parties and revolutionary tendencies would emerge rapidly. The situation would spin out of control for the national and international bourgeoisie. This is why the democratic demands must be connected with the question of the regime itself and with the question of Socialism.

As soon as the movement for democratic change in Egypt assumes a real mass character, the democratic slogans will and must be connected to demands for price controls, for wage increases, for better education, for re-nationalisation of privatised industries, for workers' control and finally the question of the abolition of capitalism that is the root cause of all the problems of Egyptian society.

These facts must be stated clearly in order to prepare and arm the best elements of the movement for what lies ahead. A declaration of war against the dictatorship means to call for the downfall of the ruling elite. This means revolution, not minor reforms. This is what the activists must prepare for. Committees must be organised in every factory, in every neighbourhood. A serious campaign must be organised.

The dynamics of revolution

"Revolution is our aim, victory is our first stage" – Sheikh Imam (1918-95)

The situation in Egypt is pregnant with revolution. It has already started at the top. The divisions on the question of the presidential succession are just the beginning of a more open split in the regime. A ferocious fight will open up within the ruling elite. The noises of opposition to Gamal Mubarak on the part of the army tops are an indication of this.

Different wings of the ruling elite are trying to solve their problems and save the regime with different methods. One wing of the regime trusts only the old methods of repression to curb opposition. Another wing wants to give concessions and reforms in order to save the regime. Both will fail. The regime cannot tolerate ElBaradei to stand – in the presidential elections – not because of ElBaradei himself, but because of the radicalised masses that stand behind him and are pushing him forward.

For the masses, the situation is becoming still more acute and unbearable. There exists a burning desire for a fundamental change in society. At the present stage, there are big illusions in democracy – but this is connected to the masses' anticipation that democracy will bring about an improvement in their living conditions. These illusions will be broken down by events themselves.

The overthrow of dictatorship in Egypt will not solve all issues. On the contrary, it will mostly serve to pose them even more sharply. No form of bourgeois democracy will be able to solve the question of price hikes, poverty, unemployment, military regime and in fact even the very question of bread. These are only questions that can be fully solved only when the whole system of capitalism and private property is abolished.

The middle classes are fed up with the regime. Before, the regime could trust the lower ranking state officials, the lawyers and intellectuals to back up the regime. This is no longer the case. Again and again, even these layers have come out against the regime. University professors have led strikes on campuses. The tax collectors have formed their own independent union. These layers are looking to the working class for a lead, but for the moment the focus is on the campaign of ElBaradei.

The workers took the road of industrial action in the period from December 2006 onwards when 27,000 textile workers in Mahalla struck and occupied their factory. But the road of relatively isolated industrial action has shown its limits – hence the importance of a national political focal point for the political struggle against the regime. There will without doubt be many turnarounds and shifts in the situation. Industrial action will come to the forefront at a later stage. At the present stage, all focus is on how to use the boycott campaign to build up national organisations. This process has its own, revolutionary dynamics.

The events looming in Egypt will shake the entire region. They will have a big impact throughout the entire Middle East where a revolutionary dynamic has already started. The period up to the presidential elections will be one of preparation for the revolutionary events which are to come. The Egyptian revolution will dramatically change the course of events in the Middle East, North Africa and on a world scale.

Thursday, 28 October 2010

UPRISING IN EGYPT: THE REVOLUTION IS SPREADING!

Alan Woods

Dramatic events are unfolding in the Middle East. Today Egypt was rocked by a wave of nationwide demonstrations demanding the end of the Mubarak regime, which has oppressed the people of this proud nation for nearly 30 years. This was the biggest protest movement Egypt has seen for decades. In Cairo and other cities thousands of anti-government protesters demonstrated on the streets and fought with police.

After the overthrow of Tunisia's strongman Zine El Abidine Ben Ali on January 14, observers wondered aloud if the dramatic events in the North African nation could provoke insurrections in other apparently entrenched Arab regimes. Now they have their answer! The revolutionary flames that have swept through the Arab world from Tunisia have reached Egypt.

The first indications of the impact of the Tunisian uprising on the popular consciousness surfaced last week in Egypt when several people set themselves on fire or attempted to do so outside parliament and the prime minister's office. Their actions sought to imitate the example of the young Tunisian vegetable vendor whose self-immolation helped spark the protests that forced Tunisia's authoritarian president to flee the country.

As in Tunisia, the demonstrations in Egypt came against a backdrop of growing anger over widespread poverty and unemployment. Nearly half of Egypt's 80 million people live under or just above the poverty line set by the United Nations at US$2 a day. Poor quality education, health care and high unemployment have left large numbers of Egyptians deprived of basic needs.

But the economic discontent is only part of a wider political discontent. There is a deep-seated anger at the injustices, inequalities and corruption of the Mubarak regime. The question is raised of how long the aged dictator will cling to power. Nobody knows whether Mubarak will run again in presidential elections later this year or perhaps position his son to run in his place. But the people of Egypt will accept nothing less than a fundamental change.

The government tried to play down self-immolation attempts, with Prime Minister Ahmed Nazif telling reporters on Monday that those who committed the act were driven by "personal issues". But nobody believed this. As in Tunisia the calls for rallies went out on Facebook and Twitter, with 90,000 saying they would attend. On all sides Tunisia was on everyone's lips. "We want to see change just like in Tunisia," said Lamia Rayan, 24, one of the protesters.

The call for protests was initiated by The Martyr Facebook page, set up in the name of a young Egyptian man, Khaled Said, who was beaten to death by policemen in the Mediterranean port city of Alexandria last year. His case has become a rallying point for the opposition. Two policemen are currently on trial in connection with his death. Yet by one of those strange ironies with which history is so rich, the protests coincided with a national holiday honouring the country's hated police.

There were remarkable scenes in Cairo today as thousands and thousands poured onto the streets, marching with apparent freedom in three major demonstrations in different parts of the Egyptian capital. Things began peacefully, with police showing unusual restraint. The noisy crowd was joined by cars driving alongside and honking their horns. People cried: "Long Live a Free Tunisia" and waving Tunisian and Egyptian flags while police initially stood on the crowd's periphery. Riot police at first seemed uncertain as to what to do, as each of the marches broke through police cordons.

An eyewitness wrote the following lines: "I'm downtown outside the offices of the government newspapers where hundreds are chanting 'Mubarak, your plane is waiting' and appealing for passers-by to join them, many of whom are taking up the offer.

"Ahmed Ashraf, a 26 year old bank analyst, told me this was his first protest, and that he had been inspired by events in Tunisia. 'We are the ones controlling the streets today, not the regime,' he said. 'I feel so free – things can't stay the same after this'."

If the police seemed to have no idea what to do, on the other side there also seemed to be little coordination between protest leaders about what to do next. It resembled the commencement of a wrestling match, with each of the two contenders circling warily, eyeing his opponent and trying to guess the next move. They did not have to wait long.

In the past demonstrations were violently dispersed. Now, however, the police had clearly received orders from the government to avoid anything that could provoke a Tunisia-like mass revolt. But such things have a life and a law of their own. As the numbers of demonstrators continued to build up, filling Cairo's main Tahrir Square, the security forces got nervous. They suddenly changed tactics and the protest turned violent as police attacked demonstrators with water cannon, batons and tear gas.

Acrid clouds of smoke filled the streets of Cairo. In the past people would have fled in panic from the feared police. But this time things were different. The people stood their ground and fought back. Defiant protesters clashed with riot police in the centre of Cairo. They threw stones and some even climbed on top of an armoured police truck. On January 25, 2011, *The Washington Post* described the scene:

Demonstrators attacked the police water cannon truck, opening the driver's door and ordering the man out of the vehicle. Some hurled rocks and dragged metal barricades. Officers beat back protesters with batons as they tried to break cordons to join the main downtown demonstrators.

To the north, in the Mediterranean port city of Alexandria, thousands of protesters also marched in what was dubbed a 'Day of Rage' against Mr. Mubarak and calling for an end to the country's grinding poverty.

[...] The demonstrators in Cairo sang the national anthem and carried banners denouncing Mr. Mubarak and widespread fraud in the country's elections. The organizers said the protests were a 'day of revolution against torture, poverty, corruption and unemployment'.

Mothers carrying babies marched and chanted 'Revolution until Victory!' while young men parked their cars on the main street and waved signs reading 'OUT!' inspired by the Tunisian protestations of 'DEGAGE!' this week. Men were seen spraying graffiti reading 'Down with Hosni Mubarak'.

The regime is in a state of panic. Eyewitnesses report that the internet, Twitter and phone calls were all blocked in Egypt, but they are returning intermittently now. The latest reports show that the insurrection is continuing and advancing to new levels. An eyewitness report states:

As darkness begins to fall, the thousands who have occupied Cairo's central square are pouring forward towards the parliament building, prompting running battles with armed police. The air is filled with teargas and some youths are hurling rocks at the police lines; many of the rocks are being thrown back by security officers.

A few moments ago a huge charge from demonstrators sent the riot police running, but they have now regrouped and are launching fresh assaults on the front wave of protesters, who are currently picking up the metal barricades installed by police and using them to set up barricades themselves. Large explosions are shaking the square, though it's not clear where they're coming from.

Reports are spreading of protesters attacking the council of ministers building downtown, while several thousands are said to be marching towards Mubarak's presidential palace in Heliopolis. In Dar El Salaam, a densely-populated neighbourhood in southern Cairo, demonstrators claim to have taken over the police station.

There's a feeling of intense excitement on the streets here in Shubra, northern Cairo, as the police continue to stand back and allow protesters to pass – but some of the security forces are wearing bullet proof vests, and some fear this is the calm before the storm.

One former television news presenter told me she hadn't seen anything like this since 1977, when an uprising over bread prices almost brought down the government of President Sadat. But demonstrations remain cut off from each other and it's still too early to say how this will play out.

It is true that nobody knows how this will end. But one thing is certain. Egypt will never be the same again. The genie is out of the bottle and it cannot be pushed back inside. The masses have had a taste of freedom and they have felt their collective power on the streets. If they possessed an organization and a leadership that was adequate to the task, they could move to take power. But in the absence of leadership and a clear plan and perspective, the situation can go in different ways.

As I write these lines, the fate of the uprising is in the balance. The regime is now on very shaky ground. The hesitation shown by the police at the start of the protest shows that they are not confident of using the apparatus of repression to put down the movement. There will be splits in the regime between those who want to crack down and those who want to make compromises to gain time.

Can the regime drown the uprising in blood? Such an outcome is not impossible, but it would be a victory purchased at a very high price. The hatred and resentment towards the regime would be long-lasting. It would poison the political life of the country and rule out any kind of compromise solution. Mubarak is an old man and cannot last long. His son, who he hopes will replace him, will be completely delegitimized. The economy will decline still further, aggravating the problem of unemployment and poverty. New explosions would follow.

However, that does not seem the most likely variant. The mass movement is gathering strength by the hour. In Alexandria there are reports of old ladies throwing pots and pans on the police from the balconies of their houses. The key to the situation is the powerful Egyptian proletariat, which has organized strike after strike in recent years. Now the workers are on the streets. In Mahala, the scene of the big textile workers' strikes, there is news of 20,000 on the streets. The police station has been overwhelmed.

The revolutionary people are occupying the central squares and refusing to leave. Every inch has been conquered by the masses and they do not intend to surrender what they have conquered to anyone. Faced with a mass movement on such a scale, the forces of state repression, which before seemed so formidable, have suddenly become vulnerable. In many places the police have been simply swamped by sheer numbers. Their cordons have been broken by the protesters. The faces of the ordinary policemen betray nervousness and their officers even more so.

There have been many cases of fraternization. A French TV news channel showed pictures of a police officer being carried shoulder high by demonstrators. They are shouting anti-government slogans, and the police officer is shouting them as well. This little incident says it all. All history shows that once the masses have lost their fear, once an entire people stands up and says "no", there is no force on earth that can stop them.

Whatever we will read in tomorrow's newspapers, we may be sure of one thing: the Arab revolution has begun. It will be greeted with every enthusiasm by the workers and youth of the whole world. Let us mobilize in support of our Arab brother and sisters! Demand an immediate end to repression! Break off all relations with the criminal Mubarak regime! Demand full rights for the people of Egypt!

- Victory to the workers and youth of Egypt!
- Down with Mubarak!
- Long live the Arab socialist revolution!

Tuesday, 25 January 2011

THE CALM BEFORE THE STORM

Alan Woods

Atense calm settled over Cairo after yesterday's street demonstrations. But if there is a truce, it will not last long. Last night some 15,000 protesters decided to stage a vigil in Liberation Square in protest against police violence. News reports speak of three people killed yesterday, of which one was a policeman. The real figure may be higher.

Sources Cairo report that the organizers plan to continue the protest until Mubarak is gone. This moment may not be so far away. Arabic internet sites were reporting today that at the peak of anti-government protests, Hosni Mubarak's son and chosen successor as Egyptian president, Gamal Mubarak, secretly took himself and his family out of the country on Tuesday by way of the military airfield in West Cairo. Twitter also carried an unconfirmed report that Suzanne Mubarak, Egypt's first lady, was identified by airport workers on arrival at Heathrow airport, London.

Twitter's service was blocked in Egypt this morning. This shows that the government is panicking. But this measure did not stop the opposition calling for the demonstrations to continue. They were heartened by their success on Tuesday in getting hundreds of thousands out onto the streets to demand the president's resignation and they have been further encouraged by reports of Gamal's desertion.

However, no source was cited and such reports must be treated with caution. In this kind of situation there is always a proliferation of rumours, mostly baseless. But if Gamal Mubarak's defection is confirmed, it would point to deep cracks in the 82-year old president's regime.

This is precisely the opposite of the sanguine opinions that have been constantly repeated in the West. We are assured that Egypt is not Tunisia; the regime is in no danger of being overthrown by the protest movement, and so on.

A good example of this was an article from a BBC "expert" on January 17, who said that no revolt would happen in Egypt because people there are apathetic: "Unlike Tunisia, the population has a much lower level of education. Illiteracy is high, internet penetration is low." The article, signed by Jon Leyne in Cairo was entitled: "No sign Egypt will take the Tunisian road." Incredibly, the same lines were left in yesterday's report about the mass demonstrations on the BBC website.

Even on Tuesday, when the people of Egypt had already taken to the streets, Hillary Clinton said she believed the government was stable: "Our assessment is that the Egyptian government is stable and is looking for ways to respond to the legitimate needs and interests of the Egyptian people," Ms. Clinton said.

But her optimistic view is evidently not shared on Wall Street. Today, the Egyptian pound fell sharply against the US dollar and the Egyptian stock market tumbled more than 4 per cent. Clearly the hard-headed men of business are better informed than the US Secretary of State. Today's editorial of the *Washington Post* shows a far more serious grasp of the situation. It is worth quoting at length:

> The secretary's words suggested that *the administration remains danger-ously behind the pace of events in the Middle East.* It failed to anticipate Tunisia's revolution; days before President Zine El Abidine Ben Ali was driven from the country Ms. Clinton said the United States was 'not taking sides' between the dictator and his protesting people. Last week President Obama called Mr. Mubarak but said nothing about the political situation in Egypt – including the regime's plan to hold a one-sided presidential 'election' this fall that would extend Mr. Mubarak's mandate for another six years.

> Tuesday's events suggested that the Cairo government is not at all stable. Three people were killed in the occasionally violent demonstrations, and thousands of protesters remained camped in Cairo's central Tahrir Square overnight. They will not be easily satisfied – because Mr. Mubarak in fact is not trying to 'respond to legitimate needs and interests.' Instead the gov-ernment is seeking to perpetuate itself in power by force, and pave the way for an eventual dynastic succession to power by Mr. Mubarak's son."

Here we have the authentic voice of the serious strategists of Capital, as opposed to the superficial Washington politicians and the BBC "Middle East experts", whose expertise consists mainly in drinking gin and tonics in a Cairo hotel and listening to gossip and the propaganda put out by the regime to calm the nerves of western governments and investors.

The serious strategists of Capital tend to come to the same conclusions as the Marxists although with a slight delay and naturally from their class point of view. In this case, they have understood what we pointed out long ago: that the reactionary Arab regimes like Egypt and Jordan are hanging by a thread and can be overthrown at any time.

The *Washington Post* understands that there is a serious danger of a revolution in Egypt, which will have far more serious consequences for the economic and strategic interests of the USA than the Tunisian uprising:

> Egypt has been a vital ally of the United States, and a potential change of regime there is frightening to many in Washington, especially given the strength of the country's Islamist movement. Those concerns are legiti-mate. But blind U.S. backing for Mr. Mubarak makes a political disaster in Egypt more rather than less likely. Instead of stressing the government's

stability, Ms. Clinton and Mr. Obama need to begin talking about how it must change.

These are serious people. Unlike Ms. Clinton, they realise that Mubarak is finished and any attempt to prop him up will only make things worse. Change is necessary, and Washington must try to control it and steer it into safe channels. The first step must be to get rid of Mubarak, but here they hit a number of problems. In the first place, Mubarak and his family have their own interests and they do not wish to surrender power.

The second problem is even more serious. If Mubarak is removed, who will replace him? They express concern about the Islamists. But their real concern is what they call "the Arab street", that is to say, the Arab masses. The Islamists have so far been conspicuous by their absence. In Tunisia they have played little or no role. In Egypt the real reactionary face of the fundamentalists is shown by their attitude to the protest movement. The Islamic parties led by the Muslim Brotherhood did not play any role in the organisation of this action and *originally they even opposed it*. Only at a later stage were they forced to allow their members to attend. That is a devastating comment on those sorry "Marxists" in Europe who have been tail-ending the Islamists and who have given uncritical support to the Muslim Brotherhood.

The Mubarak regime has lost its momentum. Grave domestic problems and economic hardships have been piling up for 30 years. Now the day of reckoning draws near. The spark from Tunis was sufficient to ignite a powder keg that was prepared in advance. Egypt has not seen such stormy demonstrations for more than a quarter century: not since 1977 when mass riots forced Anwar Sadat to back down from bread price rises. And the protests will not be silenced by batons and tear gas. Tension is running high in Cairo. New explosions are being prepared.

On Tuesday, the authorities announced that Mubarak's supporters would mount a counter-demonstration the following day. This is playing with fire. A collision between the two camps might well lead to further upheavals and end in civil war – a civil war that Mubarak is not likely to win. Yesterday exposed cracks in the state apparatus that were already there. These cracks will grow and undermine the whole edifice.

The movement has scarcely begun, and yet it has already acquired a nationwide character. There were mass protests not just in Cairo but also in Alexandria with thousands more in the cities of the Delta and along the Suez Canal. And this is just the beginning. The real motor force of the movement on the ground is not the Islamists but left wing activists – and the masses: the workers, the unemployed, the urban poor, the peasants and the revolutionary youth. We received this short report about the situation this morning:

> The police have evacuated the Tahrir square with a real bombardment of tear gas. The demonstrators have fled to the neighbouring streets. Every-

thing depends now in the next days of: 1) if the demonstrators come back *en masse* on the streets, 2) do this in different cities, 3) if the transport and industrial workers in the cities of Mahalla, Suez, Tanta, Helwan, etc can be convinced to organise a general strike. If this is the case the regime will not last long. (This was the problem during the so-called 'green revolution' in Iran in 2009). Although the spontaneity is very big, the organisation of the protest is weak and in more importantly still 'virtual'.

These few lines go straight to the heart of the problem. The masses show tremendous courage and élan. But they lack proper organization and leadership. This can complicate the whole process and give it a convulsive and protracted character. Already in relation to the mass revolutionary movement in Iran after the rigged election, we pointed out that the spontaneous character of the movement was both its strength and its weakness. Despite all the heroic efforts of the Iranian masses, the regime was able to hold on to power – at least for a time.

It is inevitable that the movement in Egypt (which has many common features with the movement in Iran) will pass through a series of phases. There will be ebbs and flows, defeats as well as victories. But in the course of struggle the masses will learn many lessons. They will learn which leaders are to be trusted and which are to be rejected. They will develop the adequate tactics and seek out the programme and ideas that can guarantee victory.

That task would be immeasurably easier if there were in existence a genuine revolutionary party like the Russian Bolsheviks under Lenin and Trotsky. Unfortunately, such a party does not yet exist. It has to be built in the course of the struggle itself. But the masses, and especially their most advanced elements, and the youth will learn quickly on the basis of events.

The decisive element in the equation, as our correspondent points out, is the mighty Egyptian proletariat, which in recent years has shown its fighting spirit in a wave of strikes. These strikes were a preparatory school for the present revolutionary movement. The task now is to generalize the strike movement under the slogan of a national, all-out political general strike. This must be prepared by action committees in every locality. The absence of a representative organization can be compensated for by the formation of such committees in every working class district, every factory, every village. Once the committees are linked up on a local, regional and national basis, they would form an alternative power that could challenge the rotten and corrupt Mubarak state.

At the present stage the main demands are of a revolutionary-democratic character. Down with the government! No to sham elections! For a Constituent Assembly to work out a new and democratic constitution! For full democratic rights now! But for the workers and peasants, the unemployed and homeless, democracy is not an end in itself but a means to an end.

A genuinely democratic regime would sweep away the corrupt politicians and gangsters. It would arrest and punish those guilty of oppressing and robbing the people. It would confiscate the fortunes of the rich and expropriate the property of the imperialists who have looted the wealth of Egypt for years. Such a policy can only be carried out by a workers' and peasants' government. That must be our aim.

The imperialists are worried that the overthrow of Mubarak will deprive them of a key "ally" in the Middle East. Of course it will! The people of Egypt will put an end to the shameful policy of Mubarak that subordinates the proud Egyptian nation to the interests of the robbers in Washington and their Israeli henchmen.

The whole Arab world is being shaken to its foundations. Anti-government outbreaks have occurred in the streets of Tunisia, Algeria, Yemen and Jordan. For the first time in decades, the Arab masses are taking to the streets to fight corrupt and unpopular regimes and overthrow them. Tunisia has shown that this is possible. The coming Egyptian Revolution will be a far more important event.

A revolutionary government will pursue a revolutionary foreign policy. It is time that the vast wealth of the Arab lands was used for the benefit of the people, not for the enrichment of a handful of wealthy parasites and their western backers. The revolutionary overthrow of these stooges of imperialism will lay the basis for a Socialist Federation of the Middle East and a Socialist Federation of the Maghreb. That is the only way forward.

Wednesday, 26 January 2011

THE REVOLT CONTINUES

Alan Woods

The mass demonstrations demanding the resignation of President Hos Mubarak have continued to rage since Tuesday across several cities, ii cluding Cairo and Suez. *Debkafile's* sources report that the situation Cairo Wednesday was extremely tense after thousands of demonstrators pour(into the streets and made for the Tel Talat Harb Square on the way to Liberatic Square city centre, where 30,000 protesters demonstrated on Tuesday.

Violent clashes are continuing in different parts of the country, particular Suez where anti-government demonstrators set fire to the local headquarters the ruling NDP party and continue to clash with security forces. There have bee some reports of workers joining in. There was a protest in front of a metro statiç in Helwan, south of Cairo, in which workers from Helwan factories and othe participated. The Helwan workers have organised strikes in defence of heal and safety in the last period, and some are now being tried by military tribunal

All three protesters killed in demonstrations to date were in Suez, where tl movement appears to have gone furthest. There are reports of other demonstr tions in Ismailia and Alexandria, yesterday and today. Around 600 proteste clashed with police in demonstrations across the Egyptian eastern city of Ismail today, witnesses said. They said the police dispersed the crowds using tear gas.

The reports from Twitter, despite their incomplete and fragmentary chara ter, give the definite impression of a developing national uprising. The preside: who has not been seen in public since the movement broke out on Tuesday, h: placed four armoured divisions on emergency standby and cancelled all leav(– two on operational preparedness outside Cairo and two near the towns on tl banks of the Suez Canal. Officers and men on furlough were ordered back to the bases.

Mubarak is clearly desperate. After initial vacillation, he has decided to clir to power and lean on the army to crush the rebellion. The situation in the Army contradictory. Security forces have made some 2,500 arrests of opposition acti· ists so far. But all this has failed to quell the unrest.

The appeal to force has come too late. On the streets the demonstrators ha\ learned their collective strength. The police have failed to stem the advancir tide. The army's reliability is increasingly in doubt. In Suez it is reported th the soldiers are refusing to repress the people. The growing desperation of tl regime is shown by the treatment of journalists, some 500 of whom are lock(in the building of the press association in the capital, including many foreig correspondents. Security officers burst into the building, collected the journalists in the lower floors of the building and prevented them from covering events, reporting or taking photos.

The situation in Suez

In Suez city the situation is particularly explosive. On Wednesday night, *Debkafile* reported: "The level of anti-government protest and violence escalated in the streets of Egyptian cities Wednesday night, Jan. 26 even after President Hosni Mubarak ordered a million security officers to back up the police and for the first time open fire on rioters in the town of Suez, leaving scores of dead and wounded. Western sources told *Debkafile* that security forces lost control of the situation in the main Suez Canal port after protesters managed to break through a line of police defending the suburb housing government institutions and set them on fire."

The same report states that the demonstrators torched police headquarters and the regional premises of Mubarak's ruling NDP. A report on Twitter adds: "Large protests in Mahalla now. Suez is boiling. Our people say it is no longer protests, it is a typical war zone between bare-handed protesters and armed police. They will get tired soon. Protesters come and go but police can't. I think and hope that it is happening."

A *Reuters* witness said police fled the post that was burned on Thursday when the protesters hurled petrol bombs over the killing of protesters in anti-government demonstrations earlier in the week. On Wednesday they had set a government building and another police post on fire, as well as trying to burn down a local office of Egypt's ruling party. The fires were put out before they engulfed the buildings. But dozens more protesters gathered in front of the second police post later on Thursday morning demanding the release of their relatives who were detained in protests.

Most important of all, there have been reports that some army units in Suez refused to support the police to confront the demonstrators and did not intervene until now. According to reports the police were forced to withdraws from Suez city, which was said to be "burning, but in hands of the protesters". Again: "Protests have renewed in Ismailiya as well (another city along the Suez Canal), to take the pressure off protesters in Suez."

Obama's dilemma

In Washington all the alarm bells are ringing. The earlier false optimism has given way to something close to panic. A top US senator called Egypt "an extremely important ally" on Wednesday but kept silent on support for President Hosni Mubarak. "All I could say this morning is that Egypt has been an extremely important ally of ours since Anwar Sadat, and we're all watching these developments in Cairo very carefully," said Republican Senate Minority Leader Mitch McConnell.

> White House spokesman Robert Gibbs told reporters aboard Air Force One that it was important for the Egyptian government of President Hosni Mubarak to demonstrate 'responsiveness' to its people. Asked whether the Egyptian interior ministry ban on demonstrations should be lifted, Gibbs said: 'Again, yes. We're supportive of the universal rights of assembly and speech. Those are universal values.' 'We have a close and important ally in Egypt and they will continue to be,' Gibbs said. (*Al Arabiya*)

In a further sign of desperation, Mubarak has sent his defence minister Field Marshal Mohamed Hussein Tantawi to Washington with an urgent request for US backing for his embattled regime. *Debkafile's* Washington sources report that in secret meetings, the Egyptian defence minister put the situation before President Barack Obama and top US political, military and intelligence officials.

According to *The Independent*: "He warned them that by advocating a soft hand with the demonstrators and responsiveness to their demands, American officials were doing more harm than good. Without a crackdown, he said, the regime was doomed."

Tantawi tried to frighten the Americans by warning that the Muslim Brotherhood, which initially stood aside from the opposition protests, was merely biding its time for the right moment to step in and take over. He asked the Obama administration for an urgent airlift of advanced riot control equipment.

We do not know what the American response was. Probably he was greeted with the usual smiles and handshakes and sent away with words of encouragement. As we know, words are cheap and smiles cost nothing at all. But behind his back his hosts must have shaken their heads and wondered aloud whether it was wise to back an 82-year old man who shows every sign of falling over. Question: what do you do when you see a man falling over? Answer: Give him a push!

By dispatching his agent to Washington on the first plane Mubarak was showing everybody where the real power lies. He was also making a public confession of his own impotence. These things will not have gone unnoticed either in the White House or on the streets of Cairo and Suez. This also places Washington in a very awkward position. They do not want their faithful stooge to be overthrown. But if they are seen to openly come to his assistance, it will add fuel to the fires of disaffection burning in cities across Egypt.

The protesters are proud of their Arab and Egyptian identity. Part of the hatred felt for the Mubarak regime is precisely its slavish collaboration with imperialism. Any sign that a foreign power is propping him up will only heighten their resolve to fight the regime to the death. Slogans of "US out" and "Death to the US" have already begun to appear on anti-Mubarak placards.

A palace revolution?

The bourgeoisie is increasingly worried. Egypt's stock exchange halted trading until 11:30 am (09:30 GMT) on Thursday after the benchmark index slid more than 6 per cent for a second day following the protests. The EGX30 index was down 6.2 per cent before the suspension, adding to a 6.1 per cent fall on Wednesday. By 11:33 GMT today the stock market was down 11 per cent to 5648. The selling frenzy continued despite the briefly halting of trading to calm nerves.

Something must be done! But what? Rachid M. Rachid, Mubarak's minister of trade had to withdraw from Davos and hurry back to Cairo. Rachid has been one of the engineers of the so-called neoliberal reforms. These have contributed to the hardship of the masses: high and rising prices, unemployment and poverty. No good whatever can be expected from his return. There are also rumours of a Cabinet reshuffle. But that only means to reshuffle the same old ministers. That will solve nothing. New faces are needed to calm the situation and soothe the nerves of the investors!

In the old days, when the author of a play needed a dramatic change in his plot, he produced a "deus ex machina", or as we say in English, a rabbit out of a hat. In the midst of these titanic upheavals, a modest, neatly dressed gentleman suddenly makes an unannounced appearance on stage. Resembling an aging university professor, Mohamed ElBaradei, the former UN nuclear weapons chief is returning to Egypt, announcing his intention to gracefully place himself at the head of the democratic opposition.

If it were not so serious, it would be comical. The thousands who have taken to the streets in the last two days have risked their lives, while ElBaradei sat comfortably abroad, thinking beautiful thoughts about democracy. The self-appointed Saviour of the Nation offered only lukewarm support for the protests before they began. Now there is a realistic prospect of their succeeding in overthrowing Mubarak, he suddenly announces his is prepared to play a role.

Not surprisingly, some of the protestors are angry. They suspect – not without reason – that this gentleman is acting in collaboration with the US State Department. The Americans are now deeply concerned about the situation and fear that Mubarak may not last. They need a suitable replacement, and Mr. ElBaradei fits the bill perfectly. With his reputation as a dissident rival to President Mubarak, he may get some support among the respectable middle classes in Egypt, and his ideology is not at all "extreme". It is safe, respectable, reliable, liberal. In other words, it is *bourgeois*.

ElBaradei has not lost time in appealing to his future electorate. This is, however, not the people of Egypt, but the important people: the ones in the White House, Wall Street and the Pentagon. He speaks to them in terms of endearment, like a would-be lover wooing a shy maiden:

> Of course, you in the West have been sold the idea that the only options
> in the Arab world are between authoritarian regimes and Islamic jihad-

ists. That's obviously bogus. If we are talking about Egypt, there is a whole rainbow variety of people who are secular, liberal, market-oriented, and if you give them a chance they will organize themselves to elect a government that is modern and moderate. They want desperately to catch up with the rest of the world.

ElBaradei, then, is a rainbow politician: a man whose views are as variable and elusive as the colours of the rainbow. To lay hold on these views is indeed like trying to embrace a rainbow, for they are equally as insubstantial. But this is just what is required! In order to deceive the revolutionary masses, to soothe their anger, to pacify them, to lull them to sleep, what is required is not a clear programme but vague expression about human rights, freedom and democracy.

Such "democratic speeches" are effective because they are all things to all men and women. They arouse the hope of improvement in the dim and distant future without doing anything to change the existing order and solve the immediate problems of the masses in the here and now. In the legends of old people imagined there was a pot of gold at the end of the rainbow. But as everyone knows, to actually arrive at the end of the rainbow is an impossible task. There is no pot of gold at the end of the rainbow, and there is absolutely nothing at the bottom of the empty "democratic" phrase mongering of ElBaradei.

Washington is watching the situation very closely. They will wait to see whether Mubarak can suppress the movement by force. If he succeeds, they will continue to back him. If he fails – which is the most likely outcome – they will conspire with the heads of the Egyptian army and security forces (who are infiltrated by the CIA) to organize some kind of palace coup. Mubarak will be put on the next convenient flight to Saudi Arabia, where he can spend the rest of his days reminiscing with his Tunisian counterpart about the good old days when they ruled the roost.

Even now intrigues will be taking place. Plots are being hatched. The purpose of a palace revolution will be to change the outward appearances of things so as to leave the fundamentals just as they were before. However, the situation is not decided by what is being planned in the corridors of power. The decisive element in the equation is not the intrigues at the top but what happens on the streets. It was announced that there will be mass protests after Friday prayers. This could well represent a vital turning point in the whole situation. The next few days will be decisive.

Thursday, 27 January 2011

THE EGYPTIAN REVOLUTION

Alan Woods

The flames of anger are spreading through all Egypt and nothing can stop them. The fate of the Mubarak regime hangs in the balance. Today there were violent clashes on the streets of Cairo and other Egyptian cities as the struggle for power entered a new stage. The call went out for mass protests after Friday prayers. The regime warned that any protests will be met with the full force of the state. The stage was set for a dramatic confrontation.

The situation has become explosive with extraordinary speed. In the last few days, hundreds of thousands of people went on to the streets demanding freedom. With admirable courage they braved the batons, bullets and tear gas of the police. Today they faced a real baptism of fire. The protests that used to be predominantly made up of students have now been swelled by the army of the poor and disinherited from the slums of Cairo and other cities. Robert Fisk wrote in *The Independent*, January 28, 2011:

> There are various clues that the authorities in Cairo realized something was afoot. Several Egyptians have told me that on 24 January, security men were taking down pictures of Gamal Mubarak from the slums – lest they provoke the crowds. But the vast number of arrests, the police street beatings – of women as well as men – and the near-collapse of the Egyptian stock market bear the marks of panic rather than cunning.

Can repression succeed?

On the face of it the Revolution faces a daunting challenge. The regime has a million and a half soldiers in its security apparatus, upon which it lavishes millions to keep them loyal. The purpose of this fearsome apparatus is not to defend Egypt against foreign aggressors. It is not to fight Israel. It is to keep the Egyptian people down. But can it succeed?

On paper it is a formidable force, against which the people have no chance of success. But one could say the same of every tyrannical regime in history. Louis XVI of France, Tsar Nicholas of Russia and the Shah of Iran all possessed an apparatus of repression that was a hundred times stronger than the one at the disposal of Hosni Mubarak. Yet in the moment of truth these mighty monsters collapsed like a house of cards.

But such a display of naked force revealed not strength but weakness: save for the police force and the army, the government is powerless. Napoleon once observed that one can do many things with bayonets, but you cannot sit on them.

In the final analysis the army and police is too narrow a base to sustain an unpopular regime. To their shock and astonishment the authorities are finding the repressive apparatus cannot stop the protests. Their spontaneous character itself provides a certain protection against the state, although it is a weakness that will have negative effects later on.

Today the regime mobilized its full strength to abort the revolution. Members of an elite counter-terrorism police unit were ordered to take up positions in key locations around Cairo in preparation for a wave of mass rallies. From the early hours of the morning the security forces were already taking possession of all the key points in an attempt to stop demonstrators from coalescing.

But all these measures were in vain. The protestors poured onto the streets in greater numbers than before. There were 80,000 protestors in Port Said, 50,000 Beni Suef, 100 kilometres south of Cairo, and big demonstrations in Alexandria and Suez City and elsewhere. As in Iran last year, it is impossible to arrest the organizers when demonstrations have been organised through Facebook and Twitter. The army of informers is powerless to combat this.

The state tried to block Facebook. They closed down the internet and disabled mobile phones. But the people proved to be one step ahead. Bloggers passed on ways to bypass the controls and information was spread by word of mouth. By midday (in London) the television screens were already showing scenes of massive conflict on the streets of the Egyptian capital. The police lines were unable to contain the demonstrations. The television coverage shows masses of protestors pushing against the police lines and the police retreating in disorder.

After chasing the police, thousands of protesters were able to flood into the huge Tahrir Square downtown after being kept out most of the day by the heavy police presence. Few police could be seen around the square after the confrontation. At a certain point even the violence of the state security services becomes counterproductive. Instead of fear, it arouses indignation and anger. In Suez City people rose up against police who shot demonstrators and burned a police station. And when this point is reached, cracks always appear in the ranks of the state forces. Most ordinary soldiers and policemen are reluctant to kill fellow citizens and will refuse to carry out orders to fire on unarmed demonstrators. In Suez there have been reports of such incidents.

Role of the youth

The protestors who have poured onto the streets all over Egypt in recent days are mainly young Egyptians, unemployed and without any future. One young Egyptian told the BBC: "We are poor. We have no work, no future. What should we do? Should we burn ourselves?" The only hope these young people have is to fight for a fundamental change in society. They have cast aside all fear and are prepared to risk their lives in the fight for freedom and justice.

Many of the protesters are university students who are unable to find work, and are therefore unable to marry and raise a family. They are motivated by a deep sense of injustice and a burning anger and resentment towards a system that denies them a future and a corrupt regime that has enriched itself at the people's expense.

On 27 January 2011, *The Guardian* correspondent in Cairo, Alaa Al Aswany, who participated on the big demonstration last Tuesday, was profoundly impressed by the "dazzling bravery" of the protesters, and impressed by their determination to do one thing – change the regime:

> I will always be in awe of these revolutionaries. Everything they have said shows a sharp political awareness and a death-defying desire for freedom. They asked me to say a few words. Even though I've spoken hundreds of times in public, this time it was different: I was speaking to 30,000 demonstrators who were in no mood to hear of compromise and who kept interrupting with shouts of 'Down with Hosni Mubarak', and 'The people say, out with the regime'.

> I said I was proud of what they had achieved, and that they had brought about the end of the period of repression, adding that even if we get beaten up or arrested we have proved we are not afraid and are stronger than they are. They have the fiercest tools of repression in the world at their disposal, but we have something stronger: our courage and our belief in freedom. The crowd responded by shouting en masse: 'We'll finish what we've begun!'

The decisive factor is that the masses have acquired a sense of their collective strength and are losing their fear. Beginning with the youngest, most energetic and determined elements, the mood of defiance has transmitted itself to the older, more cautious and inert layers of the population. The same edition of *The Guardian* reports a significant instance of this:

> More ordinary citizens are now defying the police. A young demonstrator told me that, when running from the police on Tuesday, he entered a building and rang an apartment bell at random. It was 4am. A 60-year-old man opened the door, fear obvious on his face. The demonstrator asked the man to hide him from the police. The man asked to see his identity card and invited him in, waking one of his three daughters to prepare some food for the young man. They ate and drank tea together and chatted like lifelong friends.

> In the morning, when the danger of arrest had receded, the man accompanied the young protester into the street, stopped a taxi for him and offered him some money. The young man refused and thanked them. As they embraced the older man said: 'It is I who should be thanking you for defending me, my daughters and all Egyptians.'

What now?

One thing is clear. Today has ended in a catastrophic defeat for Hosni Mubarak. As I write these lines events are moving with lightening speed. Rumours spread thick and fast. A Cairo daily has been claiming that one of President Hosni Mubarak's top advisers has fled to London with 97 suitcases of cash, but other reports speak of a furious President shouting at senior police officers for not dealing more harshly with demonstrators.

As night fell, the protestors remained on the streets, defying the curfew that the government has proclaimed throughout Egypt. They have begun to storm public buildings. According to Al Jazeera a few minutes ago, the Ministry of Foreign Affairs in Cairo has been stormed and taken over by protestors and set on fire. For the first time an office of the ruling National Democratic Party was set on fire, and the fire brigade made no attempt to douse the flames.

There is growing alarm in Washington. This afternoon Hillary Clinton admitted that the US is "deeply concerned about the use of force" against protestors. She called on the Egyptian government to restrain security forces but also says protesters should refrain from violence. She said: "These protests underscore that there are deep grievances within Egyptian society and the Egyptian government needs to understand that violence will not make these grievances go away." And she added: "As a partner we strongly believe that the Egyptian government needs to engage immediately with the Egyptian people in implementing political, social and economic reforms."

Translated into plain English this means: "Don't be a fool Mubarak. If you try to use the military to crush the rebellion it will break in pieces. The movement is too big to drown in blood. You must use cunning instead. Make some changes, or at least, give the impression that there will be change. In the end, of course, you may have to go. That is unfortunate, but we all have to make sacrifices from time to time. You are an old man and have outlived your usefulness. You can have a comfortable retirement and save capitalism. Or you can cling to power and end up like Sadat, dead. That would be too bad for you. But if you provoke the masses too much there will be a complete revolution and that would be too bad for us."

But Mubarak does not seem to be listening. Shut off from the real world in his palace, surrounded by yes-men and sycophants, he is clinging to power even as power ebbs away. He declares a curfew, but people remain on the streets. He calls in the army "to help the security forces" but the people applaud the army and call on the soldiers to join them. Here and there we hear of reports that the fraternization is having an effect. Associated Press reported on the scene in Cairo's central plaza. One of their reporters saw the protesters cheering the police who took off their uniforms and joined them. The triumphant protestors hoisted them on their shoulders.

Is this just an isolated incident? Or does it show a more widespread tendency? In such a rapidly changing, dramatic and chaotic situation, the mood can swing violently in minutes. In Alexandria the army is on the streets, but the soldiers are giving the thumbs up sign to the demonstrators. In Suez also the people are cheering the soldiers, who they see as their allies. There are unconfirmed reports that the army and the police are clashing. If this is true, Mubarak is in serious trouble.

Robert Fisk is one of the few western journalists who show a serious understanding of the real situation in the Middle East. In today's *Independent* (January, 28th 2011), he writes:

> Already there have been signs that those tired of Mubarak's corrupt and undemocratic rule have been trying to persuade the ill-paid policemen patrolling Cairo to join them. 'Brothers! Brothers! How much do they pay you?' one of the crowds began shouting at the cops in Cairo. But no one is negotiating – there is nothing to negotiate except the departure of Mubarak, and the Egyptian government says and does nothing, which is pretty much what it has been doing for the past three decades.

The Egyptian Revolution

Whatever the outcome of today's protests, one thing is clear: the Egyptian Revolution has already begun. Those sceptics and intellectual snobs who constantly harp on the alleged "low level of consciousness" of the masses now have their answer. Those western "experts" who talked contemptuously of the Egyptians as "apathetic" and "passive" and "indifferent to politics" must now eat their words. The masses, whether in Egypt, Iran, Britain or the USA, can only learn from experience. In a revolution, they learn much faster. The Egyptian workers and youth have learnt more in a few days of struggle than in thirty years of "normal" existence.

Only a few months ago the President and his ruling clique imagined they had everything under control. They were so confident that they were already grooming the youngest son of Mubarak, Gamal, to occupy his father's post. A former investment banker, Gamal was educated at the elite American University in Cairo, and worked for the Bank of America. He was heavily involved in the economic "liberalization" of Egypt, which delighted the rich while the poor suffered. This information is sufficient to make clear his political allegiances. Last year posters were plastered across Cairo calling for Gamal to stand for president in elections scheduled for later this year.

The protesters showed their attitude towards the chosen son, chanting "Gamal, tell your father Egyptians hate you" and tearing up his picture.

With lightening speed everything has turned into its opposite. On the streets of Cairo and other Egyptian cities people are not just talking of revolution. They are carrying out a revolution. That is now an indisputable fact. The question is posed of who or what is to replace Mubarak's regime? But this question is not uppermost in the minds of the protestors. Maybe the young people on the streets do not know exactly what they want. But they know precisely what they do not want. And that is sufficient for now.

The immediate task is to carry out the overthrow of Mubarak and his rotten regime. That will open the flood gates and allow the revolutionary people to push their way through. They are daily discovering their strength on the streets, the importance of organization and mass mobilization. That is already a tremendous conquest. Having gone through the experience of a thirty year dictatorship, they will not allow the imposition of a new one, or any intrigue to recreate the old regime with a new name. Tunisia is sufficient proof of this.

Despite attempts by the media to play up the role of the Muslim Brotherhood, it is abundantly clear that the Islamist element has been largely absent from these protests, which have taken place under the banner of revolutionary democracy. The overwhelming majority of the activists are young people from the schools and universities, who are not at all under the influence of Islamic fundamentalism. It is not even clear whether the belated participation of the Muslim Brotherhood in today's demonstrations had any real effect in increasing the number of protesters on the streets.

Now the masses have had a taste of their own power, they will not be satisfied with half-measures. They know that what they have achieved they have conquered with their own hands. Mohamed ElBaradei, an opposition leader and Nobel prize-winning former UN official, flew back to Egypt last night, but no one believes – except perhaps the Americans – that he can become a focus for the protest movements that have sprung up across the country without the aid of any bourgeois "leader". Today the foreign television cameras made a feeble attempt to highlight ElBaradei's participation on the demonstration. But all they achieved was to show pictures of a bewildered old man who scarcely seemed to know where he was or what he was doing.

The struggle for complete democracy will permit the construction of genuine trade unions and workers' parties. But it will also pose the question of economic democracy and the fight against inequality. Democracy would be an empty phrase if it refused to lay hands on the obscene wealth of the ruling elite. Confiscate the property of the ruling clique! Expropriate the property of the imperialists who backed the old regime and exploited the people of Egypt! The fight for democracy, if it is pursued to the end, must inevitably lead to the expropriation of the bankers and capitalists and the establishment of a workers' and peasants' government.

World revolution

In 1916 Lenin wrote these lines:

> Whoever expects a 'pure' social revolution will *never* live to see it. Such a person pays lip service to revolution without understanding what revolution is...

The socialist revolution in Europe cannot be anything other than an outburst of mass struggle on the part of all and sundry oppressed and discontented elements. Inevitably, sections of the petty bourgeoisie and of the backward workers will participate in it –without such participation, mass struggle is impossible, without it no revolution is possible – and just as inevitably will they bring into the movement their prejudices, their reactionary fantasies, their weaknesses and errors.

But objectively they will attack capital, and the class-conscious vanguard of the revolution, the advanced proletariat, expressing this objective truth of a variegated and discordant, motley and outwardly fragmented, mass struggle, will be able to unite and direct it, capture power, seize the banks, expropriate the trusts which all hate (though for different reasons!), and introduce other dictatorial measures which in their totality will amount to the overthrow of the bourgeoisie and the victory of socialism, which, however, will by no means immediately purge itself of petty bourgeois slag. [28]

These lines could have been written yesterday. The whole world situation has changed decisively and the events in Egypt show this in a very dramatic way. We have decisively entered the epoch of world revolution. Nowhere is the international character of the revolution clearer than in North Africa and the Middle East. It spreads ceaselessly from one country to another: from Tunisia to Algeria, from Jordan to Egypt, from the Yemen to Lebanon.

The Tunisian events were of course inspiring. People could now see with their own eyes that even the most powerful security apparatus could not prevent the overthrow of a hated dictator. People on the streets of Cairo even imitated the French slogan of the Tunisian protesters: "*Dégage*, Mubarak".

Tunisia showed what was possible. But it would be entirely false to assume that this was the only, or even the main, cause. The conditions for a revolutionary explosion had already matured in all these countries. All that was required was a single spark to ignite the powder keg. Tunisia provided it. The revolutionary uprising has already reached other Arab states such as Yemen. As in Tunisia, the people of Egypt, Algeria, Jordan and Yemen were living in poverty under dictatorial ruling elites which lived a luxurious life by plundering the nation.

These movements have striking similarities to the mass movements that led to the overthrow of the regimes in Eastern Europe. Again, on paper these governments had a powerful state apparatus, big armies, police, and secret police. But that did not save them. The bourgeoisie was overjoyed at the overthrow of "communism". But their rejoicing was premature. In retrospect the fall of Stalinism will be seen as only the prelude to a far more dramatic development: the revolutionary overthrow of capitalism. Everywhere, including the United States, the

---

28 Lenin, *The Discussion on Self-Determination Summed Up.*

system is in crisis. Everywhere the ruling class is trying to place the full burden of the crisis of its system on the shoulders of the poorest layers of society.

In Tunisia and Egypt the system is breaking at its weakest links. They will tell us that such things cannot happen here, that the situation is different and so on and so forth. Yes, the situation is different, but only in degree. Everywhere the working class and the youth will be faced with the same alternative: either we accept the systematic destruction of our living standards and rights – or we fight.

The argument "it cannot happen here" is without any scientific or rational basis. The same thing was said of Tunisia only a couple of months ago, when that country was considered to be the most stable in North Africa. And the same argument was repeated in relation to Egypt even after Ben Ali was overthrown. Just a few weeks were sufficient to expose the hollowness of those words. Such is the speed of events in our epoch. Sooner or later the same question will be posed in every country in Europe, in Japan, in Canada, in the United States.

Revolutionary developments are on the order of the day. The process will advance at a greater or lesser speed according to local conditions. But no country can consider itself immune from the general process. The events in Tunisia and Egypt show us our own future as in a mirror.

Friday, 28 January 2011

REVOLUTION IN EGYPT – POWER IS ON THE STREETS

Alan Woods

Day five of the revolution and the movement continues to grow in size and intensity. Last night's curfew was ignored, and today there are more people on the streets than yesterday. A new curfew was called for four o'clock Egyptian time, but this is no more effective than the previous one. Even before the curfew came into effect, larger numbers of protestors were gathering on the streets.

"The street is not being organized by the parties, it is not being organized by the state. It is not controlled by anybody." (Al Jazeera)

Following the events hour by hour I recalled the following incident from the French Revolution. On the 14th of July 1789, shortly after the fall of the Bastille, the French king, Louis XVI, asked the Duke of Rochefoucauld-Liancourt: "Is this a revolt?" To which the Duke delivered the immortal reply: *"Non Sire, c'est une révolution!"* – "No, sir, it's a revolution!"

In Egypt we are witnessing a revolution in full swing. After five days of colossal struggles, this fact has penetrated even the most obtuse skulls. The popular revolt is spreading by the hour. It is like a mighty river that overflows its banks and sweeps away all barriers that were erected to contain it.

Overnight all police have disappeared from the streets of the capital. Tanks and armoured personnel carriers are on the streets of Cairo, where fires from the previous day's violence are still smouldering. Mobile phone services have been restored in the city, but the internet remains down.

Meanwhile, the death toll has reportedly risen to 53 since the January 28 protest. In Suez, where at least twenty people have been killed, the bodies of the martyrs were carried through the streets as the people shouted revolutionary slogans. In Cairo the political prisoners have taken control of a jail. In Giza the people have burnt the police station and are attacking the police. Burning police vehicles have become a common sight on Egyptian streets. In one case, a group of protesters tried to push an armoured vehicle into the River Nile.

After the withdrawal of the police there have been many reports of looting. The people suspect that this has been deliberately organized by the regime in order to create the impression of anarchy and chaos. It is clear that the prisons have been opened to let out the criminal elements, who have been armed for this purpose. Egyptian television has shown scenes of destruction of precious artefacts in the historic Cairo museum.

It is an open secret that this is a manoeuvre to destroy the revolution. The large numbers of armed police who yesterday were shooting at unarmed demonstrators are now nowhere to be seen as armed lumpenproletarians go on the rampage. Several of the looters who were caught by protestors turned out to be undercover policemen.

In response, neighbourhood committees have been set up in Suez and Alexandria to keep order and prevent looting. In some places the committees are even directing the traffic. There is an urgent need to generalise the committees and to arm the people. We must remember the slogan of the French Revolution: "Mort aux voleurs!" (Death to thieves!)

Mubarak's speech

"Power tends to corrupt," the saying goes; "Absolute power corrupts absolutely." The President is suffering from the same delusions of grandeur that affected the mental capacities of every Roman emperor and Russian tsar in the past. Last night's speech of President Mubarak, far from calming the situation, has thrown petrol on the flames.

The people's message is loud and clear. But the President does not hear it. He is blind and deaf and has lost the use of reason. A man who has got used to being surrounded by a camarilla of servile courtiers hanging on his every word loses all contact with reality. He begins to believe in his own omnipotence. The border line between reality and fantasy is blurred. Such a state of mind is akin to madness.

Watching Mubarak speak, one had the impression of a man who has lost all contact with reality and is playing out his own fantasies. He promises that everything will be better from now on, if only the people will trust him. He will dismiss his government and he will graciously appoint another one. He will make the necessary changes. But he will not tolerate chaos and disorder. Anyone who disobeys can expect no mercy.

This is the voice of the Father of the People, the harsh but benevolent Pharaoh who decides every question for the benefit of his children. But the people of Egypt are not little children and have no need of a Pharaoh who has to send his army onto the streets to keep them obedient.

The government has duly resigned and a "new" government has been appointed (by Mubarak). The prime minister will be Rachid Mohamad Rashid – a millionaire and the former minister of investment, commerce and industry. Rashid is identified with the so-called neoliberal reforms that have contributed to the hardship of the masses: high and rising prices, unemployment and poverty.

This appointment is sufficient to reveal the precise physiognomy of the "new" government. It is a provocation to the people on the streets. Since then Omar Suleiman, the 74-year old head of the state intelligence services, has been named vice-president. Since Suleiman is one of Mubarak's main stooges, this is an even more blatant provocation to the masses. It shows how far out of touch with reality Mubarak is.

If the President's speech was intended to calm things down, it had the opposite effect. Last night BBC television spoke on the telephone to a man who had been on the streets all day: "I intended to go to bed for a few hours and then continue demonstrating tomorrow, but after I heard Mubarak's speech I immediately phoned all my relations to come out and demonstrate, and I went back on the streets."

The "Islamist menace"

The western media is constantly repeating the idea that the Moslem Brotherhood is behind the protests, and that they are the only alternative to Mubarak. This is false. The fact is that, just like all the other political parties, the Moslem Brotherhood has been completely caught unawares by this movement. Initially they did not even support it, and their role in organizing the protests has been minimal.

The Muslim Brotherhood recently subtly changed its message ahead of the latest protests. The deputy leader Mahmoud Izzat spoke encouragingly of the protests: "People are demanding freedom, the dissolution of this invalid parliament. From the beginning this is what the young people have been shouting and we are with them," Mr Izzat told the Al Jazeera news channel. And he went on to criticise "the excessive force" of the security services.

However, the Brotherhood did not organize the protests and on the demonstrations one sees very few bearded fundamentalists. The majority of the activists are young, many of them students, but there are also many unemployed youth from the slums of Cairo and Alexandria. They are not fighting for the introduction of Sharia law but for freedom and jobs.

The fact of the matter is that these reactionaries did not want this revolutionary movement and are mortally afraid of it. The people who streamed out of the mosques to demonstrate on the streets of Suez after Friday prayers did so in spite of the fact that the imam told them not to participate in the protests. The reactionary role of the fundamentalists is shown by the influential Islamist al-Qaradawi who, according to Al Jazeera, "urges people not to attack state institutions."

The Brotherhood itself is split and has declined. Hossam el-Hamalawy told Al Jazeera:

> The Brotherhood has been suffering from divisions since the outbreak of the al-Aqsa intifada. Its involvement in the Palestinian Solidarity Movement when it came to confronting the regime was abysmal. Basically, whenever their leadership makes a compromise with the regime, especially the most recent leadership of the current supreme guide, it has demoralised its base cadres. I know personally many young brothers who left the group. Some of them have joined other groups or remained independent. As the current street movement grows and the lower leadership gets in-

volved, there will be more divisions because the higher leadership can't justify why they're not part of the new uprising.

International repercussions

If the government and all the political parties have been taken by surprise, this is still more the case with western governments. Having denied any possibility of an upheaval in Egypt only one week ago, the leaders of the western world in Washington now stand with their mouths open.

Obama and Hilary Clinton seem to be having difficulty keeping up with the situation. Their public declarations show that they have not yet grasped the realities on the ground. They express sympathy with the protestors but are still in favour of maintaining a friendly dialogue with the government that is shooting and gassing them. This desire to ride both horses at the same time may be understandable, but it is a little difficult to do when both horses are running in opposite directions.

President Obama, as everybody knows, specializes in facing all directions at once. But his chief speciality is in saying nothing but saying it very nicely. He advises Egypt to introduce democracy and provide its citizens with work and a decent living standard. But neither he nor any of his predecessors had any problem about collaborating with Hosni Mubarak, although they knew he was a tyrant and a dictator. Only now, when the masses are on the point of overthrowing him, do they suddenly begin to sing the praises of democracy.

Obama's request for more jobs and improved living standards in Egypt sounds particularly hollow. It was the United States that was behind the economic "reforms" of 1991 that pushed Egypt into the kind of "liberalism" that resulted in huge inequality; obscene wealth for a few and poverty and unemployment for the vast majority. More than anything else that is what has created the present explosive situation in Egypt. In this context, Obama's advice is the worst kind of cynicism.

Washington's concern is not motivated by humanitarian or democratic considerations. It is motivated by self-interest. Egypt is the most important Arab country in the Middle East. By comparison, Tunisia is a small and relatively marginal country. But historically whatever happens in Egypt tends to communicate itself to the entire region. That is why all the Arab ruling cliques are worried and that is why Washington is worried.

They are right to worry. But the Israeli ruling circles are even more worried. Mubarak was a useful tool of Israeli foreign policy. As a "moderate" (that is, a western stooge) he helped to keep up the illusion of a fraudulent "peace process" which kept the Palestinian masses in check while the Israelis consolidated their positions. He propped up the equally "moderate" Abbas and the other leaders of the PLO, who have betrayed the aspirations of the Palestinian people. He supported the so-called war on terror.

He was thus very useful to both the Americans and the Israelis. His services were well rewarded. The USA subsidized his regime to the tune of around $2 billion a year. Egypt is the fourth largest recipient of American aid, after Afghanistan, Pakistan and Israel. Most of this money went on arms expenditure, a fact that will have been painfully brought home to the protestors when they read the labels on tear gas canisters with the words "Made in the USA" written on them. These messages from Washington speak to the protestors with far greater eloquence than the speeches of Mr. Obama.

The removal of Mubarak will therefore remove one of the most important elements of US foreign policy in the Middle East. It will further undermine the "moderate" (pro-American) Arab regimes. Already the mass protests are growing in Jordan and Yemen. Others will follow. Saudi Arabia itself is not safe.

The imperialists look on aghast. Overnight all their schemes are coming undone. Malcolm Rifkind, a former Conservative British Foreign Secretary, when asked for his view of the situation on BBC television, said: "Well, this has been prepared for a long time. Whatever government comes to power in Egypt will not be pro-western. But there is not a lot we can do about it."

The army

The army is now all that separates Mubarak from the abyss. How will the army react? The army has now replaced the police on the streets. The relationship between the soldiers and the protestors is uneasy and contradictory. In some cases there is fraternization. In other cases, there have been clashes with protestors.

In order to put an end to the revolt, it would be necessary to kill thousands of protesters. But it is impossible to kill them all. And there is no guarantee that troops would be prepared to obey the order to fire on unarmed demonstrators. The army officers know that one bloody incident would be sufficient to break the army in pieces. It seems very unlikely that they would be prepared to take the risk. Today the BBC website speculated about the army's role:

> Broadly speaking, Egyptians respect their army, which is still seen as a patriotic bulwark against their neighbour Israel, with whom they went to war in 1967 and 1973.
>
> But the black-clad riot police, the Central Security Force (Amn al-Markazi), belongs to the interior ministry, and has been in the forefront of much of the violent confrontations with protesters.
>
> Poorly paid and mostly illiterate, they number around 330,000 when combined with the Border Force. They themselves rioted over low pay in the early years of President Mubarak's rule and had to be brought under control by the army.
>
> The army has a similar strength – around 340,000 – and is under the command of Gen Mohammad Tantawi, who has close ties with the US (he has just been visiting the Pentagon).

When Mr Mubarak ordered the army onto the streets of Cairo and other cities late on Friday, his aim was to back up the riot police who have been heavily outnumbered by the protesters.

But many of them are hoping the army will take their side or, at the very least, act as a restraining force on the police who have been acting with excessive brutality throughout this protest.

Hence the cheers that greeted the columns of army vehicles as they drove through Cairo on Friday night.

Up until now, President Mubarak has enjoyed the support of the armed forces.

He was, after all, a career air force officer suddenly catapulted to the presidency when Anwar Sadat was assassinated in 1981.

But if these protests continue and intensify there are bound to be senior voices within the military tempted to urge him to stand down.

The days of the Mubarak regime are numbered and this must be clear to the army chiefs, who must think of their own future. Even if security forces manage to put down protests today, how will they put down the ones that happen next week, or next month or next year? Power is, in effect, lying in the street, waiting for somebody to pick it up. But who will do so? If a party like the Bolshevik Party of Lenin and Trotsky were present, the conquest of power by the working class would be on the order of the day. The problem is that such a party does not yet exist.

In the absence of a revolutionary party and leadership, the present situation can end in deadlock. In such situations the state itself, in the shape of the army, tends to raise itself above society and become the arbiter between the classes. In Egypt and other Middle Eastern countries there is a long history of such things, beginning with Abdel Nasser. It is possible that a section of the army leaders will decide to dump Mubarak.

The mass movement is strong enough to overthrow the old regime. But as yet it lacks the necessary level of organization and leadership to constitute itself as a new power. Consequently, the revolution will be a protracted affair, which must go through a series of stages before the workers are in a position to take power into their hands. There will be a series of transitional governments, each more unstable than the last. But on a capitalist basis none of the fundamental problems can be solved.

However, the fall of Mubarak will open the floodgates. The working class has been awakened to struggle. For the last four years there has been a wave of labour strikes in Egypt. The workers will take advantage of democracy to press their class demands. The struggle for democracy will open the way for the fight for socialism.

Saturday, 29 January 2011

REVOLUTION KNOWS NO FRONTIERS

Alan Woods

The popular uprising against the Hosni Mubarak government continues. On Sunday morning the sun rose over another tense day following a night of mass defiance and anti-government protests that turned the curfew into a dead letter. This fact strikingly exposes the real situation.

It is the first working day in the Egyptian capital since protests peaked on Friday. Yet, in the words of Al Jazeera's Dan Nolan, it is a "long way from business as usual". Main roads in the capital have now been blocked by military tanks and armoured personnel carriers. Extra military roadblocks have been set up in an apparent attempt to divert traffic away from Tahrir Square, the focal point for demonstrators. "It's still a very tense scene to have so much military in the capital city of the country," he says.

The President, who on paper enjoys enormous power, makes decrees. The army is ordered to carry out his orders. Those who defy the curfew are threatened with dire consequences. But nobody obeys and nothing happens.

The BBC correspondent in Cairo summed up the real situation. Standing before a huge building from which flames and smoke are belching, visibly astonished, he says: "The headquarters of the ruling party is on fire and there is no fire brigade in sight. And of course there are no police. The state here has disappeared."

This is not the only case. Several key government buildings in the capital continue to smoulder this morning, visible proof of the way the rebels have attacked the state. A crowd of people tried to storm the hated Ministry of the Interior, where people are taken for torture. They were beaten back by police snipers firing from the roof, leaving three dead.

Unidentified men on Sunday came out of the interior ministry compound in a car and dumped a body on a street. They then opened fire on people present in the area and fled. There were no immediate reports of casualties in that attack.

People are risking their lives every day on the streets. The death toll is now said to be over one hundred and fifty, and at least 4,000 injured. But nobody knows what the real figure is. Yet no amount of repression can halt the movement. People have lost their fear. Thousands of protesters remain camped out in the city's Tahrir Square. They are not afraid to die. That is their main strength, and the main weakness of the forces that confront them.

Al Jazeera's sources have indicated that the military has now also been deployed to the resort town of Sharm el Sheikh. Sherine Tadros, Al Jazeera's correspondent in the city of Suez, said the city had witnessed a "completely chaotic night", but that the streets were quiet as day broke. She reported that in the absence of police and military, people were "taking the law into their own hands", using "clubs, batons, sticks, machetes [and] knives" to protect their property.

The "international community"

The "international community" is terrified at this turn of events. Caught by surprise, the US has been a mere spectator over the last several weeks, as people took to the streets in Tunisia and Egypt. Washington understands all too well that the events in Egypt will have far reaching implications on other countries in the region.

The Americans and Europeans are now urging Mubarak to refrain from violence against unarmed protesters and to work to create conditions for free and fair elections. They realize that what Mubarak has offered is too little and too late. The US told Mubarak on Saturday that it was not enough simply to "reshuffle the deck" with a shake-up of his government and pressed him to deliver "genuine reform".

"The Egyptian government can't reshuffle the deck and then stand pat," State Department spokesman PJ Crowley said in a message on Twitter after Mubarak fired his government but made clear he had no intention of stepping down.

"President Mubarak's words pledging reform must be followed by action," Crowley said, echoing Obama's appeal on Friday. These words are echoed by the leading governments of Europe. In a statement released in Berlin on Saturday, the leaders of Britain, France and Germany said they were "deeply worried about the events in Egypt".

"We call on President Mubarak to renounce any violence against unarmed civilians and to recognise the demonstrators' peaceful rights," the joint statement said.

"We call on President Mubarak to begin a transformation process that should be reflected in a broadly based government, as well as free and fair elections."

The Europeans appealed to Mubarak to respond to his people's grievances and take steps to improve the human rights situation in the country: "Human rights and democratic freedom must be fully recognised, including freedom of expression and assembly, and the free use of means of communication such as telephone and internet."

But they leave out of account one small detail. The only "genuine reform" the people want is the immediate resignation of Mubarak and all his cronies. This is one reform Mubarak is not prepared to contemplate. In all these declarations the word democracy is conspicuous by its absence. All the emphasis is on *stability*. That goes to the heart of the matter.

The Americans and Europeans have no right whatsoever to speak of human rights. For decades they have supported the bestial regime of Hosni Mubarak. They have financed his army and police force and turned a blind eye to repression, brutality and torture. In return, he has supported their policies in the Middle East. He was a pivotal figure in the ugly farce of the "peace talks" and the betrayal of the Palestinians. This beautiful relationship was not based on democracy and human rights but on cynical self-interest.

For years these same imperialists have dictated the economic policies of supposedly "independent" governments. In the past many Arab governments called themselves socialist. They carried out nationalizations and measures in the interests of the workers and peasants. But for the last three decades these policies were reversed. In 1987, at the height of the debt crisis, the left nationalist government of Habib Bourguiba was replaced by a new regime, firmly committed to "free market" reforms.

So-called market reforms have led to growing inequality, poverty and unemployment. The food price hikes in Tunisia were not "dictated" by the Ben Ali government. They were imposed by Wall Street and the IMF. Ben Ali's government slavishly carried out the IMF's deadly economic medicine over a period of more than twenty years. This served to destabilize the national economy and impoverish the Tunisian population. That is the real basis for the Tunisian Revolution.

The same was true of Egypt when Sadat reversed the policies of Abdel Nasser and turned Egypt into a satellite of US imperialism. His faithful lieutenant Hosni Mubarak continued and deepened these policies, especially after the economic reform of 1991, which was dictated by the Americans. These governments slavishly obeyed and effectively enforced the diktats of the IMF, while serving the interests of both the US and the European Union. This pattern has occurred in numerous countries. Now all this is threatened.

The real "concern" in Washington, London, Paris and Berlin is that the imperialists are facing a catastrophic collapse of all their strategies for controlling the Middle East and its huge resources. This was clearly spelled out in the European statement: "We recognise the balanced role that President Mubarak has played for many years in the Middle East. We call on him to adopt the same moderate approach to the current situation in Egypt."

The "moderate approach" and "balanced role" of Hosni Mubarak consisted in blatant support for the policies of the imperialists. That is why he was an invaluable ally of the USA and Israel. That is why they are desperate to prop him up. But they have already failed. No force on earth can save him now.

The domino effect

The fears of the imperialists are well grounded. Revolutions are no respecters of frontiers. The revolutionary events in Tunisia and Egypt are shaking the whole Arab world to its foundations. From the day that President Ben Ali fled to Saudi

Arabia, the question was never just what would happen next in Tunisia, but whether the popular uprising there would become a catalyst for discontent elsewhere. Now we have the answer.

Immediately following the Tunisian insurrection there were mass protests in neighbouring Algeria. There have been mass demonstrations in Yemen and Jordan. Last week the BBC reported that a group of former Jordanian army officers produced an open letter to the king asking him to introduce reforms before something worse happened. Interviewed by the BBC, the Jordanian deputy prime minister replied that there were only a few such officers: "not more than 150 or 200".

The corrupt oil states in the Gulf have been sitting on vast wealth for decades while millions of people in the Arab world are suffering terrible poverty, unemployment and deprivation. These rotten regimes are unpopular and base themselves on repression as much as Mubarak. His overthrow would destabilise one pro-western Arab regime after another.

The Gulf Cooperation Council, a loose economic and political bloc of states in the Arabian Gulf, said on Sunday that it wanted a "stable Egypt".

"We are looking for a stable Egypt and hoping things will be restored soon," Abdulrahman al-Attiyah, the GCC's secretary general, said on the sidelines of a Malaysian investment forum. He also downplayed concerns about the possible economic fallout of the unrest.

The recent revelations concerning the secret deals between the PLO leadership and Israel will have provoked a crisis in the ranks of the Palestinians. The masses and the rank and file of the PLO will be shocked and disgusted by this blatant collaborationism. The so-called peace process is now dead in the water. The faith of the masses in the leadership will be severely shaken. In such a context the events in Tunisia and Egypt will have a very serious impact on the thinking of ordinary Palestinians.

The tactic of so-called armed struggle has led nowhere. The rockets of Hamas do not even dent the armour of the powerful Israeli state. But the policies of the so-called moderates have also failed miserably. Neither Hamas nor Abbas have anything to offer the Palestinian people. They must trust only themselves, in their own strength. The prospect of a new Intifada is growing stronger by the day. And Tunisia and Egypt provide them with an inspiring example.

This lesson has not been lost on the Israeli ruling circles. No government is more terrified than that of Israel of the Arab revolution. When the first protests erupted a senior Israeli government source described the events in the Middle East as an "earthquake". Israel was monitoring the situation in Egypt closely, he added, but he foolishly believed the Mubarak regime was strong enough to withstand the protests. "We believe Egypt will overcome the current wave of protests," he said. "But it reflects the fragile situation in the region."

Egypt is one of the closest collaborators of Israel in the region. It has a border with Gaza and Mubarak has actively collaborated with the Israelis in strangling the Gaza Strip. He has provided invaluable support for Abbas and the right wing leadership of the PLO. His fall would be a catastrophe for Israel and transform the situation throughout the Middle East and beyond. However, the Israelis are powerless to intervene. They must be very careful about what they say about Egypt, for fear of making a bad situation (from their point of view) even worse.

Benyamin Netanyahu, the Israeli prime minister told cabinet ministers that Israel was "closely monitoring" events in Egypt, adding: "Our goal is to maintain stability and ensure that peace between us and Egypt continues to exist with any development." He continued:

"The cause of instability ... has no connection with the Israeli-Palestinian conflict", but was being driven by economic factors. The protests were being fuelled by social media, he said – "it's what connects the dots" – pointing out that in the past Arab regimes were able to maintain a tight grip on news and communications. Al Jazeera, he said, was "playing a more significant role than a regular TV station in the West". There were many differences between Egypt and Tunisia, where protests forced the president and his wife to flee the country. "Mubarak's regime is well-rooted in the military."

The Israeli ruling clique is not worried by suicide bombers and Hamas' rockets. On the contrary, every rocket that falls on a Jewish village, every bomb that blows up a bus is excellent news for the Zionists. It serves to convince ordinary people in Israel that "they want to kill us", and pushes the population behind the government. But this is something different. The revolutionary movement of the Arab masses poses a serious threat to them.

What now?

What happens when an irresistible force meets an immovable object? For Egypt there is no way back. Mubarak has opted for more of the same old and bankrupt ways of dealing with national uprising, making promises of change and cosmetic alterations in order to cling to power. It will not work. Everything depends on two things: the momentum of the popular uprising and the role of the military.

There are tanks on the streets. But they are surrounded by the revolutionary people. The protesters climb on the tanks, appeal to the troops who often reply with the thumbs up sign.

In Liberation Square the troops opened fire yesterday, probably above the heads of the people. This was real fire. But the people did not flinch. On the contrary, when they heard the gunfire people ran towards the place where the firing was taking place. In other words, they were running towards danger, not away from it. This little detail is extremely important. It shows the limits of military power.

The movement has not been intimidated by a show of force. The continued momentum of the uprising poses the need to remove Mubarak, his family and his political leadership from the helm. The tops of the army will make their calculations on the basis of a delicate balancing act. Their need to insure their own influence and privileges is far more important to them than the preservation of Mubarak.

The revolt continues to expand and gain momentum in major Egyptian cities and protestors demand the removal of Mubarak and his regime. The masses know that the position of the regime is untenable. They feel they have already won a victory. On the streets there is a mood of joy, of euphoria. This euphoria is being transmitted to every layer of the population. It is a far more powerful stimulant than wine.

An elderly middle class man who had fled from the disturbances in Cairo was asked by the BBC if he thought that the demonstrations have gone too far. With a voice trembling with emotion, he answered: "The demonstrations are wonderful! I have been waiting for this all my life!"

New and dramatic events are being prepared that will shake the world.

Sunday, 30 January 2011

THE MOMENT OF TRUTH

Alan Woods

The Great Pyramid of Giza has lasted for 3,800 years. Hosni Mubarak has lasted somewhat less, but he would like to survive for a little longer. The difference between his regime and the Pyramid of Khufu is that his is an inverted pyramid. All its strength is at the top, but there is only a tiny point at the bottom. The laws of gravity and architecture tell us that such a structure is inherently unstable. The slightest push can bring the whole structure crashing down.

The whole of Egypt is now in a precarious balance. That same precariousness applies to the role of the armed forces, the sole remaining fulcrum of the regime. On paper it is a formidable force, as solid as the aforementioned pyramid. But armies are composed of human beings, and are subject to the same pressures as any other social stratum or institution.

From one minute to the next the protesters awaited the order from the President for the army to disperse the crowds. "The soldiers are not out here for the people, they are out for the president," said a middle-aged man. As darkness fell, the loud whirring of military helicopters could again be heard above central Cairo. Despite this, the rebels continued to chant angrily for President Hosni Mubarak to step down, some waving the Egyptian flags. Air force jets made multiple passes overhead. But on the ground the troops made no attempt to break up the protests.

The tanks that rolled into Tahrir Square were meant to intimidate. But they were immediately surrounded by a human mass that impeded their progress. There have been shows of solidarity with protesters sharing their food with soldiers and in one case, carrying a young officer on their shoulders. The longer the army is in contact with the revolutionary masses, the greater will be the effect and the more difficult it will be to use it to crush the revolution.

The display of military might was meant to have a psychological effect on the tens of thousands of protesters gathering in Tahrir Square. However, the tanks have failed to stop the protests. Mubarak, a former air force officer, decided that fighter planes might get better results, since it is difficult to fraternize with a high-flying pilot. Yesterday fighter jets flew low over the protesters in an attempt to cause panic. But just as they had quickly adjusted to the presence of tanks on the streets, demonstrators were undeterred.

Instead of fear, however, this intimidatory gesture caused anger. "Look! They are sending the air force against us. From this moment we have no President. We will get rid of Mubarak or we will die here." That was the reaction of one protester. "At first, I was frightened from the sound of the planes, but now it's as if I'm listening to music," commented a student who had come out to protest for the first time. "It's okay, they're not going to kill us," she said, then added, "although some people do say the president might kill all the country just to stay on."

In a revolution, as in a war, timing is of the essence. The same is true of a counterrevolution. Decisive action is necessary if order is to be imposed by force of arms. But here there is no decisive action, only hesitation, prevarication and indecision. Mubarak is "willing to wound, and yet afraid to strike". This is a sure recipe for undermining any authority he may still have had. Machiavelli said that it was better for a ruler to be feared than to be loved. Just one week ago Mubarak was not loved but he was feared. Now he is regarded with contempt. He has lost the initiative and it will be impossible to regain it.

General strike

It is obvious that society cannot continue like this. Either the old order will re-impose its authority – a perspective that is becoming increasingly unlikely – or the masses will impose a new order. There is talk of a general strike. Groups of protesters camped out in ·the capital overnight, determined not to leave until Hosni Mubarak goes. The momentum of the movement continues to grow as we write these lines. Thousands rallied over the weekend in Alexandria and there were also sizeable demonstrations in Mansoura, Damanhour and Suez.

Crowds are again building in Cairo's Tahrir Square, despite army checkpoints designed to limit access. A march billed as the "protest of the millions" is taking place today (Tuesday). More than a million people are out in Tahrir Square, 300,000 in Suez, 250,000 in Mahalla, 250,000 in Mansoura, and 500,000 in Alexandria. Protesters are out in every single city and town in Egypt, approximately four million all over Egypt. It is the moment of truth.

Even without a general strike normal economic life has already ground to a halt. The Japanese car maker Nissan has announced that it is halting production at its Egypt plant for a week, and it has urged non-Egyptian employees to leave the country. The impact is already being felt in global markets. The Nikkei fell in early trading in Tokyo as the Egyptian unrest prompted investors to dump risky assets.

Most shops and businesses in Cairo are closed. The middle classes are rushing to withdraw money from bank cash machines. The few supermarkets that are open are stripped bare by shoppers, stocking up with food. In the poor areas, the bakeries are running out of the small round loaves of bread that are a staple of the national diet. Streets are said to be piling up with rubbish as shops and hotels run out of basic supplies as infrastructure breaks down due to the unrest.

In a further vacillation the police have been ordered back on the streets again. State television has warned there are gangs on the rampage, although some believe it is exaggerating the threat to scare people. The regime is trying to create an atmosphere of tension to justify a clampdown. Security forces in plainclothes are engaged in destroying public property in order to give the impression that many protesters represent a public menace. A recent *Stratfor* report indicated that plainclothes police from Egypt's internal security apparatus are the main drivers behind the growing insecurity in the streets over the past few days. It says:

> It is important to keep in mind that historically, animosity has existed between Egyptian police and army officers. The Interior Ministry, according to *STRATFOR* sources, wanted to prevent the military from imposing control in the streets. It appears that the absence of police on the streets Jan. 29 was (at least in part) encouraged by the outgoing interior minister, who was sacked the same day along with the rest of the Cabinet. Egyptian plainclothes police allegedly were behind a number of the jailbreaks, robberies of major banks and the spread of attacks and break-ins in high-class neighbourhoods. The idea behind the violent campaign was to portray the protesters as a public menace and elicit a heavy-handed army crackdown to embroil the military in an even bigger crisis.

The reaction of the people has been to begin to take over the running of their areas. The protester are forming people's committees to protect public property and also to coordinate demonstrators' activities, including supplying them with food, beverages and first aid. In some neighbourhoods, residents are erecting makeshift checkpoints. They arm themselves with sticks and pistols against looters. Some use equipment left by police officers after they abandoned their usual positions.

Images of the scenes unfolding are being broadcast into homes across Egypt and the Arab world, and large audiences are watching and waiting to see what happens. The authorities are attempting to get a monopoly over the means of communication by restricting the printed media and the internet. The information ministry has closed the local Al-Jazeera office in a fresh attempt to control the message. However, such efforts seem futile. The ever-resourceful Egyptians are continuing to tune in to satellite television to hear the news.

An "orderly transition"

Amid growing fears in London and other European capitals that "extremists could try to exploit the situation", British premier David Cameron spoke to King Abdullah of Jordan on Sunday about the situation in the Middle East and North Africa[29]. British foreign secretary William Hague told the BBC: "It's to avert

---

29 No doubt Cameron was advising the King of Jordan on what to do to placate the masses. The latest news is that King Abdullah II of Jordan has now sacked his government. This has come after huge street protests inspired by the revolutions in Tunisia and Egypt. This is confirmation that, after the protests in Yemen, Algeria and other countries, what started in Tunisia could engulf the whole of the Arab world

those risks and meet the legitimate grievances and aspirations of the Egyptian people that we are urging the Egyptian authorities... to create a more broadly-based government." He said reforms should be "real and visible" and elections "free and fair".

But there is one small problem with all this well-meaning advice. Mubarak seems determined not to run away as Ben Ali did. And in fact the Americans don't wish that either. They can see that the resulting power vacuum would be very dangerous for them. The Americans have warned President Mubarak urgently that there must be no more killings. They know that one bloody clash would be sufficient to split the army in pieces. Then the floodgates would open. That is why the army has stated that it will not use force to suppress the demonstrations. This is the kiss of death for Mubarak.

ElBaradei and the other "reformers" are pleading with the Americans to intervene: "It is better for President Obama not to appear that he is the last one to say to President Mubarak: 'It's time for you to go'." But Obama has not said this – not yet anyway. The masses want a complete transformation. But Barack Obama wants only an "orderly transition". An orderly transition – to what? We do not know. But we do know that Obama has called for Mr Mubarak to initiate it. That is to say, he is willing to give the old dictator a key role in making arrangements for the future of Egypt. We know also that Washington sees Egypt is a key "ally" in the Middle East. It has given it billions of dollars of aid, and it wants value for its money.

The White House says Mr Obama made a number of calls about the situation over the weekend to foreign leaders including Turkish Prime Minister Recep Tayyip Erdogan, King Abdullah of Saudi Arabia and British Prime Minister David Cameron. The protests in Egypt are top of the agenda of a meeting of European Union foreign ministers in Brussels on Monday. All are terrified about the effect of "contagion" from Egypt.

The BBC correspondent John Simpson says: "From the American point of view, the best thing that could happen would be a peaceful end to the protests, the retirement of Mr Mubarak and the continuation of some part (at least) of the system which he has created – shorn, hopefully, of its corruption." But he adds a warning: "It won't be easy and it won't appeal greatly to the demonstrators, who have condemned Mr Mubarak's entire political structure and want to bring it down."

The strategists of Capital are relying on the fact that people will be tired, and that there will be a general desire to get back to ordinary life, and this will bring a gradual end to the protest. Then the system if not the president himself might survive. But everything depends on the demonstrators: if they hold out, an "orderly transition" will not be possible, and the movement could go far further than anybody suspects.

Last night on (British) Channel Four News there was a debate between an American and a British "expert". The American – a typically bone-headed right winger – was optimistic about a "managed transition to democracy". His British counterpart was not impressed. "This is a revolutionary situation," he replied with icy sarcasm. "You cannot hope to manage a situation like that." There can be no doubt that the latter evaluation is the correct one.

Meanwhile, China has added its voice to the chorus calling for a return to "order". A Chinese foreign ministry spokesman said on Sunday: "Egypt is a friend of China's, and we hope social stability and order will return to Egypt as soon as possible". The Chinese regime is interested in global economic stability because it wants to continue to earn a lot of money from exports. But it is also afraid of anything that could provide an impetus for strikes and protests in China itself. That explains why the Chinese regime has blocked the use of search engines to find news on the events unfolding in Egypt!

The masses fight, the politicians intrigue

The Americans are desperately manoeuvring behind the scenes. For the last week there have been intense discussions with senior U.S. officials, the government and the tops of the army. The military is preparing the time for Mubarak's political exit. Until this happens, the unrest in the streets will continue. But who and what will take his place?

In its search for an "orderly transition", the western media is trying to build up the figure Mohamed ElBaradei. The television cameras somehow always manage to locate him among a mass of demonstrators. But it brings to mind the following anecdote. A man was seen wandering aimlessly behind a crowd of demonstrators. When someone asked him who he was, he answered: "Me? I'm their leader."

Although he played no role in organizing the protests, he is nevertheless presented as the leader of a mysterious "opposition coalition", which apparently includes the Islamist Muslim Brotherhood, which also played no role in organizing the protests and at first did not even participate in them. This "coalition" is calling for a national unity government to be set up. Who will be in this government? Nobody knows. Who elected this "opposition coalition"? Nobody knows. Yet behind the backs of the masses, these gentlemen are already making plans to seize the reins of power.

The leaders are jockeying for power. The opposition is unified in its hatred against Mubarak, yet divided on almost everything else. Already there were signs of disunity within the "united" opposition. The Muslim Brotherhood is having second thoughts about its endorsement of leading figure Mohamed ElBaradei as a negotiator with Mr Mubarak. A spokesman for the Muslim Brotherhood, Mohamed Morsy, told the BBC:

"The people have not appointed Mohamed ElBaradei to become a spokesman of them." That is quite true. The people have not appointed Mohamed ElBaradei, but neither have they appointed the Muslim Brotherhood. They have not appointed anybody because they have not been consulted. They are fighting and dying on the streets, and their objective is not to further the careers of opportunist politicians but to change their lives.

The revolts in Tunisia and Egypt are largely secularist and democratic, and often deliberately excluding the Islamists. The conventional wisdom that only the Muslim Brotherhood can organise grassroots opposition movements in the Middle East is false, as is the idea that it is the 'only real opposition'. The protests indicate the extent to which Egyptians have rejected jihadist ideology. They prove that Islamists do not have a monopoly on grassroots movements. The basic demands of the Egyptian demonstrators are for jobs, food and democratic rights. This is nothing to do with the Islamists and is a bridge to socialism, which has deep roots in the traditions of Egypt and other Arab countries.

The moment of truth

Tensions are growing between the army and the police and between the police and protesters. The revolution has provoked a crisis in the state. There are reports of a major confrontation that has been played out behind the scenes between the Interior Ministry and the military. The army must try to end the protests on the streets. But it will not be easy, now that the masses have got a sense of their own power.

The political structure of the state is crumbling, forcing the army to assume direct responsibility for the running of society. The military is supposed to be the guarantor of the state. But the military is not a monolithic entity. The army in Egypt is not like the army in Britain or the USA. The lower and middle ranks of the officer caste reflect the pressure of the masses. The entire history of Egypt places the possibility of a colonel's coup on the agenda. The result could be a nationalist regime like that of Gamal Abdel Nasser, a colonel in the armed forces, who overthrew the British-backed monarchy in 1952.

In the present situation, it is possible that history will be repeated. But whatever "transitional" government is formed will be under close scrutiny. It will feel the hot breath of the masses on its neck. The key to the whole situation is the mass movement. All the contradictions are coming to a head. The coming hours will be decisive. The moment of truth has arrived.

Tuesday, February 1, 2011

EGYPT ON THE BRINK OF CIVIL WAR

Alan Woods

The revolution in Egypt is reaching a critical point. The old state power is collapsing under the hammer blows of the masses. But revolution is a struggle of living forces. The old regime does not intend to surrender without a fight. The counterrevolutionary forces are going onto the offensive. There is ferocious fighting on the streets of Cairo between pro- and anti-Mubarak elements.

Yesterday's "protest of the millions" surpassed all expectations. More than a million people thronged Cairo's Tahrir Square. There were 300,000 on the streets of Suez, 250,000 in Mahalla, 250,000 in Mansoura, and an impressive 500,000 in Alexandria. This mighty movement has no precedent in Egyptian history.

Protesters took to the streets in every single city and town. According to some estimates four million demonstrated all over Egypt. By contrast, the numbers who took to the streets to voice their support for the President yesterday were small and undoubtedly made up of members of the security forces, bureaucrats and their families, all those who have something to lose if Mubarak is overthrown.

The Revolution has enormous reserves of support. However, there are weaknesses in the revolutionary camp. As we pointed out from the beginning, the spontaneous character of the movement was both its main strength and its principal weakness. The forces of the counterrevolution are numerically weaker (this was shown yesterday). But numbers are not everything in revolution as in war. Many times in history a large army composed of valiant soldiers has been defeated by a smaller professional army with good officers.

The revolutionaries have determination, courage and morale. But the counterrevolutionaries have a lot to lose: their jobs, positions, power and privilege. Desperation will give them the courage to resist. And they are organized and well trained. There is not the slightest doubt that the shock troops of the mob that attacked the demonstrators in Tahrir Square today were policemen out of uniform. This was not a spontaneous demonstration of loyalty to the President but a carefully prepared action that corresponds to a worked out plan.

Mubarak's strategy

In Tunisia President Ben Ali decided relatively quickly that the game was up and took a plane to exile together with his wife and a large amount of loot. President

Mubarak of Egypt is tougher and more stubborn. He has decided to ignore the millions of demonstrators shouting for his downfall in the streets. He does not care what happens to Egypt. Still less is he concerned with the preoccupations of his former friends and allies in Washington. His only programme is survival. His only perspective is the age-old slogan of despots: "*Après moi le deluge*" – "After me, the flood!"

Everyone must now realise that the only way of calming the country is for the president to go. The self-appointed "leaders of the opposition" have made it clear that they will not even talk unless Mubarak disappears. They have no choice, since the masses on the streets are vigilant and will not tolerate any compromise.

The immediate removal of Mubarak was therefore the only hope to secure the "orderly transition of power" that the US so fervently desires. But John Simpson – the editor of BBC News World Affairs, an intelligent bourgeois commentator – correctly points out: "The only trouble is no-one has told the crowds in Tahrir Square about this. Their slogan is 'Mubarak out now' not 'Mubarak out with honour in a few months and the continuation of his system slightly improved'."

In last night's speech, Mr Mubarak promised to leave at the next polls, and promised constitutional reform, but he announced that he would like to stay on until September to oversee the change. In his address on Tuesday, Mr Mubarak said he would devote his remaining time in power to ensuring a peaceful transition of power to his successor (he did not mention his son Gamal). He criticised the protests and said his priority was to "restore peace and stability". "This is my country. This is where I lived, I fought and defended its land, sovereignty and interests, and I will die on its soil," he said.

The speech was seen by the protestors as a provocation. Far from calming things down it again poured petrol on the flames. The reaction of the protesters to Mubarak's statement was first disbelief, and then indignation. "The speech is useless and only inflames our anger," one protester, Shadi Morkos, told Reuters. "We will continue to protest." This was a universal reaction.

Last night the protesters remained camped out on Tahrir Square saying Mr Mubarak's promise was not enough, and chanting: "We will not leave! He will leave!" The masses do not want to give Mubarak time to manoeuvre. They want him overthrown and put on trial. On the demonstrations yesterday they hanged him in effigy. That shows the real frame of mind on the streets.

Everyone knows it was he who gave the order to shoot down the demonstrators last Friday. The television showed the father of a young man killed on a demonstration weeping as he cried: "They are killing our children". Now the regime is attacking unarmed people with murderous intent. Unarmed people are being beaten, stoned and gassed in Tahrir Square. With this regime there can be no truce, no peace and no forgiveness.

An historical precedent

Egypt is in the grip of a titanic battle between revolution and counterrevolution. Until this moment the demonstrations had been completely peaceful. This had lulled the masses into a false sense of security. Now all the illusions have been dissolved. The masses are receiving their baptism of fire. Mubarak's plan is to regain control of Tahrir Square and thus to seize the initiative, which has hitherto been in the hands of the revolutionaries. The struggle for power has begun in earnestness.

The whole thing has been carefully prepared in advance. The anti-government protestors are unarmed and were unprepared for the conflict. The pro-government forces are armed and have used tear gas, thrown into crowds including children. They have entered the Square mounted on horseback and camels. With the advantage of surprise and superior weapons and tactics, as I write these lines, the counterrevolutionaries are slowly forcing the revolutionaries back. They have arrested protestors who are then handed over to the army. Their fate is unknown.

In the context of these actions it is clear that Mubarak's speech last night was an integral part of a plan to push the Revolution back step by step. By promising concessions and offering to stand down in September, he was hoping to win the support of the wavering elements: the middle classes who fear instability and long for "order"; the bourgeoisie who fear a revolution like the plague and would like business to return to normal; the backward, politically inert layers who understand nothing and gravitate to the big names, the strong men and whoever is in power; the depraved criminal classes and lumpenproletariat who sell their political allegiance to the highest bidder. These are the social reserves of the counterrevolution that are now being mobilized against the Revolution.

There is a clear historic precedent. On 17 October 1905 (30 October in the new calendar) in response to the Russian Revolution of 1905, Tsar Nicholas II issued the October Manifesto. The regime was in what seemed to be an impossible position. It was confronted with a colossal revolutionary movement and a general strike. In many areas the revolutionary committees of workers were taking control of society.

The Manifesto pledged to grant civil liberties to the people: including personal immunity, freedom of religion, freedom of speech, freedom of assembly, and freedom of association; and the convening of an elected parliament – the Duma – under universal male suffrage. On paper this was a major victory, but in practice the democratisation was insignificant. The Tsar remained in power and exercised a veto over the Duma, which he repeatedly dissolved.

The Manifesto was a gigantic fraud, just as the promised reforms of Mubarak, but it was sufficient to buy off a layer that had previously supported the Revolution. The bourgeois Liberals immediately supported it, broke with the Revolution and made their peace with the Tsar. They desired "stability", as did a large part of the middle classes. Their defection prepared the way for a counterrevolutionary backlash.

At the same time as the Tsar announced his reforms, he unleashed the "dark forces" on the masses: the lumpenproletariat, the scum of the slums, the anti-Semitic pogroms, to drown the Revolution in blood. Mubarak is attempting to do the same. In Russia the pogroms were organized by the tsarist police. In Cairo the counterrevolutionary attacks are organized by plainclothes police posing as "pro-Mubarak demonstrators".

At the same time as his henchmen crack skulls in Tahrir Square, Mubarak has announced that the banks and shops will reopen on Sunday, the first working day after the Islamic weekend. The intention is to create an impression of a return to normality. But normality will not return to Egypt for a long time.

Washington worried

In Washington they are getting increasingly nervous. The longer Mubarak clings to power, the greater the risk of what they call "chaos". The latest developments have confirmed their worst fears. Egypt may be sliding towards civil war. The Americans would not be too worried about that, but the problem is that it would destroy all their plans for a "managed transition".

In a statement after Mr Mubarak's address, Obama said the US would be happy to offer assistance to Egypt during the transition process. He modestly declared that it was *not his country's right* to dictate the path for Egypt, but that any transition must include opposition voices and lead to free and fair elections: "It is my belief that an orderly transition must be meaningful, it must be peaceful and it must begin now."

Despite Mr. Obama's soothing words about having no right to choose the leaders of other nations, we seem to recall that Washington had something to do with the removal (and trial) of Slobodan Milosevic, and was somehow instrumental in the removal (and execution) of Saddam Hussein. We also recall the eagerness with which the USA proclaimed the policy of "regime change" as the best way to get rid of dictators and usher in "democracy" (under American control).

Here the cynical reality of bourgeois democracy stands out in all its uncouthness. US imperialism always considers it to be their country's right to remove leaders that are disobedient and replace them with more pliant leaders. To this end, "democracy" is as good an excuse as any other. But when it comes to those regimes that are friendly to US interests, all scruples about democracy and human rights instantly vanish. The world's policeman is suddenly afflicted by an attack of scrupulous legality: "it is *not our country's right* to dictate the path for Egypt" – or, of course, for Saudi Arabia, Jordan, Morocco, or any of the numerous unsavoury regimes that are America's good friends in the world.

Obama said he had told Mr Mubarak all this during a 30-minute phone call. It would be interesting to know the precise content of this telephone conversation, but we imagine it would not have been very cordial. When the present occupant of the White House says that an orderly transition "must begin now", this is as near as the Americans dare to come to saying to Mubarak: "For God's sake, go!"

There is very good reason why Obama cannot tell Mubarak to go, at least in public. The Americans have to choose their words very carefully because they are being carefully followed by the rulers of Jordan, Morocco and Saudi Arabia who feel the ground trembling underneath their feet. Simpson, again, explains:

> President Mubarak's offer to stand down will cause shock waves right across the Middle East. Until recently the regime in Egypt seemed pretty much rock solid.

> Now autocratic governments in North Africa right through to Yemen, Syria and maybe even Saudi Arabia will be looking for ways to buy off discontent at home.

The shock waves from Egypt continue to shake all the neighbouring countries. Turkey's Prime Minister Erdogan is the latest to proffer friendly advice to the embattled Mubarak. In the kind of obscure utterance we associate with Ottoman diplomacy he advised his friend in Cairo to take a "different step". He omitted to add the small detail that it was a step over a very steep cliff.

What now?

John Simpson adds the following: "In every revolution, popular or otherwise, there comes a critical moment – a tipping point – at which the future is decided. [...] The fact is we are still not at the tipping point quite yet. But we will know it when we see it."

Suddenly there is an answer to the basic question: Are the protesters too strong for the power structure or can the country's leaders face them down?

He continues: "All popular revolutions share certain basic similarities. The vast crowds, often gathering for the first time, believe that they are bound to win because there are so many of them and their determination is so great. But if the political structure refuses to take the hint and keeps the support of the army and the secret police then it can survive. It all depends on how strong and resilient the structure of government is."

Simpson compares the situation in Egypt with the overthrow of the Stalinist regimes in Eastern Europe two decades ago. I made the same comparison in an article last week. The parallels are instructive. On paper these regimes seemed solid and unchallengeable. They possessed powerful armies, police and secret police. But in the moment of truth, they were shown to be brittle and wafer-thin.

The case of Russia in 1991 is even more striking. The demonstrators who brought down the old regime were few in number and nervous of the government reaction, but the government was even more feeble and collapsed without a fight. Now we see a similar phenomenon. In Eastern Europe the crowds kept on demonstrating until the old regime simply caved in. That is what we are seeing before our very eyes in Egypt. But there is a difference. Mubarak refuses to go.

The masses are on the streets in large numbers, but Mubarak has unleashed the forces of the counterrevolution against them and the army looks on. What is to be done? The people have correctly concluded that if a week of demonstrations has pushed the president this far then there's every incentive to keep up the pressure on him. The next flashpoint will be on Friday, when another mass demonstration will take place after Friday prayers. The word is going round that the next step will be a march on the President's palace.

The people demand justice and revenge. Those who are guilty of crimes against the people must be handed over to popular tribunals to answer for their crimes. That is applicable not only to the police who fire upon unarmed demonstrators but also to the man who issued the orders. Insurrection is in the only way out. In order for it to succeed, the workers' movement must play a key role.

It was the long wave of workers' strikes and protests that played a key role in weakening the regime and creating this movement. Workers are now setting up independent unions. They have the power to paralyse the country and also to organise the economy. There has been talk of railway workers refusing to transport troops and security forces to be used in repression.

The calling of a nationwide general strike is the only fitting answer to the use of thug tactics against unarmed demonstrators. In order to prepare for this and keep order, action committees should be set up everywhere (workplaces, neighbourhoods and barracks) and linked up at local, regional and national level. This way the revolutionary people can take power and elect their own representatives, not those who are self-appointed "leaders" or people put in place by the US ambassador.

What we are seeing is a desperate rearguard action of the old regime. The old order is like a wounded animal that refuses to die and is thrashing about. The new order is struggling to be born. The outcome of this life-and-death conflict will determine the immediate fate of the revolution. The Revolution must defend itself. It must arm itself to resist the attacks of the counterrevolutionaries. But the best form of defence is attack. It is time for the movement to go beyond mass rallies.

The only way to kill a snake is to knock it on the head. Passivity is the death of the Revolution. Power will not fall into your hands like a rotten apple. Instead of remaining in Tahrir Square, the masses should go onto the offensive, march on the presidential palace and take power. The revolutionary masses should trust only their own forces. That is the only way to save the Revolution and win a decisive victory.

Wednesday, 02 February 2011

THE BATTLE OF TAHRIR SQUARE

Alan Woods

66 The sky was filled with rocks. The fighting around me was so terrible we could smell the blood." With these words Robert Fisk describes the dramatic events in Tahrir Square, where the forces of the Revolution met the counter-revolution head-on. All day and all through the night, a ferocious battle raged in the Square and the surrounding streets.

This pogrom was presented to world public opinion as a spontaneous response by ordinary citizens who have had enough of the disorder. It was described in the media as a clash between two rival political movements. On both sides tens of thousands of young men fought, and both sides sang the national anthem and waved Egyptian flags. It was described as "chaos" and a "battle of Egyptians with Egyptians".

But there was a fundamental difference. On the one side stand the representatives of the workers and youth, of the democrats and progressive intelligentsia, that is, of all the living forces of Egypt. On the other side of the barricades stand the representatives of a reactionary and corrupt regime, the oligarchy and the bureaucracy, the gangsters and torturers. One side is fighting for the future, hope and freedom. The other side is fighting to defend a shameful and barbaric past.

The "dangerous class"

There was nothing spontaneous about this vicious and bloody encounter. It was highly organized and well planned, a final desperate effort to prop up the Mubarak dictatorship. Huge posters of Mubarak were distributed by officers of the National Democratic Party and held in the air by men carrying cudgels and police batons. The indiscriminate use of tear gas by the latter was further proof (if any were needed) that these pro-government "demonstrators" were in fact policemen out of uniform.

Of course, the police did not act alone. They emptied the prisons of common criminals, who they armed and organized, and they used their contacts in the criminal underworld to mobilize thousands of other young men from the slums of Cairo to do the fighting for them. These are the lumpenproletariat, the "dark forces" of which Marx and Engels wrote in *The Communist Manifesto*:

> The 'dangerous class', [*lumpenproletariat*] the social scum, that passively rotting mass thrown off by the lowest layers of the old society, may, here and there, be swept into the movement by a proletarian revolution; its con-

ditions of life, however, prepare it far more for the part of a bribed tool of reactionary intrigue.

That is exactly what we are seeing on the streets of Cairo. Fisk bears witness to this: "The problem is that the Mubarak men included some of the very same thugs I saw then, when they were working with armed security police to baton and assault the demonstrators. One of them, a yellow-shirted youth with tousled hair and bright red eyes – I don't know what he was on – carried the very same wicked steel stick he had been using on Friday. Once more, the defenders of Mubarak were back. They even sang the same old refrain – constantly reworked to take account of the local dictator's name – 'With our blood, with our soul, we dedicate ourselves to you'."

This brutal attack was Hosni Mubarak's real reply to the demand of the Egyptian people for democracy. An army of thugs recruited from the jails and slums and bussed into the capital from every part of Egypt descended on the capital. Here was a motley coalition of the most ignorant, venal and retrograde elements in society. The men on horseback and camels who galloped into the Square were, it seems, recruited from the wretches who earn a living hiring their animals to tourists near the pyramids.

Fisk writes: "As far away as Giza, the NDP had rounded up the men who controlled voting at elections and sent them hollering their support as they marched along a stinking drainage ditch. Not far away, even a camel-owner was enjoined to say that 'if you don't know Mubarak, you don't know Allah' – which was, to put it mildly, a bit much."

Armed with cudgels, iron bars, knives, rocks and Molotov cocktails they attempted to storm the Square. The counterrevolutionaries appeared on the roofs of neighbouring apartments from where they threw slabs of concrete and Molotov cocktails on people below. By the end of the day there were reports of five deaths in Cairo. In the end there will be many more.

The army

Many are asking: what of the army? The army encouraged the protesters by calling their demands legitimate and promising not to fire on them. But it has remained inactive when they have been attacked. In other words the army has acted in collusion with the counterrevolutionaries. They opened the barriers to allow the thugs free entry into the Square, then sat back and did nothing.

Hundreds of those protesting in the square wore bandages and other signs of being hurt, while the army looked on. Robert Fisk writes: "The Egyptian Third Army, famous in legend and song for crossing the Suez Canal in 1973, couldn't – or wouldn't – even cross Tahrir Square to help the wounded." Such treacherous "neutrality" amounts to support for the counterrevolutionaries.

Mohamed al-Samadi, a doctor who had been treating people complained the troops were not helping. "When we come here, they search us for weapons, and then they let armed thugs come and attack us," he said. But he remained defiant: "We refuse to go. We can't let Mubarak stay eight months."

Many observers have found this conduct of the army strange. But there is nothing strange about it. Lenin long ago explained that the state is armed bodies of men in defence of property.

It is very likely that there are divisions within the army. The top generals have a vested interest in preserving the status quo. They are an integral part of the regime and have got their share of the loot. The ordinary soldiers will be under the pressure of the masses but are also subject to army discipline. The middle layers of the officers will be divided: some more inclined to the status quo, but others sympathetic to the protesters.

The majority of the troops are bewildered and do not understand what is happening. Fisk cites the following incident: "And there was the soldier on an armoured personnel carrier who let the stones of both sides fly past him until he jumped on to the road among Mubarak's enemies, putting his arms around them, tears coursing down his face".

In launching a counter-offensive, Mubarak is pursuing a very risky strategy. Undoubtedly he is being encouraged to stand firm by the Saudis and other reactionary Arab regimes, terrified of "contagion" from a successful revolution in Egypt. But these actions will put the Egyptian army under unbearable pressure. How far the inner cohesion of the army can resist these pressures is an open question.

The strategy of the counterrevolution

The result is a complicated equation that can only be resolved by the struggle of living forces. That is why the battle for possession of Tahrir Square was so important. If the counterrevolutionary forces had prevailed, it would have marked a turning point in the whole process. Victory for the counterrevolutionaries would have had a demoralizing effect because of the symbolic importance of the Square.

Egyptian Vice-President Omar Suleiman on Wednesday urged the demonstrators in Tahrir Square to "leave and observe a curfew to restore calm". He said the start of dialogue with the reformists and opposition depended on an end to street protests. But once the masses are off the streets the regime will be in no hurry to talk to anyone.

Once the revolutionaries have lost the initiative, it would be relatively easy to suffocate revolutionary trends in the army and restore discipline. The next step would have been to clear the streets of the capital inch by inch, one by one, driving the Revolution back. "Order" would be restored. The shops and banks would reopen on Sunday, giving an impression of "business as usual". Gradually, the momentum of the movement would be lost and people would sink back into the daily routine.

The police would reappear on the streets and arrests would be made. They would include a few criminal elements but would be overwhelmingly anti-Mubarak supporters, starting with the key activists. This would serve to terrorize the "moderate opposition", who would be forced to accept whatever minor crumbs the regime offered them or go into exile. Mubarak would remain in his palace. The counterrevolution would be in the saddle. But all these plans have been upset by the bravery and determination of the rebels.

Taken by surprise and initially outnumbered by the counterrevolutionaries, they fought back. The army allowed Mubarak's men to enter the Square (it was clearly pre-arranged). They started to throw stones and attack the protesters. But the latter refused to be intimidated and began breaking stones to hurl them back.

Bravery of revolutionaries

As the news spread thousands of Egyptians came to the Square. As Fisk writes, they "swarmed towards each other like Roman fighters, they simply overwhelmed the parachute units 'guarding' the square, climbing over their tanks and armoured vehicles and then using them for cover."

Mubarak's supporters almost crossed the entire square but in the end were driven out by the courage of the rebels. Robert Fisk was with Mubarak's supporters as they charged into Tahrir Square and provides a very graphic image of what happened:

"The sky was filled with rocks – I am talking of stones six inches in diameter, which hit the ground like mortar shells. On this side of the 'line', of course, they were coming from Mubarak's opponents. They cracked and split apart and spat against the walls around us. At which point, the NDP men turned and ran in panic as the President's opponents surged forward. I just stood with my back against the window of a closed travel agency – I do remember a poster for a romantic weekend in Luxor and 'the fabled valley of the tombs'.

"[...] Of course, it would be an exaggeration to say that stones cloaked the sky, but at times there were a hundred rocks soaring through the sky. They wrecked an entire army truck, smashing its sides, crushing its windows. The stones came out of side roads off Champollion Street and on Talaat Harb. The men were sweating, headbands in red, roaring their hatred. Many held white cloth to wounds. Some were carried past me, sloshing blood all over the road."

Fisk continues: "I saw young women in scarves and long skirts on their knees, breaking up the paving stones as rocks fell around them – fought back with an immense courage which later turned into a kind of terrible cruelty.

"Some dragged Mubarak's security men across the square, beating them until blood broke from their heads and splashed down their clothes."

What do you expect? When unarmed men and women are subjected to a violent assault, are they not entitled to defend themselves by violent means? The right to self defence is universally recognized in every civilized nation. And if subsequently they took revenge on the paid thugs who showed no mercy on old people, women and children, we see nothing reprehensible in that. These monsters got what they deserved. Under the circumstances they got off lightly.

The Egyptian revolutionaries acquitted themselves well yesterday. They withstood the initial onslaught and fought back, bravely pushing back the enemy all along the line. They finally won the Battle of Tahrir Square. But there was a heavy price to pay. Five are reported dead in Cairo and 1,500 injured, but nobody knows the true figures. And though the revolutionary people have won an important battle, the central question – the question of power – remains unresolved.

Hypocrisy about "violence"

The Egyptian Revolution has thrown western governments into confusion. They did not expect these events and do not know how to react. The latest trick is to "deplore violence" and call on all parties to "show restraint". Ban Ki-moon, UN Secretary-General, said if the regime sponsored violence, "that is completely unacceptable". Similar comments have come from Washington and London: "*if* the regime is responsible", "*if* it can be shown that the government has organized the attacks" or "*if* it has done nothing to prevent it". And so on and so forth.

Everybody knows who was behind the bloody assault on peaceful and unarmed demonstrators. Yet Obama, Cameron and Ban Ki-moon put on a hypocritical act, pretending they do not know who is responsible. They place the victim on the same level as the assailant. And even if the government of Egypt is found to be responsible, what do you propose to do? The answer is clear: nothing at all.

Robert Gibbs, Obama's spokesman, said on Wednesday: "If any of the violence is instigated by the government it should stop immediately." He urged "restraint on all sides". This is hypocrisy at its most repulsive. Until yesterday the movement in Egypt was entirely peaceful. The masses who gathered in Tahrir Square have acted in an orderly and disciplined manner. They protected the treasures of the National Museum from looters. They directed the traffic. They have even cleared litter from the streets.

Yesterday these peaceful demonstrators were viciously attacked by armed thugs, organized and directed by Mubarak's secret police. This vicious attack was entirely unprovoked. Imagine the following scenario: a vicious bandit who is armed to the teeth attacks an unarmed man in the street and tries to kill him. The victim of the unprovoked attack tries to defend himself by kicking and punching. Then a policeman appears and does nothing to stop the attack but issues a stern lecture advising both unarmed victim and armed assailant to "show restraint". What would we say of such behaviour?

The violence is making life increasingly difficult for Mubarak's former friends internationally and among those Egyptians who had accepted his pledge to step down in September. Along with the United States, France, Germany and Britain have also urged a speedy transition. Their minds have been concentrated by the international effects of the events in Egypt – both economically and politically.

Oil prices have climbed on fears the unrest could spread to other authoritarian Arab states including oil giant Saudi Arabia or interfere with oil supplies from the Red Sea to the Mediterranean through the Suez Canal. Brent crude surpassed US$103 a barrel on Thursday.

Meanwhile the revolutionary tide is flowing in all directions. On Thursday, thousands of anti-government protesters gathered in the Yemeni capital Sanaa demanding a change in government and saying President Ali Abdullah Saleh's offer on Wednesday to step down in 2013 was not enough.

For all these reasons the imperialists need stability in the Middle East. But how are they to get it? That is the question! From the beginning the US has been struggling to find a coherent response to events that are changing by the day, even by the hour. In reality the strongest power in the world has been reduced to the role of a helpless onlooker. An article in today's *Independent* by their correspondent in Washington, Rupert Cornwell, carried the interesting title: *Washington's strong words underline US impotence.*

It says: "In reality, those words merely underline the helplessness of the administration, at this point reduced to watching TV like everyone else, and keeping its fingers crossed about how events unfold – in Egypt most immediately but also in other friendly countries in the region, most notably Saudi Arabia and Jordan."

Obama does not dare call on Mubarak publicly to resign because of the effects in these other states. He is obliged to speak in carefully calculated code. "An orderly transition must be meaningful, it must be peaceful and it must begin now," the US President said, hours after the Egyptian leader had spoken on Tuesday. The operative word was supposed to be "now". This was supposed to make clear where Obama stood.

But nobody on the streets of Cairo got the message. Even worse, Mubarak immediately called his bluff by calling out his supporters on the streets to attack the protesters. If anything, the latest weasel words of Obama are more shameful and repugnant than the openly reactionary policy of Bush. The protesters' "passion and dignity" was "an inspiration to people around the world", the President declared. "We hear your voices."

Somebody said last night that even the language could not be translated into a comprehensible Arabic. That is hardly surprising, since it can barely be understood in English. The purpose of diplomatic language in any case is not to convey ideas but to disguise them. The problem Obama has is that it is very difficult simultaneously to hunt with the hounds and run with the hare.

Every American administration has supported, armed and financed the Mubarak regime. Obama and Clinton are no different to Bush and Reagan in this respect. They all backed this faithful ally of America and Israel. They were all silent about the numerous crimes of his brutal regime. Clinton in November 2010 said: "The partnership between the United States and Egypt is a cornerstone of stability and security in the Middle East and beyond, and we look to Egypt for regional and global leadership on a wide range of issues. This is a relationship rooted in mutual respect and common interests and a history of cooperation and a shared vision for the future."

Today Tony Blair, Bush's chief partner in crime in Iraq, had this to say about Mubarak: "Where you stand on him depends on whether you've worked with him from the outside or on the inside. I've worked with him on the Middle East peace process between the Israelis and the Palestinians so this is somebody I'm constantly in contact with and working with and on that issue, *I have to say, he's been immensely courageous and a force for good.*" (My emphasis, AW.)

These words were spoken after the murderous attack on the demonstrators. It shows that the record of the European governments in the Middle East is no better than that of the USA. They are all complicit in these crimes and their hands are equally stained with blood.

A crafty politician, Mubarak is hoping that the White House will tacitly put up with the crackdown in the hope that stability can somehow be maintained in Egypt and the other states in the region. But this is a vain hope. It would only delay the inevitable, and would enormously increase hostility to the US in Egypt and across the region.

Granted that America's policy makers are not particularly bright, even the stupidest among them must dimly grasp the fact that it is not good policy for Washington to sacrifice its long-term interests for the sake of short term and illusory gain. Thus far, anti-American slogans have not played a big role on the streets of Cairo. But that could change very quickly.

No matter what happens in the next days and weeks, the Egyptian people will never forget the crimes of Hosni Mubarak. His name will forever be branded with infamy. And they will never forgive or forget those western governments who to the very last provided support and aid to the hangmen in Cairo. The very words "democracy" and "human rights" in the mouth of Obama and his European counterparts stink of hypocrisy.

For a revolutionary programme!

While the imperialists talk of an "orderly transition" the counterrevolutionaries are shooting down people in the streets. By daylight there was a lull, with troops with tanks still looking on. But by mid-morning groups of pro-Mubarak gangs were seen moving again toward the Square with knives and sticks. Reuters reports that Mubarak supporters opened fire on protesters, killing at least five people.

The firing began around 4 a.m. (02:00 GMT) while hundreds of anti-government protesters camped out in the square. The authors of this new crime are well known. A senior U.S. official also said on Wednesday it was clear that "somebody loyal to Mubarak has unleashed these guys to try to intimidate the protesters".

It is no use begging the army to intervene to stop the murders. It is even more futile to appeal to the "international community", that is, to the same western governments that have been behind Mubarak and his regime all along.

There is a power in society that is stronger than any state. That power is the people. But it must be organized. When the police were taken off the streets in order to cause chaos and disorder, the people set up committees to protect their areas from criminal elements. The same idea must now be taken up and generalized: *form defence committees everywhere!*

The threat from the counterrevolutionary gangs of criminals can only be answered if the people are armed for self defence. Pacifism is no use when confronted with armed thugs. It is necessary to arm the people! If they attack you with sticks and stones, arm yourselves with sticks and stones. If they attack you with Molotov cocktails arm yourselves with Molotov cocktails. If they attack you with guns, arm yourselves with guns.

The only way to defeat the counterrevolution is by stepping up the mass action and carrying it to a higher level. That means organizing an all-out general strike. Deprive the regime of transport, petrol, telephones and post, light, heat and water, and you will soon show them that the working class is more powerful than all their armed thugs and policemen put together.

An *all-Egypt general strike* would show who really has the power in the land. In order to organize it in the most effective manner it is imperative to set up elected committees for the defence of the Revolution in every factory, street and village. The revolutionary committees should link up on a local, regional and national level. This would be the embryo of a future democratic people's government – a real alternative to the rotten dictatorial regime.

If there is one lesson to be drawn from the experience of the last few weeks it is this: the people can trust nobody but themselves: *trust in your own strength, your own solidarity, your own courage, your own organization.*

Thursday, 03 February 2011

THE EGYPTIAN REVOLUTION: "THE PEOPLE WANT THE DOWNFALL OF THE SYSTEM"

Alan Woods

The masses have once again taken to the streets in the biggest demonstrations yet seen in Egypt. They call it the "Day of Departure". Already this morning Al Jazeera showed an immense crowd of people thronging Tahrir Square. The mood was neither tense nor fearful, but jubilant. The very instant Friday prayers finished the masses erupted in a deafening roar of "Mubarak out!" The few Mubarak supporters who were slinking on the streets outside the Square like impotent jackals could do nothing.

In Alexandria there was a massive anti-Mubarak demonstration of over a million. There were no pro-Mubarak people in sight and no police or security forces of any kind on the streets. There were demonstrations on Thursday in Suez and Ismailia, industrial cities where inflation and unemployment are rife, and although I have not yet seen any reports today, there can be no doubt that there will be very big demonstrations today all over Egypt. The Egyptian people have spoken and the message is unmistakable.

The class dynamics of the Revolution

Marx pointed out that the Revolution needs the whip of the counterrevolution. This is the case here. The brutal onslaught of the counterrevolutionaries yesterday created the conditions for a new advance of the Revolution today. A revolution is characterized by violent swings of public opinion. We have seen this in the last 24 hours. Yesterday the mood of the protesters was grim. Today the revolutionary masses scent victory in the air.

This represents a complete turnabout in a few hours. But how can this transformation be explained? To understand what has happened it is necessary to understand the class dynamics of the Revolution. Different classes move at different speeds. The advanced layers – especially the youth – are the first to move into action. They draw the most advanced conclusions. But they are a minority. The mass of the people lag behind. Their consciousness has been moulded by past defeats. They are weighed down by decades of routine, habit and tradition.

The father of modern physics, Isaac Newton, explained that objects at rest tend to stay at rest. The phenomenon of inertia applies not only to the physical world but to society. To overcome the resistance of inertia a powerful external force is necessary. The present epoch is preparing shocks that will shake the masses out of their inertia. But this does not happen all at once. Mubarak has tried to play on the innate conservatism of the population, the fear of sudden change and the danger of chaos.

Mubarak mobilized the forces of the counterrevolution in an attempt to crush the Revolution by force. At the same time he made soothing speeches offering peaceful reforms. This speech had an effect on the minds of the inert mass of the population, especially the middle class who are fearful of disorder. "If you remove me there will be chaos, like Iraq," he tells them. Such arguments can have an effect on the more backward strata of the masses. They have not yet begun to move. They are not on the streets. They are watching events on the television and they are worried. By promising reform and a return to normality, the President was telling these people what they wanted to hear.

After the speech many of people who were initially sympathetic to the protesters were saying: "That is enough! You have got what you wanted. The old man is going to stand down in September. Why can't you wait a few months? We are tired of all this. We want a peaceful life, with the shops and banks open and business as usual." This was a dangerous moment for the Revolution. The mood of the middle classes was swinging towards the President. The counterrevolutionaries were gaining ground on the streets. The army was passive. At this point, the whole process could have begun to go into reverse.

At this critical point, the fate of the Revolution was determined by the courage and determination of the advanced guard. It is true that the active forces of the Revolution were a minority. But it is equally true that the shock troops of the counterrevolution were a minority. In order to defeat the Revolution, Mubarak summoned every last ounce of his support. He bussed in people from the provinces and they concentrated their strength outside Tahrir Square.

This was the decisive turning point. If they had succeeded in driving the protesters from the Square the whole process could have been thrown into reverse. But they failed. Not only were they driven back by the heroic resistance of the revolutionaries. After seven hours of fighting for every inch, the revolutionaries finally got Mubarak's thugs on the run. This was a decisive turning point. This produced a change in the psychology of the wavering elements. The ferocious violence of the counterrevolutionaries produced a new swing in public opinion that may well prove fatal to Mubarak's cause.

The battle was live on Al Jazeera, and millions of people could see what was happening. The scenes of a police van hurtling down the street at top speed, mowing down demonstrators said it all. The same people who had illusions in Mubarak's promise of reform could now see they had been deceived. The smiling mask of the Father of the People slipped to reveal the ugly physiognomy of a cruel and despotic Pharaoh.

So it was all lies, after all! Mubarak's warning of chaos if he stepped down was contradicted by these images. The chaos already exists, and the President is responsible. Down with the President! Al Jazeera reported one case that explains the process whereby the consciousness of the masses is transformed in a revolution. A man came to Tahrir Square and said: "I believed that the protesters were paid by foreign powers, but now I have come here and seen for myself I have understood that it is not true." And this man, who only yesterday was supporting the counterrevolution, joined the demonstration.

Crisis of the regime

The defeat in Tahrir Square has provoked a crisis in the regime. In a clear expression of weakness the government is publicly apologising for bloodshed on Wednesday. There are signs of divisions at the top. Ahmed Shafiq, the new prime minister, said he did not know who was responsible for the bloodshed. That is exceedingly strange because everyone else in the world knows that it was the work of undercover police. He also said the Interior Minister should not obstruct Friday's peaceful marches. For his part, the Interior Minister denied that his men ordered their agents or officers to attack the demonstrators, although not even his own mother believes him.

There are indications that the 82 year old President, who remains hidden inside his heavily guarded palace, is tired and partly demoralized. Yesterday he told the American TV network ABC News.: "I am fed up. After 62 years in public service, I have had enough. I want to go." But he immediately added: "If I resign today, there will be chaos."

Speaking in the presidential palace, with his son Gamal at his side, Mubarak said: "I never intended to run [for president] again," Mr Mubarak said. "I never intended Gamal to be president after me." Since everybody in Egypt knows that these were precisely his intentions, this shows that the old man at least does not lack a sense of humour. He then repeated his long-held assertion that the Muslim Brotherhood would fill the power vacuum left by his absence.

The government gives the impression of struggling to regain control of events that are slipping out of its hands. It also does not seem to know what it is doing. While Mubarak utters dark warnings about the Muslim Brotherhood, his prime minister is inviting the Muslim Brotherhood to talks, a very kind offer which the latter have politely declined. They are not so stupid as to offer a hand to a drowning man who only wishes to pull them into the water to keep him company as he goes under.

The Americans are constantly repeating this argument that this is an Islamist movement led by the Muslim Brotherhood and that if Mubarak goes the *jihadis* will take over. That is a lie, although American diplomats and politicians are stupid enough to believe it. This movement has nothing to do with *jihadi* fundamentalism or Islamic politics. *The New York Times* correctly pointed out: "For many, the Brotherhood itself is a vestige of an older order that has failed to deliver."

This great revolutionary movement was not organized by the Muslim Brotherhood or any of the bourgeois political parties. The Muslim Brotherhood is well organized and has a strong apparatus and money. Its leaders are manoeuvring behind the scenes. But the youth movement is the largest and most determined component of the revolution. It is they who have played the leading role from start to finish.

When these courageous young men and women went to the streets on 25th January, all the political parties including the Brotherhood were taken by surprise. The Muslim Brotherhood did not support them. The youth of 6 April are the ones calling for action. They are the ones who called today's demonstration. And today, when the revolutionary people marched in their millions, every political party including the Brotherhood were negligible.

The revolutionary people are not fighting for Islam or any religion. They are fighting for their democratic rights and for national and social liberation. Under Mubarak Islamic extremists murdered Christians. But on the demonstrations Christians and Muslims march together. In Tahrir Square there are Muslims and Christians, believers and unbelievers – all united in the same struggle against the same oppressors. The Revolution has cut across all sectarian divisions. That constitutes its great strength.

A "meaningful transition" – to what?

The immediate threat of counterrevolution has been defeated by the courage and determination of the revolutionary people. But victory has not yet been won. The ruling class has many ways of defeating the people. When state violence fails, it can resort to trickery and deception. The situation is very clear. Mubarak cannot control Egypt. Either he will leave, or the Revolution will sweep all before it. This prospect is what fills the Americans with terror.

Washington has lost its grip on events. Taken by surprise at every stage, they lack even the semblance of a coherent policy. The CIA, Saudi Arabia and the Israelis want Mubarak to stand his ground, not out of any personal loyalty, but to prevent the Revolution from spreading to other Arab countries. But the Americans are playing a double game. Obama and the State Department can see that Mubarak's days are numbered and are manoeuvring behind the scenes to maintain the old regime under another name.

It has emerged that the White House has been in talks with the Cairo government about how Egypt can begin making a "meaningful transition". US Vice-President Joe Biden spoke to his Egyptian counterpart on Thursday; one day after Suleiman had similar talks with Secretary of State Hillary Clinton. According to *The New York Times* among the proposals was a plan for Mubarak to resign immediately and hand power to a military-backed interim government under Mr Suleiman.

Neither the White House nor the State Department have directly denied the report. But a spokesman for President Barack Obama's National Security Council said it was "time to begin a peaceful, orderly and meaningful transition, with credible, inclusive negotiations". However, the BBC's Mark Mardell in Washington says other reports suggest the US plan *has already been rebuffed in Egypt*, and that the administration has been "surprised" by the attitude of the military and Suleiman.

The Americans know very well that Suleiman was involved in the attacks on the opposition, and yet they consider that he is the right man to lead an interim government. Everybody knows Omar Suleiman is the man of the CIA and of Israel. This is just a means of maintaining the system while giving the impression of a change. It would be the negation of all the democratic aspirations of the people: a lie and a cynical deception.

What the people want

In Tahrir Square today there is a placard that reads: "THE PEOPLE WANT THE DOWNFALL OF THE SYSTEM." Note the exact wording: *not just the downfall of Mubarak, but the downfall of the entire system upon which he rests.* The people read out a list of all the present political leaders and after each name shouted out: "Illegitimate!" That is a warning to the politicians that they will not accept any deals that involve the inclusion of any figure from the old regime. This shows an absolutely correct political instinct.

The problem is one of leadership. The bourgeois liberals cannot be trusted. The men who are trying to usurp control are like merchants in a bazaar who will use the Revolution as a bargaining piece with which they can haggle with the regime to win positions and careers. They will always betray the people to further their own selfish interests. The Wafd party and other liberals immediately accepted Mubarak's "concessions" and ended their participation in the revolution. ElBaradei is a stooge of the Americans who Washington wishes to put in power as a replacement of Mubarak. How can we place any confidence in men like these?

The revolutionaries must be on their guard! The people of Egypt did not fight and die to allow the same old oligarchy and their imperialist backers to stay in power. The movement must not be demobilized. It must be stepped up. The Revolution must be carried on to the end! No deals with Suleiman or any other figure of the old regime! Not a single one must remain!

The revolutionary people must take a big broom in their hands and sweep out the entire political establishment. For a wholesale purge and the dismissal of all the old officials! Those guilty of corruption must be put on trial and their property confiscated and used for the benefit of the poor.

As long as the old apparatus of state repression remains in being the Revolution will never be safe. The people can accept nothing less than the complete dismantling of the old state apparatus. For the immediate disbanding of the repressive apparatus! For the establishment of popular tribunals to try and punish all those guilty of repressive acts against the people!

The Revolution must be organized. It needs structured, democratic, popular organizations and a fighting machine able to defend it against any aggression. For popular committees for the defence of the Revolution! For a people's militia! Once the people are armed, no force on earth can oppress them.

The armed people are the only force that can guarantee the conquests of the Revolution defend democratic rights and convene genuinely free elections to a Constituent Assembly.

A proud people awakes

The New York Times yesterday published interviews that reveal the real content of the Revolution: "I tell the Arab world to stand with us until we win our freedom," said Khaled Yusuf, a cleric from Al Azhar, a once esteemed institution of religious scholarship now beholden to the government. "Once we do, we're going to free the Arab world."

"For decades, the Arab world has waited for a saviour – be it Gamal Abdel-Nasser, the charismatic Egyptian president, or even, for a time, Saddam Hussein. No one was waiting for a saviour on Wednesday. Before nearly three decades of accumulated authority – the power of a state that can mobilize thousands to heed its whims – people had themselves.

"I'm fighting for my freedom," Noha al-Ustaz said as she broke bricks on the curb. "For my right to express myself. For an end to oppression. For an end to injustice."

Mubarak is justly regarded as a traitor and an American and Israeli stooge. The same sentiment is shared by many parts of the Arab world. The same conditions that provoked revolution in Tunisia and Egypt will cause a domino effect across other Arab states. That is why the demands of the Egyptian people have found an echo in the streets from Algeria to Morocco, from Palestinian camps in Jordan to the slums of Baghdad's Sadr City.

Cynical western observers have often described the Egyptian people as apathetic and passive. Now this stereotype, the product of superficial thinking and feelings of racial superiority, has been stood on its head. Where is the apathy now? This is an ancient, proud and noble people who were exploited, oppressed, insulted and humiliated for generations by foreign masters and their corrupt local agents. They are in the process of breaking with the past and building a new and better future.

The Revolution has given a voice to those who had no voice, it has articulated the sense of hopelessness, the frustration, the humiliations at the hands of the police and the outrage of the youth who do not have enough money to get married and raise a family. The masses are not just fighting for bread and elementary human rights. They are fighting for human dignity. Thanks to the Revolution, the people of Egypt have stood up and raised themselves to their true stature.

"From minute-by-minute coverage on Arabic channels to conversations from Iraq to Morocco, the Middle East watched breathlessly at a moment as compelling as any in the Arab world in a lifetime. For the first time in a generation, Arabs seem to be looking again to Egypt for leadership, and that sense of destiny was voiced throughout the day."

These words of *The New York Times* show the real situation. All this is having a tremendous impact that extends far beyond the Middle East and North Africa. Revolutionary Egypt can now begin to occupy its real place in world history.

Friday, 04 February 2011

EGYPTIAN REVOLUTION REVERBERATES THROUGHOUT ARAB WORLD

Fred Weston

The Egyptian revolution, following on rapidly from the Tunisian uprising, has sent shockwaves across the whole of the Arab world. All the serious strategists of capital are discussing the "domino effect" of the events unfolding in Egypt. None of them, however, had anticipated any of this.

One week before Ben Ali was forced to flee *The Economist* magazine denied that Ben Ali would be overthrown, or that his regime would even be shaken. Then, once Ben Ali was ousted, they compounded the error by reassuring their readers that the Tunisian revolution would not spread to countries like Egypt, because Egypt was "different", of course. Within a few days Egypt erupted.

The imperialist powers, in particular the United States, thought that they had the situation under control, and that the regimes under their patronage were stable. An interesting comment that highlights the thinking of the bourgeois appeared in an article in the *Financial Times* on January 28th. This is how they saw the situation until not too long ago: "Before 2007, developments in the global economy appeared so calm and predictable the period was sometimes dubbed the age of 'great moderation'."

This idyllic period, however, was suddenly shattered by the crisis in 2008. And the events in the Middle East came as even greater shock. The article continues: "...investors now live in a world that is increasingly unpredictable in both an economic and political sense. Or to use market jargon, what the Middle East is now demonstrating is the potency of 'fat tails' (for events that seem so unlikely to occur that they are usually ignored until they suddenly strike with a vengeance)." The article quotes Simon Williams, an HSBC Middle East analyst, thus: "What happened in Tunisia took everyone by surprise. It has forced us all to re-examine the old certainties [in the region]."

The problem with these so-called bourgeois "experts" is that they failed to detect what was happening in the lower layers of society, among the millions of downtrodden workers and poor. That is because, as they live in their ivory towers, they usually ignore these layers. And because apparent calm can last even for decades, they began to think that is how things would always be. That reveals extreme short-sightedness on their part.

The foresight of Marxism

Marxism, on the other hand, because it has a "long view of history" and takes into account all the contradictions and how these will impact on the situation over time, was a tool which allowed us to understood perfectly well what was happening. Compare the lack of understanding that the above quotes reveal to the following: "The reactionary Saudi monarchy is now hanging by a thread. This corrupt gang is increasingly unpopular and are trying to cling to power..." (*The Middle East, Annapolis and the Palestine problem: More talks about talks*, Alan Woods, 6 December 2007). Note the date: 2007!

And what about the article we published on 7th April 2008, *Egyptian April 6th – a dress rehearsal for bigger events in the future*, by Jean Duval and Fred Weston: "The Mubarak regime is facing its most severe crisis ever. The most significant thing is that the workers have lost their fear of the regime. (...) All the conditions are maturing for revolution."

More recently, back in October we explained that: "The tensions in Egypt are reaching boiling point. [...] Revolution is developing just beneath the surface." [30]

We were able to write all this long before the present revolutionary upheaval began because we understood the effects decades of oppression, compounded by economic crisis and growing social polarisation, were having. But when we raised the prospects of revolution in the Middle East we were answered with a deafening cacophony of cynicism and scepticism that denied that revolution was possible. Now revolution has erupted in Tunisia, Egypt and is spreading to Yemen, Jordan and many other Arab countries.

Western imperialists are now scrambling to try and make up for lost time. The response of US imperialism and their west European allies has been to call on Mubarak for moderation and to prepare a transition to a more democratic regime. They do this for fear of the revolution spreading from one country to another until every rotten, despotic regime in the Middle East and North Africa comes tumbling down. That possibility they now can see!

However, not all the world "leaders" are pushing for this outcome. There is another side to the story! Should Egypt – the key country in the Arab world go the way of Tunisia, and Mubarak is finally ousted, it would have an even bigger impact than the events that led to the downfall of Ben Ali. After Egypt countries like Jordan, Yemen, and Algeria and so on could all see revolutionary upheaval. This would directly threaten powerful material interests in the region.

So while Obama is calling for "transition", behind the scenes we can be sure that other Arab leaders have been encouraging Mubarak to resist. If he can hold back the tide, there is hope still for these despotic leaders. The Israeli ruling class also does not wish to see revolution next door. Although they pride themselves at

---

30 *Egypt: The gathering storm*, by Hamid Alizadeh and Frederik Ohsten, 28th October 2010.

being the "only democracy" in the Middle East, it seems they are not too keen to see the dictatorships that surround them come tumbling down.

These leaders all have good reason to be worried. The same conditions that exist in Tunisia and Egypt also exist in all the Arab countries. And in these conditions, the spreading of the revolution from one Arab country to another is also facilitated by the fact that a common language is spoken in all these countries (without ignoring the various minorities that do exist in these countries, and who are also participating in the movement), there is a common cultural heritage, a common religion (at least for 90 per cent of the population), territorial continuity (despite the artificial state borders drawn by colonialism), the perception that they all have the same problems, the resistance to capitalist and imperialist domination. All this has created a powerful force in the minds of the masses. And like causes have like effects. The whole region is pregnant with revolution.

The tempo of the events unfolding in the Middle East and North Africa in part depends on what happens in Egypt in the coming days and weeks. Should the present movement fail to topple Mubarak in the short-term, this could slow the process down. Should he be brought down soon, this in turn would accelerate the process elsewhere. As the outcome is determined by a struggle of living forces, one cannot say in advance how fast or how slow this will be. But the direction of the process is very clear. Sooner or later Mubarak will have to go and a new period will open up, in which the class struggle in Egypt will rise to a higher level. There is no escaping from this, and it will have an impact on the whole region.

The following brief outline of the situation is an indication of the international impact that the Egyptian revolution, following from the Tunisian, is already having.

Jordan

Jordan is a prime candidate to follow the Egyptian road. Protests over growing poverty, rising food prices, unemployment, and corruption have been going on for weeks. Unemployment is officially 14 per cent in a country of six million. Seventy per cent of the population is young, under the age of 30 and 25 per cent of the population lives below the poverty line.

Thousands of people in Jordan have been out on the streets in protests, demanding the prime minister's resignation and for prices to be brought down. This is the result of the ongoing economic crisis. Jordan has a record deficit of US$2bn this year. Inflation has risen to 6.1 per cent.

In an attempt to appease the masses, King Abdullah has promised some "reforms", particularly on a controversial election law. The Prime Minister also announced US$550 million of new subsidies for fuel and basic products such as rice, sugar, livestock and cooking gas. He also announced a wage rise for civil servants and security personnel.

But all this has been to no avail. That explains why on February 1, King Abdullah II announced he was sacking Samir Rifai, the prime minister and with him the entire cabinet – and replacing him with Maruf Bakhit giving him the task of forming a new government that should "take practical, quick and tangible steps to launch true political reforms." The King is promising an immediate programme of democratic reform, as he tries desperately to cut across the growing protest movement and avoid an Egyptian type scenario. Bakhit, however, is not fundamentally different from the outgoing premier. He is remembered for overseeing local and parliamentary elections in 2007, when he was last in government, where blatant electoral fraud took place.

Activists on Friday's, [February 4th] demonstration in Amman outside the prime minister's office, in fact chanted "Down with the government", showing that they will not accept any half-measures. A failure to meet the demands of the people could threaten the very survival of the monarchy and bring the whole regime down.

Yemen

Widespread poverty in Yemen, with 45 per cent of the population living on less than US$2 a day, is at the root of the present protest movement there. The latest news from the Yemen is that Thursday [February 3rd] more than 20,000 people – the largest turnout so far marched through the streets of Sanaa, demanding that the President Ali Abdullah Saleh should go.

As in Egypt counter-revolutionary pro-Saleh demonstrators met the immense anti-Saleh protest which led to some physical clashes, broken up by the police. In the city of Aden, in the south tear gas and live ammunition were used to break up the demonstrators. No doubt this will have the same effect as in Egypt: to stiffen the resolve of the revolutionary movement.

On Wednesday, President Ali Abdullah Saleh had announced he would no longer be standing in 2013 and added that his son also would not be standing. Again, this is similar to what Ben Ali announced before he was ousted, and seems almost a photocopy of the behaviour of Mubarak in Egypt. He is attempting to appease the masses with the promise that he will go, but this is only a ruse to get the masses off the streets in order to regain control of the situation.

He has also announced wage increases and tax cuts, the creation of a fund to provide jobs for university graduates, the extension of social security coverage, and exempted university students from paying the rest of their tuition fees for this academic year, and has also called for the cost of a degree to be reduced.

These are all clearly manoeuvres to try and avert the protest movement from growing and becoming like that in Tunisia and Egypt. But the protestors have indicated that this is not enough. The 20,000 people on the streets on Thursday were chanting: "The people want regime change", "No to corruption, no to dictatorship" and "Change the regime and out with the president."

Algeria

Algeria saw protest movements against the rising cost of basic foodstuffs at the end of December around the same time that protests erupted in Tunisia. On December 30th there were reports that at least 53 people had been injured and 29 others arrested as police clamped down on protests against bad housing conditions in a district of Algiers, the capital. How determined the fight back of the protestors was can be seen by the fact that of the 53 injured, apparently 52 were members of the security forces.

Riots erupted again in early January over rising food prices and lack of jobs. The regime responded with a combination of repression. Five days of street protests left five people dead and more than 800 wounded. This led to cuts in prices, reducing the prices of oil, sugar and other basic necessities, and buying a million tonnes of wheat to build up stocks and the regime also promised that subsidies on essential foodstuffs like flour would continue. In this way they hoped to appease the masses and stop the revolutionary upsurge that was beginning to unfold. But the underlying problems that led to the revolt in the first place have not been resolved. Unemployment, especially among the youth, who make up half the population, remains high. According to government it stands at about 10 per cent, but more realistic figures put it at closer to 25 per cent.

Anger has continued to simmer below the surface, waiting to erupt at any moment. On January 22nd, for example, several people were injured as they were attacked by police during a pro-democracy demonstration in Algiers against a law that bans public gatherings. Hundreds defied the ban and came out on the streets only to face heavily armed police forces.

On February 1st, thousands responded to the call to demonstrate issued by the Coordination locale des étudiants (CLE, Local Student Coordination Committee) of the University of Tizi Ouzou. According to the organiser, 15,000 took part in the protest action. Significantly, some of the protestors were carrying the Tunisian flag, a clear indication that they wish to see a movement in Algeria that can overthrow the hated Bouteflika regime. One of the slogans was "Bout-Ali dégage!" a play on words mixing Bouteflika and Ben Ali.

On February 3rd, President Bouteflika announced that the country's state of emergency would be removed in the "very near future". The state of emergency has been in place since 1992, originally put in place to "fight terrorism". As he made this announcement, Bouteflika apparently called on his cabinet to adopt policies that would create jobs and also announced that national TV and radio should air the views of all political parties.

So far, these remain just promises. They are words aimed at appeasing the protest movement, of making it believe that "democratic reform" is on its way. No date was given for when the lifting of the state of emergency would take place. And as for jobs, how they are going to be created in the present economic climate is anyone's guess.

A new day of action is now planned for February 12th. Such ongoing protests indicate that the people in Algeria are restless and could move again, following the example of their Tunisian neighbours.

Morocco

Hundreds of students demonstrated in the Moroccan city of Fes on Sunday, January 30th, in a protest against price increases and worsening social conditions. The demonstrators chanted slogans linking the fate of King Mohammed VI to that of Ben Ali. This follows an earlier protest in the northern city of Tetouan, on January 20th, organised by the local Committee against prices increases and attacks on public services, with the participation of the Communist Action League (Moroccan section of the IMT). The Tetouan rally, which attracted 300 people, was also called in solidarity with the Tunisian revolution.

In the last few days, the Spanish media has published reports that army and anti-riot units of the security forces have been moved from the Sahara to Morocco's main cities, in preparation for major disturbances. The Moroccan government has strongly denied such reports, but it is clear that they are very worried about the possibility of revolution spreading to their own country. A Day of Rage, called by the "Movement for Freedom and Democracy Now" has been announced for February 20th, which could also become the focal point for protests around the country.

And just as *The Economist* was attempting to soothe the nerves of its readers that Egypt "was different" and could not go the way of Tunisia, the Spanish Foreign Affairs Minister, Trinidad Jiménez, recently stated: "I sincerely believe that the situation in Tunisia and Egypt is clearly different to that in Morocco", the reason being that Morocco has already undertaken the road of "democratic opening up". No doubt, the Spanish government would not be too keen to see revolution erupt just across the Strait of Gibraltar!

Someone much closer to the Moroccan King, however, his first cousin, Prince Moulay Hicham, has a very different opinion. In an interview with *El País*, he said that "Morocco will probably not be an exception... Almost all authoritarian systems will be affected by the great wave of protests."

Gaza and the West Bank

Right across the eastern border of Egypt in the Gaza Strip, where the reactionary Hamas have control, the movement of the Egyptian people is affecting the Palestinians. Some so-called Marxists in the past had portrayed Hamas as somehow a progressive force that merited the support of the left. In fact it is an utterly reactionary force that has merely filled a vacuum because of the corrupt nature of the PLO leadership that has governed the Palestinian Authority.

Hamas tries to portray itself as "revolutionary" and "anti-imperialist". If that were so then one would have expected them to be in support of the unfolding revolution in Egypt. On the contrary! Last week Hamas police broke up a small rally in Gaza City in support of the revolutionary movement in Egypt, arresting several women.

Hamas is as concerned about the revolutionary developments in Egypt as the government of Israel. Extra security forces have been placed on the Egypt-Gaza border, not on the Egyptian side but on the Palestinian. The fact is that Hamas does not want the movement in Egypt to spill over into the Gaza Strip. If anyone is looking for an answer to the accusation that what is happening in Egypt is an Islamic uprising then simply look at the reaction of Hamas.

Hamas is right to fear contagion from Egypt. An indication of the mood is the fact that several thousand Palestinians living in the Gaza Strip have joined a Facebook group that called for a protest against Hamas rule for Friday February 4th. This is the answer to all those sceptics who see only Islamic reaction in Gaza. The real voice of the Palestinians who inhabit this small strip of land is now being raised.

Something similar is being organized in the West Bank. Palestinian leaders in the West Bank in fact acknowledge the fact that the protests in Tunisia and Egypt could spill over into the Palestinian Territories. And the police there have similar concerns to that of Hamas. On February 5th, 2011 the police of the Palestinian Authority attacked a rally in solidarity with the Egyptian uprising, in Ramallah on the West Bank.

They are right to fear that protest could erupt in the West Bank. Let us not forget that it was only very recently that The Palestinian Papers revealed the secret collusion between PLO Palestinian Authority leaders and the Israeli state, even discussing the assassination of a Palestinian fighter.

Fearing unrest, and trying to cut across any possible protest movement, Palestinian Authority Prime Minister Salam Fayyad has just announced municipal elections in the near future, and there is talk of a general election as well. Palestinian Authority President Mahmoud Abbas, is considered to be close to Mubarak, and should the latter fall this would further damage his standing among the Palestinian people.

All the conditions are brewing in the Palestinian Territories for another Intifada, this time on a much larger scale, and as part of an All-Arab movement, not an isolated uprising. Let us remember that the Intifada had a far greater impact on Israeli society than decades of individual terrorism. Launching a few rockets that hit working class neighbourhoods in Israel, or suicide bombers that kill innocent Israeli men, women and children on buses or in supermarkets doesn't dent one little bit the machine of the Zionist state. In fact these actions have served to strengthen the Zionist state, as they push the whole population into supporting their government as they feel threatened as a people.

Furthermore, the fact that all the Arab regimes are despotic dictatorships, that have always exploited the Palestinian question to their advantage, blaming

Israel for the ills suffered by the Arab people, has also been skilfully used by the Zionist elite to paint a picture of Israel as a country surrounded by states that want to destroy the country. A revolutionary movement of the Arab workers and youth would, at some point, no doubt have an impact on ordinary working people in Israel.

Syria

Syria was long considered a "rogue state", with its pro-Soviet past and national-ized economy. But under al-Assad the regime has gone some way to opening up the economy and allowing the "market economy" to develop. Thus we have a regime with all the trappings of the past in terms of a repressive state apparatus, but now adding to that the effects of an opening up to capitalism, which leads to growing social polarisation, growing inequality with wealth being accumulated by the elite and poverty in the lower layers of society.

Al-Assad, the dictator of Syria, in the light of the revolutions in Tunisia and Egypt has admitted that Arab rulers need to do more to accommodate the rising political and economic aspirations of the people in the region. He is planning to push through political reforms this year including municipal elections, although he has stated that stability and the economy are higher up his list of priorities than political reform. In fact he has also announced some minor economic concessions in a bid to undermine any plans to bring people out on the streets. The government has announced subsidies and aid for the poor. Teachers have granted interest-free loans for laptops, while some public officials were charged with corruption in the city of Aleppo. Recently two million government workers were also granted a 17 per cent pay raise.

What al-Assad means by stability and the economy being the priority is that he thinks that by achieving some kind of economic improvement he can maintain his grip on power. However, now unemployment in Syria officially stands at 10 per cent, but some think it may be higher, as high as 25 per cent even.

Growing social problems are contributing to a spirit of revolt brewing among the youth of the country. Using the limited internet access allowed by the regime, several pages have been set up on Facebook, with the aim of organising protests along the lines that started the movements in Tunisia and Egypt. A call was is-sued for protests Friday and Saturday [February 4th and 5th] but failed to attract any protesters. As one anonymous activist said, "It is still soon for us. We have time. The street is definitely not ready yet."

The Syrian regime is one of the most brutal in the region, when it comes to dealing with dissent. There are reports that Syrian security forces violently broke up a vigil in Damascus in support of the Egyptian uprising on Wednesday of last week. The internet is also heavily policed. Facebook, for example, has officially been blocked since November 2007, although many young Syrians get round this by using proxy servers.

The regime has combined this repressive apparatus with concessions of an economic nature in order to cut across any attempt to spark off a movement like that in Egypt. It is worth noting, however, that although the regime may not yet be facing the same level of protest as elsewhere, it has taken the precautionary measure of increasing the number of blocked sites and chat services available to internet users in the country. All this indicates that Syria too is facing growing unrest, and given the extremely brutal nature of the regime this could erupt unexpectedly and in a massive way at some point.

Sudan

Shortly after the fall of Ben Ali in Tunisia, security forces in Sudan arrested opposition leader Hassan al-Turabi. This came shortly after al-Turabi's party called for a "popular revolution" if the Sudanese government did not reverse price increases.

"This country has known popular uprisings before," Turabi said in an interview to the AFP news agency. "What happened in Tunisia is a reminder. This is likely to happen in Sudan ... If it doesn't, then there will be a lot of bloodshed. The whole country is armed. In the towns, it will be a popular uprising, but in Darfur, and in Kordofan as well, they have weapons."

Since then a movement has erupted in the country, with students on the streets last week. On Monday [January 31st] a student, Mohammed Abdulrahman, from Ahlia University, died after being beaten by police. This led to the regime closing many universities and the heavy deployment of police around the campuses. At the medical faculty of Khartoum University, the police tried to stop around 300 students from leaving the campus, but they eventually forced their way through shouting: "Revolution against dictatorship!"

The regime has attempted to silence any media outlet that reported on the student protests for fear of these having a contagious effect. In fact, in recent weeks Sudan has seen widespread social unrest, as the country sinks deeper into economic crisis with growing inflation affecting the prices of basic goods. To make matters worse, the government has cut subsidies on petroleum products and sugar, a key commodity in Sudan. Clearly, Sudan is also on the boil.

Saudi Arabia

Saudi Arabia is a key country in the region in that it is the world's largest oil exporter. The imperialists are extremely concerned that this "friendly regime" could fall, thus endangering the steady supply of oil so essential to the workings of the world economy.

The official unemployment rate stands at 10 per cent and inflation is rising. Western and Saudi analysts comfort themselves with the fact Saudi Arabia has immense oil wealth and that it can use this to defuse anger and frustration. It can increase food subsidies for instance, without too much difficulty. Saudi Arabia passed a record budget in December and plans to spend US$400bn in the five years to 2013 to upgrade infrastructure. Protests and strikes are illegal. There are no student organisations, trade unions, or political parties. And yet, the Saudi government looks with trepidation at what is happening in Tunisia and Egypt. These too were supposed to be stable and immune from revolution.

On January 31st, Banq Saudi Fransi published a document, "The wakeup call: Egypt contagion looms, but manageable". John Sfakianakis, chief economist at the Banq Saudi Fransi, explained that: "The Saudis have the means to keep subsidies in place, but they are not insulated from what is happening in Egypt... It is a wakeup call for everyone in the region. They have to keep in mind that unemployment and job creation should be a top priority in Saudi Arabia."

The Financial Times of February 5th published an interesting comment on the dilemma facing the Obama administration in Saudi Arabia: "[the US administration] must be asking itself the big question: what if Saudi Arabia, the world's largest oil exporter but also a land where a young population has not felt the benefits of oil wealth, were shaken by similar upheavals?"

Last month, in fact 200 teachers organized protests outside the Ministry of Education demanding government jobs. Such protests have been ongoing for some time now. The latest was on Friday when demonstrators who gathered in Jeddah to protest against poor infrastructure were arrested. Protesters apparently demonstrated for a few minutes after Friday prayers on a main Jeddah street before authorities broke up the protest and detained participants.

Such small protests are ongoing and are an indication of a much more deeply felt malaise among the wider population. The same Sfakianakis, quoted above, points out that, "We can no longer take for granted stability in the Middle East ... People in the Middle East are neither patient nor silent any more. After Tunisia, we thought it will never happen in Egypt, but look at what happened."

What the bourgeois analysts fail to understand is that it is not poverty alone that leads to revolution. It is an important factor, but not the only one. Egypt has many poor people, but it is not the poorest country in the world. What provokes revolutionary upheaval is the passage from one period to another, the swings up and down in the economic conjuncture. The taking away of reforms granted in the past can unleash powerful movements.

There is also another factor. The wealth in these countries is concentrated in the hands of the few. All these countries have seen significant economic growth. Egypt, for example, since 2003 has grown at an average annual rate of 5.5 per cent. But that growth is not equally distributed. So we have an army of poor facing a small elite of very rich. That in itself can trigger revolutionary developments.

And then there is the growing hatred of these corrupt, oppressive regimes. It is not by chance that many women have taken part in the recent movements in

Saudi Arabia. All this could unleash a powerful movement even in what appears as such a stable regime as Saudi Arabia.

Implications for imperialism

This sudden explosion of revolution across the Arab world has serious implications for imperialism. In the 1960s many of the Arab countries swung to the left. A prime example of this was Syria, where the economy was modelled on that of the Soviet Union. But even where the process did not reach such levels, regimes like that of Nasser in Egypt were moving in the same direction. Large parts of the economy were nationalised and with this went the development of welfare measures such as healthcare, education, subsidies on food, etc., all of which made for a better life for the masses. To this day Nasser is remembered fondly by many Egyptians. He was also widely respected across the Arab countries, as he was seen as someone who stood up against imperialism.

However, since the late 1970s and early 1980s the process began to be unravelled. In Egypt the regime under Sadat, Nasser's successor, started to move back under the sphere of influence of US imperialism. On this basis privatisations were on the order of the day. And on the international arena, Egypt, from being an enemy of Israel, signed a peace deal and has kept to it ever since. Jordan also signed such a deal. In Tunisia, when Ben Ali came to power 80 per cent of the economy was under state control. After 23 years Ben Ali had managed to dismantle that, privatising whole swathes of the economy and with it destroying many reforms of the past. A similar picture could be seen across the whole of the Middle East.

That process evolved over a 30 year period. And now we see the results: revolution across the whole region. Mubarak in Egypt and King Abdullah in Jordan are considered key allies of the US. This cosy, stable relationship is now endangered by the revolutionary movement of the masses. The problem is that there is little they can do about it. They created the conditions for revolution and now they must suffer the consequences.

Monday, 07 February 2011

EGYPTIAN WORKERS TAKE THE LEAD

Alan Woods

There are situations in which mass demonstrations are sufficient to bring about the fall of a regime. But Egypt is not one of them. All the efforts of the masses to bring about the overthrow of Mubarak through demonstrations and street protests have so far failed to achieve their principal objective.

The protests have left three hundred people dead and thousands more injured. They have forced the cabinet to resign, brought the army onto the streets and paralyzed Egypt's economy. But they have not yet succeeded in overthrowing the government. On the other hand, the latter has not succeeded in re-establishing control. By Monday the situation in Egypt appeared to have reached a kind of stalemate.

But every time the regime thinks it has succeeded in regaining the initiative, its hopes are dashed by the masses on the streets. Contrary to all expectations, the movement is continuing to advance and is reaching a new high point. Far from subsiding, the fury against Mubarak is increasing. Egyptian society is becoming sharply polarised.

All the commentators were predicting that the movement was in decline. But the dramatic entry of the Egyptian proletariat on the stage of history marks a turning point in the destinies of the Revolution. Egypt is now being shaken to its very foundations by a mighty movement of the working class. In one city after another there are strikes and occupations. The revolution is moving onto a higher level.

Yesterday *Ahram Online* reported:

> Labour protests escalated in Suez with textile workers joining in and demonstrating with 2000 others demanding their right to work. Ali Fuad, a worker at the station, said: 'We are having a sit-in today to demand our rights, which are in the text of the workers' law, our right to obtain the annual increase in salary which the management refuses to give us so we strike with all the laws that uphold the right of workers.'

> Mohamed Abdel-Hakam factory, head of the factory syndicate, confirmed workers have continued their sit-in for a third day. In the city of Suez itself, around 2000 youths demonstrated to demand the chance to work. Amid expectations of growing labour protests in Suez, officials from the local council have attempted to meet the protesters and end the crisis.

> In Mahalla, more than 1500 workers of the Abu El-Subaa company in Mahalla demonstrated this morning, cutting the road, demanding their

salaries and stating that it is not the first time. The workers have staged repeated sit-ins for two years as they demand their rights and mediation between the workers and the company's owner, Ismail Abu El-Subaa. More than 2000 workers from the Sigma pharmaceutical company in the city of Quesna have gone on strike demanding higher wages and benefits that have been suspended for years. The workers are also calling for the dismissal of managers who have ill-treated workers.

New layers are being drawn into the struggle not just by the day but by the hour. The same report says:

Around 5000 unemployed youths demonstrated this morning in front of Aswan governorate building, which they tried to storm. The protesters chanted their demand that the governor be dismissed.

In Kom Ombo, around 1000 protesters called for the president, Hosni Mubarak, as security remained absent. Dozens of liver patients gathered in the governorate of Menoufeya at noon today over the lateness of their vaccinations. They were due to receive their treatment from the Hilal hospital three days ago. Dr. Murhaf El-Mougy, Menoufeya's general director of medical insurance, stated that the governorate was late in receiving the vaccination from its manufacturer. He attributed the delay to the curfew imposed during the demonstrations in Egypt.

In Cairo, more than 1500 public authority for cleaning and beauty workers demonstrated in front of the authority's headquarters in Dokki. According to a statement by the head of the authority on Egyptian television, their demands include an increase in their monthly wages, to LE1200, and a daily lunch meal. The workers are also demanding for permanent contracts and the dismissal of the authority's president.

And in Menya, thousands demanded the removal of the ruling regime in Egypt and Mubarak's resignation. Amid heavy security, the demonstrators marched towards the governorate building.

In recent days, Menya has witnessed several demonstrations, most of them opposed to the regime. However, demonstrations in favour of Mubarak have been staged. Violence as a result of these protests has lead to 72 people being injured, demonstrators and security personnel, according to Dr Adel Abu Ziad, deputy of the ministry of health in Menya.

The regime hangs on

Up to this point, the state was attempting to regroup its forces as the regime tried to capitalise on fears of insecurity. But the new upsurge in the movement has changed everything. Within sections of the army the belief was already growing that only Mubarak's departure can calm Egypt's streets. The latest developments will have strengthened this belief.

The ruling clique would be prepared to ditch Mubarak, but so far has not dared do so. They are under conflicting pressures. On the one hand, the Saudis and Israelis are demanding that Mubarak must stay. This is also the position of the CIA, which works in cahoots with the Saudis and Israelis. On the other hand, Obama and the State Department are pressing him to leave.

At the centre of this complex parallelogram of forces is Mubarak himself. He has lost power, yet he retains power. The balance of forces cancels itself out, leaving him where he was before. The proposed "compromise", basically that he should stay in power while in practice relinquishing it, is an expression of the impasse at the top, which in turn is a reflection of the impasse of the Revolution itself.

In Tunisia, a popular uprising forced Ben Ali into exile and overthrew the ruling party, although here also the fight is not finished. The Tunisian events convinced many Egyptians that their regime might prove equally fragile. The speed of Ben Ali's flight to exile in Saudi Arabia persuaded Egypt's dissidents that the correct demand was that Mubarak must go. The problem is that Mubarak refuses to go.

Mubarak has shown that he is made of sterner stuff than Ben Ali. He is still hanging on, although with two black eyes. He has also shown a certain amount of low animal cunning. Mubarak eventually said he would go – but only at the end of his term in September. He is resigned to his fate but wishes to leave office with dignity. This promise – which is rejected indignantly by the people on the streets, was accompanied by a subtle threat: accept my offer or prepare for the worst.

Hosni Mubarak reminds one of other figures in history: Charles I of England, Louis XVI of France and Tsar Nicholas of Russia. The poet Blok described the Tsar during the last months of the monarchy as follows: "Stubborn, but without will; nervous, but insensitive to everything; distrustful of people, taut and cautious in speech, he was no longer master of himself. He had ceased to understand the situation, and did not take one clearly conscious step, but gave himself over completely into the hands of those whom he himself had placed in power." These lines could be applied precisely to Mubarak in the hour of his final eclipse.

For a man with not many cards in his hand, Mubarak has played his hand well. His calculations are quite astute. All the "concessions" offered by the regime have a fraudulent character. The "new" cabinet contained half the ministers of the previous government. Suleiman, the former head of Egyptian Intelligence, is his right hand man. As the French say: *"Plus Áa change, plus c'est la míme chose"*: The more things change, the more they stay the same.

By offering a bare minimum of concessions, Mubarak hoped to drive a wedge between the revolutionaries and the more inert layers of the population who fear chaos and want a return to "normality". On February 2 the two sides were fighting for possession of Tahrir Square. Mubarak was hoping the counterrevolutionaries would clear the square, but they failed. The revolutionaries held their ground and grew in confidence.

Hosni Mubarak is fighting for his survival. Suleiman is fighting for the survival of the regime. But the imperialists are fighting for the survival of capitalism and their puppet regimes in the Arab world. The latter are worried about where Egypt's revolt will go, and how far it will spread. These are the big questions, and they are still unanswered.

In the end the old man may announce an early retirement on health grounds. But so far Mubarak has shown himself to be extremely stubborn. He is placing his interests, and those of the clique around him, above those of the imperialists. Exactly thirty years ago Anwar Sadat was assassinated by his own guards. This could happen again. It would not be impossible to arrange for Mubarak to go in the same way. But the clique that controls the army and the state is afraid to resort to such measures. The removal of Mubarak would open the floodgates and they fear that the raging waters would sweep them all away.

"Negotiations"

The ruling class has many strategies for defeating a Revolution. If it cannot do so by force, it will resort to cunning. The old regime attempted to crush the uprising with force on Wednesday 2 February, but it failed. The defeat in Tahrir Square unnerved the ruling clique completely. Mubarak has disappeared from the scene. Behind locked doors the rulers of Egypt argued about what was to be done. And all the time the phone was ringing. Washington is demanding action in increasingly imperious tones. And Washington pays the bills.

After Wednesday the regime was staring defeat in the face, and when the ruling class faces the prospect of losing everything they will always offer concessions. Belatedly, the ruling clique realized that it would be necessary to do a deal with the leaders of the opposition. Another face must be presented to the people. Mubarak was quietly pushed into a side room. Without a word, Suleiman took the reins of power. Facing the danger of losing everything, Suleiman and all his generals and ministers are now for a compromise. But it must be a compromise that will maintain their power and privileges.

Suddenly the regime is willing to talk. Suleiman offered to negotiate with the opposition. Last week they were only prepared to talk the language of concrete slabs, clubs and Molotov cocktails; now it is all smiles, handshakes and conference tables. Following advice from Washington and London, they have not renewed the attempt to take the Square by force. Suleiman says: "We will not disperse them by force." The tanks do not move. Nor do the pro-Mubarak mobs make an appearance. Their masters have ordered them to keep out of sight, as the owner of a dog calls it to come to heel.

Since they have been defeated on the streets they are trying to strike a bargain, that is, try to fool the leaders of the opposition, so that they in turn can fool the masses. The idea is that once the initiative is in the hands of the "negotiators", the masses will become mere passive onlookers. The real decisions will be made elsewhere, behind locked doors, behind the backs of the people. And what can the people do? Remain on the Square shouting slogans? But the regime has already taken this into account.

Obama and the Europeans say to Suleiman: "Why go to the bother of using force? That has already failed and only creates public sympathy for the trouble-makers. It can split the army down the middle and then you will be in serious trouble. Better leave them alone. Close off the Square and box the protesters in there. Then you only have to wait until they get tired. The movement will collapse like a balloon that runs out of air. After a while there will only be a handful left. Then you can do what you like with them." The problem is that the movement is not prepared to give up the fight. What the regime is now counting on is that the so-called leadership of the protest movement may be able to rein in the masses for them.

What does the Muslim Brotherhood stand for?

The leadership of the protest movement, like the movement itself, contains diverse elements and different ideological tendencies. At this stage there is a lot of emphasis on unity. One of the leaders of the youth told Al Jazeera that the demands of the youth were not "classist", and that corruption and repression weigh on all layers of society. This is typical of the early stages of the Revolution.

Initially every revolution appears to be a great carnival of national unity, where the illusion is created that all classes are united in a common struggle for change. However, as the struggle proceeds, there will be changes. As the movement becomes more radicalized, some of the elements who played a leading role in the early stages will fall behind. Some will abandon it; others will go over to the enemy. This corresponds to different class interests.

The poor people, the unemployed, the workers, the "men of no property" have no interest in maintaining the old order. They want to sweep away not only Mubarak but the entire regime of oppression, exploitation and inequality. But the bourgeois Liberals see the struggle for democracy as the path to a comfortable career in parliament. They have no interest in carrying through the Revolution to the end or of disturbing existing property relations.

This process of inner differentiation has already begun. By offering to negotiate, Suleiman wished to win over the moderate (i.e. bourgeois) elements in the opposition. He even offered to negotiate with the Muslim Brotherhood, which is a banned organization. The purpose of this is to gain time, to confuse and disorient the movement and to trick the opposition into making a deal with the oligarchy and preserve the system. There is an old saying: if you sup with the Devil, use a long spoon. But these gentlemen, in their indecent haste, fell right into the soup.

A serious revolutionary leadership would understand that this was a confession of extreme weakness. It would continue to attack until the regime fell. It would give it no time to recover its nerves and rally its forces. But a section of these leaders is neither revolutionary nor serious. For them the mass movement is only a convenient bargaining chip, something with which they can threaten the government to give them a few more crumbs.

The Muslim Brotherhood had declared that it would not negotiate with the government until Mubarak steps down. ElBaradei has described pro-Mubarak demonstrations as criminal acts by a criminal regime. But the moment the regime beckoned with its little finger the leaders of the "opposition" fell over themselves to accept Suleiman's offer, forgetting all their brave words about "not negotiating until Mubarak goes".

Significantly, the leaders of the Muslim Brotherhood, after initially refusing to negotiate, changed their minds and joined this pleasant little party. One of their leaders went onto Tahrir Square, where the protestors were standing firm and preventing the tanks from occupying the Square with their bodies, appealing to them not to clash with the army. Clearly, the "hard line" Islamists are as frightened of the revolutionary masses as the regime itself.

The poor people who support the Brotherhood are one thing. The leaders are another thing altogether. In the 1980s leaders of the Brotherhood were key beneficiaries of economic liberalization – the programme of *infitah* or "opening" – under which Sadat and then Mubarak dismantled the state sector, favouring private capital. One study of Brotherhood businessmen suggests that at this point they controlled 40 per cent of all private economic ventures. They are part of the capitalist system and have every interest in defending it. Their conduct is not determined by the Holy *Qur'an* but by class interest.

Sitting next to the Muslim Brothers on the negotiating table are certain individuals who call themselves the "representatives of the youth on Tahrir Square". Since nobody ever elected them, it is hard to see who they really represent, other than themselves. But their presence around the table is important for the regime, which can present itself before the television cameras as eminently reasonable and willing to listen to "all points of view". In this way the people who remain on the Square can be presented to public opinion as "extremists", people who are not willing to engage in dialogue to solve the nation's problems.

The laws of revolution

The laws that govern revolution have many features in common with those that govern wars between nations. War is not a continuous battle. There are a series of battles, which are won or lost, or end inconclusively. But between battles there are long periods of inactivity when nothing seems to happen. But there is a constant ebb and flow. Certain layers get tired and drop out of activity. But they are constantly replenished with new, fresh layers moving into struggle. The Revolution still has considerable reserves. These reserves are now mobilizing for action.

To say that a revolution has begun is not to say that it has been completed, or even that victory is assured. It goes without saying that revolution is a struggle of living forces. The counterrevolutionaries have a lot to lose and they are acting intelligently and with decision. But the leadership of the revolutionaries is divided and does not speak with one voice. That is the main problem. The enemy noticed this hesitation and began to recover its nerve. They began to feel more confident and redouble their manoeuvres and intrigues, basing themselves on the more moderate sections of the opposition.

This was a dangerous situation. If the movement had been allowed to stagnate the confidence of the streets would have begun to ebb and the initiative would have passed into the hands of the regime. That was the aim of Suleiman when he offered to negotiate with the opposition. These "negotiations" were only a trick of the regime to gain time and to deprive the demonstrators of the initiative. That could have been fatal to the Revolution.

On Monday 7 February the banks were opened for the first time since the protests began, but the stock exchange remained closed for fear that it would lead to a rush to sell. This pessimistic perspective was confirmed the very next day. Unwittingly, by ordering a resumption of business, the regime miscalculated. This has allowed workers and students to come together, hold mass meetings, discuss the situation and take collective action. As a result, students are agitating on the campuses. Workers are staging strikes and factory occupations, driving out hated managers and corrupt trade union leaders.

The sudden entry of the workers onto the scene as an independent revolutionary force has changed everything. On Tuesday, the protesters mounted their biggest demonstrations so far. Thousands again took to the streets and squares of Egyptian towns – from the Western desert on the Libyan border up to the northern Sinai town of El Arish in the east. In Cairo, Alexandria, the Delta Cities, the industrial belt around Mahalla-el-Kebir and the steel city of Helwan, the masses came onto the streets shouting "Death to Mubarak!" and "Hang Mubarak!"

The Revolution cannot stand still

A Revolution cannot stand still. It must constantly advance, striking blows against the enemy, capturing one position after another until the old order is utterly overthrown. If it hesitates, it is lost. Marx pointed out that the Paris Commune failed because it did not march on Versailles. This gave time for the counterrevolutionary forces to regroup and prepare a decisive counteroffensive against revolutionary Paris.

At several moments during the past two weeks, power was in the streets. But having won power in the streets, the leaders of the movement did not know what to do with it. The idea that all that is necessary is to gather a large number of people in Tahrir Square was fatally flawed. Firstly, it leaves the question of state power out of account. But this is the central question that decides all other questions. Secondly, it is a passive strategy, whereas what is required is an active and offensive strategy.

It is true that in war, defence can be transformed into offense. A decisive moment was on Thursday and Friday. After the revolutionaries had defeated the attacks of the counterrevolutionaries and regained the initiative, they should have gone onto the offensive. By confining the action on Friday to a mass demonstration in Tahrir Square, they allowed the initiative to slip from their hands and into those of the enemy.

Suleiman is playing for time because time is not necessarily on the side of the Revolution. Society cannot continue indefinitely in a chaotic situation. People must live. The economy is losing 300 million Euros a day in lost tourist revenues alone. Bread becomes scarce in the shops as time goes on; people cannot get to work. Wages are not paid. People can start to blame the protesters for provoking chaos. The call for order can get an echo in these conditions. There are certain indications that this process was beginning.

An Al Jazeera report summed up the situation thus: "It was clear the government was attempting to return a sense of normalcy to the city; businesses and banks were set to open on Sunday, and the army was intent on clearing away all signs of discord but for the crowd in the square. Men in fluorescent vests even went about clearing debris and trash from the streets where protesters had died just nights before."

Fortunately, the most revolutionary wing of the opposition realized the danger. The same report from *Al Jazeera* quoted one of the youth leaders as follows: "But as high-ranking opposition figures negotiate a transition with Mubarak's right-hand man, former intelligence chief and newly appointed Vice-president Omar Suleiman, Mohammed Sohail and the men on the rooftops remain dug in, hoping for a complete overhaul. After the thugs' attack on Wednesday, they will not accept negotiation with Mubarak. He's hiding a dagger behind his back."

These words express the real situation very well.

The problem of leadership

The Revolution in Tunisia and Egypt came from below. It was not organized by any of the existing political parties or leaders. All of them were left far behind by a movement they had not foreseen and for which they were completely unprepared. The "spontaneous" character of the Revolution has inclined some observers to believe that it in some way represents a confirmation of the theories of anarchism. But the opposite is rather the case.

The argument that "we do not need leaders" does not bear the slightest scrutiny. Even in a strike of half an hour in a factory there is always leadership. The workers will elect people from their number to represent them and to organize the strike. Those who are elected are not arbitrary or accidental elements, but generally the most courageous, experienced and intelligent workers. They are selected on that basis.

Leadership is a very important element in war. This is not to say that it is the only element. Even the most brilliant leaders cannot guarantee success if the objective conditions are unfavourable. In the American Civil War the South had far more capable generals than the North, and this was an important factor in its initial victory. The Northern generals were mostly very bad, but the North had a far bigger population and was more able to sustain heavy losses. Above all it had a powerful industrial base, which the agricultural slave states of the South lacked, and it had a lot of money. The combination of financial wealth, industry and manpower ultimately guaranteed success, in spite of poor generals.

In the end it is the most determined revolutionary elements that will remain standing: those who are not prepared to compromise and are willing to go to the end. And in this it is the youth who play a key role. In 1917 the Mensheviks accused the Bolsheviks of being just a "bunch of kids", and they were not entirely wrong. The average age of the Bolshevik activists was very low. The first section to move is always the youth, who are free from the prejudices, fear and scepticism of the older generation.

In Egypt we again see the same thing. The protestors who have poured onto the streets all over Egypt are mainly young Egyptians, unemployed and without any future. One young Egyptian told the BBC: "We are poor. We have no work, no future. What should we do? Should we burn ourselves?" The only hope these young people have is to fight for a fundamental change in society. They have cast aside all fear and are prepared to risk their lives in the fight for freedom and justice.

The youth and the most revolutionary elements do not want the movement to be hijacked by the "moderates" who are bargaining with the regime like merchants haggling in a bazaar. But the question remains: how to carry the Revolution forward? What needs to be done? The demonstrators have done everything possible. They have shown great courage and determination. But the limitations of the tactics pursued up till now are becoming clearer by the hour.

In order to carry the Revolution to a higher level, another force is necessary. This can only be provided by the working class. An all-out general strike would transform the entire situation. It would demonstrate clearly who the real master of the house is.

The role of the proletariat

The economic growth of Egypt in the last years was a very positive development from the standpoint of the Marxists, because it strengthened the working class. However, it did not solve any of the fundamental contradictions of Egyptian society. The last few years have seen a sharp upswing in strike activity in Egypt, notably the heroic struggle of textile workers of Mahalla. This reawakening of the proletariat was one of the main factors that prepared the present situation. It is also the key to the situation.

Recent reports speak of large groups of workers, mainly in Cairo, rebelling against state-appointed managements and setting up "Revolutionary Committees" to run factories and other work places, including Egyptian state TV and Egypt's biggest weekly *Ros el-Yusuf*.

There is a wave of strikes, many of them involving different forms of sit-ins and factory occupations. The telecom workers in Cairo are on strike, and the strike seems to be spreading to other cities: Maadi, Opera, MisrElgedida, Ramsis, and Alexandria. The workers are protesting against corruption and low salaries.

In the key city of Suez, the workers have occupied the Suez Trust Textile plant. Around 1,000 workers in the Lafarge cement factory in Suez are also on strike. Among their demands: the forming of a union and support for the revolution. The Tora cement workers have started a sit-in to protest against their intolerable working conditions.

At the same time there is a movement to get rid of the old corrupt leaders of the unions (syndicates) who are agents of the ruling party and the bosses.

The employees at the Workers' University in Nasr City are staging a sit-in and, according to one report, there has been the kidnapping of the vice president of the official ETUF union, Mustapha Mungy, by employees of the Workers' University. In the course of a sit-in the workers detained him and demanded his removal and the opening of investigations into widespread corruption in the Workers' University.

The official *Ahram Online*, on Monday 7 February 2011, carried a report entitled "Employees detain vice-president of Egyptian workers union", which reported: "The vice-president of the Egyptian Workers Union, Mostafa Mongy, has been detained since Monday morning by employees demanding his immediate resignation."

The Centre for Trade Union & Workers' Services (CTUWS) presented a Communication to the Public Prosecutor demanding the issue of an order against Hussein Megawer, president of the ETUF, preventing him from travelling abroad and investigating the sources of his wealth.

On Tuesday 8th university professors staged a march in support of the revolution, joining the protesters in Tahrir. Also at 12 noon, journalists will gather at their union HQ, in an emergency meeting to lobby for the impeachment of their state-backed union chief, Makram Mohamed Ahmed.

The journalists are also on the move. They have attacked the state-backed head of the syndicate, shouting: "murderer, murderer!" Journalists marched from their union HQ to Tahrir Square, denouncing the government. Journalists have started collecting signatures to impeach the state-backed press syndicate head. In all the state run newspapers journalists are in revolt against their pro-government editors.

The movement is spreading like a forest fire. The railway technicians in Bani Suweif are on strike. At least two military production factories in Welwyn are on strike. Public transport workers in three garages are on strike. Thousands of oil workers are protesting in front of the oil ministry. Tomorrow more oil workers from the provinces will descend on Nasr City to join protests in front of the oil ministry, and the Ghazl Mahalla workers will also start a strike.

Many of the strikes are economic, but others are political in character. An interview with Hossam El-Hamalawy on Sunday 6 stated: "It's been two days since the workers said that they wouldn't return to work until the fall of the regime. There are four hotbeds of economic struggle: a [steel] mill in Suez, a fertilizer factory in Suez, a textile factory near Mansoura in Daqahlia (the Mansoura-España garment factory in the Nile Delta region) on strike – they have fired their CEO and are self-managing their enterprise. There is also a print shop in southern Cairo called Dar al-Matabi: there, too, they fired their CEO and are self-managing the enterprise. But, while workers are participating in the demonstrations, they are not developing their own independent action as workers. We still have not seen workers independently organize themselves en masse. If that comes, all the equation of the struggle will change." [31]

On Wednesday the three independent unions that exist in Egypt (Property Tax Collectors, Health Technicians and Pensioners' Federation) demonstrated in front of the headquarters of the state-backed Egyptian Federation of Trade Unions, in Galaa Street, calling for the prosecution of the federation chief on corruption charges, and demanding the lifting of all restrictions on establishing free unions. The civil servants then marched to Tahrir Square in support of the revolution. They are not the only ones. Delegation after delegation of workers is arriving on the Square to express their solidarity with the demonstrators and discuss the future of the Revolution.

These reports are of tremendous importance. *They mean that the Revolution is entering the factories and workplaces.* They signify that the workers of Egypt are proceeding from the struggle for democracy in society to the struggle for economic democracy in the workplace. It means that the Egyptian working class is beginning to participate in the Revolution under its own banner, fighting for its own class demands. This is a decisive factor for the future of the Revolution.

The idea of a general strike is in the air. The demands of the workers have a clear revolutionary and class character. The workers of Egypt are drawing the most advanced conclusions. This is strikingly revealed in the statement of the

---

31 *http://mrzine.monthlyreview.org/2011/hamalawy080211.html*

Iron and steel workers in Helwan, who are calling for a major workers' rally next Friday to Tahrir Square. They are advancing the following demands:

1. the immediate stepping down of Mubarak and all the figures of the regime and its symbols;

2. the confiscation of wealth and property of all the regime's symbols and all those to be proven to be corrupt, on behalf of the interest of the masses;

3. the immediate resignation of all workers from the trade unions controlled by or affiliated to the regime and declaring their independent unions now preparing their general conference to elect and form their syndicate;

4. the acquisition of public sector companies that have been sold or closed and the declaration of nationalizing them on behalf of the people and the formation of a new administration to run it, involving workers and technicians;

5. the formation of committees to supervise workers in all work sites and monitor the production and distribution of prices and wages;

6. the calling of a constituent assembly of all classes of people and trends for the drafting of a new constitution and the election of people's councils without waiting for the negotiations with the former regime.

What now?

These demands are absolutely correct. They show a very high level of revolutionary consciousness and coincide completely with the programme that has been advanced by the Marxists. This programme provides the Egyptian Revolution with all it needs to succeed.

The immediate demands are naturally democratic in character. But the fight for democratic demands, if it is pursued consistently, must lead directly to the demand for economic democracy. The poor people of Egypt do not fight for democracy in order to provide ministerial positions for careerists but as a means of solving their most pressing problems: the lack of jobs and houses, the high cost of living. These economic and social problems are too deep to be solved by any bourgeois government. *The Economist* writes:

> Some 40% of Egyptians still live on less than $2 a day. In recent years, even as Egypt's overall economy has grown apace and more consumer goods have filled even lower-income households, the poor have won little relief from relentlessly rising food prices and sharper competition for secure jobs. Such anxieties have found expression in a growing number of strikes and local protests across the country. Yet in a sense, persistent poverty has helped prop up the regime. 'People survive on a day-to-day basis,' says a young Cairo lawyer. 'They can't go for long without a daily wage and daily bread, so they can't afford to make trouble'.

The present movement cannot succeed unless it is taken to a new and higher level. This can only be done by the working class. Mass demonstrations are important because they are a way of bringing the formerly inert masses to their feet, giving them a sense of their own power. A new and higher level involves the calling of a general strike.

An all-Egyptian general strike would deal a mortal blow to the regime, which is already in crisis. The old state power is breaking up. It must be replaced with a new power. The general chaos and disorder and the persistent reports of security agents engaging in arson and thievery convinced people that the chaos was planned. This has now led to the organization of citizens' militias in many parts of the country.

Hossam el-Hamalawy, in the same interview quoted above, describes how they were formed: "Following the collapse of the police force on January 28th, people stepped in to protect their neighbourhoods. They have set up checkpoints, armed with knives, swords, machetes and sticks and they are inspecting cars that are coming in and out. In some areas, such as the province of Sharqiya, the popular committees are more or less completely running the town, and organizing the traffic."

Here we have the embryo of a people's militia – of an alternative state power.

The latest reports indicate that, in desperation, Suleiman is considering a coup. The problem he fac- - -- -hat the army is already split. In these conditions an open confrontation with the working class and the revolutionary masses would strain its internal cohesion to breaking point. If the Egyptian regime attempts to use the army, it can break in pieces in its hands. Suleiman, the new "strongman" may stand at the head of the army and the police. But if he went down the road of organising a coup he could find himself with no telephones, no electricity, no transport, no fuel, no food and no water.

The old state power is breaking up. It must be given a final push and replaced with a new power. Only the proletariat can show a way out by placing itself at the head of the Nation. The workers of Egypt have a tremendous power in their hands, but it must be organized. That can only be done through the establishment of revolutionary committees. In some areas committees exist, but they must be extended to every workplace, neighbourhood, school and college, and they must be coordinated on a national scale.

Imperialist intimidation

Faced with a revolution that continues to march forward, all the plans of the imperialists are now in ruins. The situation that they hoped was under control is out of control. *Ahram Online* yesterday reported that the Suez Canal Company workers from the cities of Suez, Port Said, and Ismailia had begun an open-ended sit-in. This threatens to disrupt shipping movements if the strike continues. Over 6,000 protesters have agreed that they will continue their protest in front of the company's headquarters until their demands are met. They are protesting against poor wages and deteriorating health and working conditions.

In desperation, Washington has sent U.S. naval, marine and air forces to the Suez Canal's Greater Bitter Lake. This is the mailed fist that is concealed within the velvet glove of Obama's "democracy". The imperialists are worried about the effects of the Egyptian revolution on the Suez Canal through which about 40 per cent of the world's marine freight passes. Should it be disrupted for any length of time it could have repercussions far beyond Egypt itself, directly affecting oil transportation and subsequently the price of oil.

In reality this is an empty gesture on the part of Washington. The U.S. burned its fingers in Iraq. A new military adventure in Egypt is highly unlikely. It would provoke a storm in the USA and on a world scale. There would not be a single U.S. embassy left standing in the Middle East and all the other pro-US Arab regimes would be faced with overthrow. However, it does represent an attempt to intimidate the people of Egypt. This attempt at imperialist bullying must receive a powerful rebuff by the international labour movement.

Let us raise our voice in support of our class brothers and sisters in Egypt:

• Hands off Egypt!
• Down with imperialism!
• Solidarity with the Egyptian Revolution!

Every class-conscious worker in the world will rejoice at this marvellous movement of the Egyptian workers and youth. Whatever happens in the next days and weeks Egypt, the Middle East and the whole world will never be the same again.

Wednesday, 09 February 2011

MUBARAK HAS FALLEN! – REVOLUTION UNTIL VICTORY!

Alan Woods

The tyrant has fallen! As I write these lines, Hosni Mubarak has resigned. This is a great victory, not just for the people of Egypt, but for the workers of the entire world. After 18 days of continuous revolutionary mobilisations, with 300 dead and thousands injured, Hosni Mubarak's 30-year tyranny is no more.

This is the result of the marvellous movement of the masses, which has faced the guns and batons of the police and courageously resisted every attack by the forces of reaction. It is the culmination of two weeks of revolutionary struggle that has been an inspiration to us all.

Yesterday the mass of demonstrators thought that they had won. But the past 24 hours convinced the masses that all the negotiations and compromises were leading nowhere. That explains why today more people than ever turned out to protest as the idea that nothing short of a popular insurrection would lead to the overthrow of a hated and despised autocrat. Last night, before Mubarak spoke on television, one demonstrator on Tahrir Square told the BBC: "I will remain here until he goes. If he does not go, tomorrow will be a very rough day for Mubarak." Tomorrow has now arrived.

Already at dawn thousands of people were converging on Tahrir Square, ready for a decisive confrontation with the regime. Events have moved with lightning speed. The movement was becoming radicalized by the hour. Protesters were "more emboldened by the day and more determined by the day", Ahmad Salah, an Egyptian activist, told Al Jazeera. "This is a growing movement, it's not shrinking." Political prisoners are being released from the jails. But there are still an unknown number of people missing, including activists thought to be detained during the recent unrest. Human rights groups have alleged that the Egyptian army has been involved in illegally detaining and sometimes torturing protesters.

The mood today became angry and defiant. Al Jazeera's Ayman Mohyeldin in Cairo reported yesterday that in the north-eastern town of Port Said at least five government buildings, including the governor's office and the office for public housing, were set alight in two continuous days of riots. People have been blocking roads, there have been clashes, and huge numbers of people poured into Liberation Square. Nobody knows the real numbers involved today but the demonstrators have been out all over Egypt in their millions.

In the provinces things went even further than in Cairo. In Suez, where the movement has been particularly radical, and where the casualties have been especially numerous, the people occupied all official buildings. In Asyut, where tens of thousands have been out on the streets, they have taken over the headquarters of the ruling party and other official buildings.

In El Arish in northern Sinai, where tens of thousands demonstrated, a crowd of about one thousand youths broke away from the demonstration and engaged in gun battles with the police, attacking police stations with Molotov cocktails.

In Alexandria a crowd of at least 200,000 people gathered outside the Ras-el-Tin palace and fraternized with the sailors, who distributed food to the protesters. Damietta, a city situated where the Nile meets the sea, has a population of around one million. Of these, 150,000 were on the streets today, surrounding the police stations and besieging government buildings. Similar reports are coming from all over Egypt.

There was fury on the streets against the lying propaganda of the media. Last night on the BBC Newsnight programme the deputy editor of *Al Ahram,* the official organ of the regime, apologized to the people and promised to print truthful reports of the demonstrations. "The people are angry with us," he admitted: "I have even received telephone calls threatening to burn the building down."

In Cairo the protesters surrounded the central television station, which was protected by paratroops. But the attitude of the troops has been friendly and fraternization was taking place. According to one eyewitness a paratrooper Major was seen smiling and shaking hands with protesters, who told the officer: "Paratroopers are OK, but we don't want the Presidential Guards." The eyewitness then describes the following scene: "He smiles back. All the soldiers on the other side of the fencing around the television building look sympathetic towards the protesters. It is a very emotional scene."

There were constant rumours about a march on the President's palace. Several hundred demonstrators left Tahrir Square in Cairo to march all the way to the palace last night – some 15 kilometres from the square. The palace was being defended by the army and the elite Presidential Guard. Some commentators speculated that, while the army would not fire on them, the Guard might do so, in which case there could have been a confrontation between the army and the Guard.

But according to the reports, instead of shooting the protesters down, the Army were serving breakfast. CNN reported that the soldiers and the crowd were cheering each other. In a gesture pregnant with meaning, the tanks turned their guns away from the demonstrators, who responded with wild cheering. A soldier climbed out of a tank and hung an Egyptian flag on the barrel of its gun.

Manoeuvres at the top

To put these developments in context: the first indication that something was going on at the top was when on Thursday 10, the military's supreme council met in the absence of its commander in chief, Hosni Mubarak, and announced on state TV its "support of the legitimate demands of the people". In reality, the real decisions were made, not by the army council, but on the streets and in the factories. After weeks of sitting on the fence, the officer caste has been knocked off its perch by the actions of the working class and the revolutionary people.

The council was in permanent session "to explore what measures and arrangements could be made to safeguard the nation, its achievements and the ambitions of its great people". AFP quoted an army source as saying: "We are awaiting orders that will make the people happy." By 3:34 pm euphoria had gripped the crowd in Tahrir Square. People were cheering loudly and once again calling for the fall of the Mubarak regime and chanting: "The army and the people stand together, the army and the people stand united."

General Hassan al-Roueini, the military commander for the Cairo area, told thousands of protesters in central Tahrir Square: "All your demands will be met today." Since the first demand was the disappearance of Mubarak, people naturally assumed that the President had been deposed.

A senior field commander who preferred to remain anonymous told *Ahram Online* that the Supreme Council had taken over authority in the country "for an interim period", the duration of which was to be determined later. Asked about what such a step might mean for the president, the vice-president and the prime minister, the armed forces commander said "these are people who have no power over the armed forces."

A senior member of Egypt's governing party told the BBC he "hoped" that President Hosni Mubarak would transfer power to Vice-President Omar Suleiman. However, there were already some indications that Mubarak was not willing to go quietly. One hour later, contradictory messages were circulating. Reuters quoted Egypt's information minister, Anas el-Fekky, as saying: "The president is still in power and he is not stepping down. The president is not stepping down and everything you heard in the media is a rumour." It was said that Mubarak was "still in negotiations over whether to hand power to Suleiman". An Egyptian official told Reuters: "It is not decided yet ... It is still in negotiation."

But what was there to negotiate?

Mubarak's little surprise

President Hosni Mubarak had a little surprise prepared. His decision not to resign evidently came as a rude shock both to the Egyptian military chiefs and to Washington. CIA Director Leon Panetta had spoken earlier as if his resignation was a done deal and a resolution to the crisis was guaranteed. Other sources in Cairo spoke in the same sense. On the other side of the Atlantic Ocean, President

Obama, with his customary sense of an actor's rhetoric, spoke of an "historic moment" that was being prepared "before our eyes".

Once again the old man tricked them all. Mubarak was pursuing his own agenda. Many asked what his motivation could be. He was under intense pressure from all sides to step down quickly. The Americans were terrified that if he did not go soon the situation, which was already getting out of control, would get much worse. Instead of merely changing a few faces at the top, the direct intervention of the masses would sweep everything away; the whole regime would go, and with it the last vestiges of US influence in Egypt.

The problem was that he was also hearing other voices. The Saudi monarchy, even more corrupt, rotten and reactionary than the Mubarak regime, is terrified and realises that, now their friend in Cairo has gone, they could be next. They have been offering large sums of money to Egypt, but on condition that at all costs Mubarak should stay. The Israelis are equally terrified of the consequences of losing their faithful Egyptian ally, the man who enabled them to sell the so-called Peace Plan – that vicious piece of deception – to the world. They were anxiously pleading with everybody to cease criticising the Egyptian President.

But the most influential voices were the ones in the President's head. They were telling him that he was great, that he was good, that he knew better than anybody what was best for Egypt. Like the Absolute Monarchs of old, he regarded himself as above all laws, parliaments, parties and generals. He considered himself the embodiment of the Nation and the supreme judge of the People's Will. As he spoke in calm and measured tones last night, his face as inexpressive and stony as the funeral mask of a Pharaoh, one got the impression of a man who had lost all touch with reality.

The people of Egypt, however, reacted to Mubarak's speech, among other things, with a kind of black humour which often disguises a serious message. Here is an example: "The Interior Minister asks Hosni Mubarak to write a Farewell Letter to the Egyptian people. Mubarak replies: Why? Where are they going?"

The crowds who gathered in Tahrir Square with Egyptian flags, waiting impatiently for news of his resignation, listened in shocked disbelief as he repeated the same old platitudes. He sympathised with the youth of Egypt, he regretted past mistakes, he wept for the blood of the martyrs and promised to punish those responsible for their deaths (at this point the Father of the People did not even blush), he promised a new and better life. But he did not resign.

Shock then turned into anger – a cold fury gripped the masses, a fury even more intense because of the high hopes that had been aroused by the earlier rumours. All the plans of the Egyptian military were suddenly in ruins. Instead of a "managed transition" Egypt was once again plunged into a revolutionary maelstrom.

Key role of strike movement

The decisive element in the revolutionary equation, that eventually forced Mubarak out, was the intervention of the working class. This is the answer to all those "clever" ladies and gentlemen who argued that the workers were not revolutionary or even that the working class did not exist. In the past few days across the country, workers and unions have been joining the protests. Nation-wide strikes gave a new and irresistible momentum to the mass demonstrations in Cairo and other cities.

All over Egypt the workers moved into action with more than 20 strikes in the railroads and also in the textile industry, among nurses and doctors, in a hospital, in both government-owned and privately owned factories. The numbers are in the region of tens of thousands and have been growing all the time. On Wednesday there was a spate of strikes in Kafr El-Zaiat, Menoufeia and the Suez Canal zone. The *CTUWS* reported that in the textile town of Mahalla, more than 1,500 strikers blocked roads and that more than 2,000 workers from the Sigma pharmaceutical company in Quesna went on strike.

In Giza, hundreds of young women and men held a protest in front of the Giza governorate's office, demanding housing. In Asyut 7,000 Asyut University employees protested, expressing their anger at not working under proper contracts, and at low wages. The protesters demanded that they be given the same rights as the permanent employees. Another 200 employees of the Assiut Petrol Company continued their protest from yesterday in front of the company's headquarters, where they had spent the night. The protesters said that they would refuse to move until they are given proper contracts.

In the governorate of Qesna, 200 employees of Siyanco went on strike for the day, demanding that financial guidelines be implemented with equality for all. Thousands of oil workers also went on strike and protested in different parts of the country. In Ismailia, employees of the Suez Canal University, Petrotrade and the general hospitals demanded better work conditions and proper contracts. In Aswan in the south of Egypt, 300 employees of the Development and Agricultural Credit Bank protested against corruption.

Egypt Telecom, one of the country's largest telecommunications companies, also saw widespread protests in front of its various headquarters throughout the country over the last two days. The workers are calling for proper contracts and better wages. In Cairo, 700 Mukattam Hospital employees, including doctors and nurses, held a protest demanding better wages and proper labour contracts.

The doctors and nurses have been striking and demonstrating. In Ain Shams hospital, 1,000 employees protested, demanding better wages, proper contracts and health insurance for hospital staff. Even the actors have been protesting against their union, demanding the resignation of its head, Ashraf Zaki and that the general prosecutor launches an investigation of corruption.

Yesterday thousands of medical students, doctors dressed in white coats and lawyers in their black robes, marched in central Cairo and were hailed by pro-democracy protesters as they entered Tahrir Square. It is well named. This is indeed *Liberation* Square. They were joined by artists and public transport workers, including bus drivers, all of whom had joined the strikes. The movement is growing.

Many of these strikes are of an economic nature. Of course! The working class is pressing its immediate demands. That is to say, they see the Revolution as a means of fighting not just for formal democracy but for better wages, for better working conditions; for a better life! They are fighting for their own class demands. And this struggle will not cease just because Hosni Mubarak is no longer sitting in the Presidential Palace.

But these are also political strikes. Mubarak has gone, but the workers have been demanding that the unjust system upon which he rested must also go. The workers are raising the question of democracy in the factories and in the unions. The official government union federation, the Egyptian Trade Union Federation (the only legal union), supported Mubarak. But they have disappeared. The strikers are demanding the removal of the old leadership. On January 30 a new federation was established, the Federation of Egyptian Trade Unions (FETU), across many cities, in both the private and the public sector.

Workers prepared the ground

Let us remind ourselves that the Egyptian Revolution was prepared by the biggest strike movement Egypt has witnessed in more than half a century. From 2004 to 2008 over 1.7 million workers participated in more than 1,900 strikes and other forms of protest. In the recent period there have been 3,000 strikes, including all sectors, both government and private. Many of them were successful, leading to wage increases. But improved living standards were no longer enough to satisfy the workers.

Thousands of workers of the Mahalla Spinning and Weaving Company went on strike on Thursday demanding better wages. According to the Centre for Trade Union & Workers' Services (CTUWS), 24,000 workers took part in the protest. The workers from the morning shift had joined their colleagues from the night shift and gathered this morning in front of the company's headquarters, where they announced their strike and their solidarity with the protesters in Tahrir Square.

The workers at government textile mills at El Mahalla El Kubra and tens of thousands more at smaller private factories, are the soul of the Egyptian labour movement. Events in Mahalla on April 6, 2008 changed everything. Tens of thousands of people in this city of half a million came onto the streets. "Our slogans now are not labour union demands," said Mohamad Murad, a railway worker, union coordinator and leftist politician. "Now we have more general demands for change."

The police opened fire, killing two people, and crowds rampaged through the streets, setting fire to buildings, looting shops and throwing bricks at the officers. Protesters tore down and stomped on a giant portrait of Mubarak in the central square. "This uprising was the first to break the barrier of fear all over Egypt," Murad said. "On that Friday, the crowds controlled the city". [...] No one can say that Egypt was the same afterward." There is no question that these strikes played a key role in breaking the fear of the rest of the people, starting with the workers themselves. The April 6 youth movement grew out of that movement of the workers.

The army

Yesterday's events already showed that the general staff was no longer interested in saving Mubarak but rather in saving itself and the regime upon which its power and privileges depend. Mubarak is 82 years old and in any case would be leaving office in September. He was a spent force and the generals knew it. Yesterday they obviously decided to ditch him. But to their immense surprise and irritation, the old man refused to go.

In theory, the final decision was made by the army, clearly shaken by the events of the past 24 hours. But the army itself was showing signs of cracking under the pressure of the masses. Al Jazeera reported yesterday of an army Major dropping his weapons and joining the demonstrators in Tahrir Square together with his soldiers. He announced that he was not alone but part of a group of 15 officers of different ranks joining the revolution. Apparently it was not as isolated case. Under these circumstances there could be no question of using the army against the revolutionary people. This, and the massive strike wave that has been sweeping Egypt, explains why in the end the army council decided to ditch Mubarak.

The army may now have taken over the government in Egypt, but they do not control the streets or the factories. Millions of Egyptians were pouring onto the streets. The military had to act quickly or lose control of the situation completely. But the generals had only a few choices. The first was to do nothing, allow the crowds to grow and let them march to the presidential palace and hope for the best. The second choice was to try to block more demonstrators in Tahrir Square. The third was to overthrow Mubarak.

The problem with the first option was that it would mean that the masses, and not the military, determined the course of events. The second option would create a situation where the army might have to fire on the protesters. But a bloody clash with the people would have lead directly to a split in the army.

That left them with only one option, which was a coup. This should already have been done last night so that it could have been announced before demonstrations started to build up after Friday prayers. The delay in acting shows that the army high command was itself divided, paralysed and incapable of decisive action. They wanted the Boss to disappear but at the same time they feared the consequences of his disappearance. Maybe Mubarak sensed this and that is why he treated them with such contempt.

The fears of the army chiefs were well grounded. Now that Mubarak has gone a heavy weight will be lifted from the shoulders of Egyptian society. The flood gates will be open and every section of society will press for its demands to be satisfied. But how could a military regime satisfy them?

"Revolution until Victory"

The overthrow of Mubarak is only the first step. The Revolution has now entered into a new phase. The fight for democracy is only the first half of the task. The second half will be the fight against the dictatorship of the rich: for the expropriation of the property of Mubarak and the entire ruling clique; for the expropriation of the property of the imperialists who backed them and kept them in power for three long decades.

Washington is watching events unfold with bated breath. Leon Panetta, the head of the CIA, said yesterday there was "a strong likelihood that Mubarak may step down this evening, which would be significant in terms of where the, hopefully, orderly transition in Egypt takes place." What the Americans understand by an "orderly transition" is a transition controlled by the CIA. But this is not going to happen.

The situation has gone too far; the masses are aroused and will take this victory, not as a signal to demobilize, but to press for their demands. By clinging to power to the bitter end, Mubarak radicalized the whole situation. Any chance of a "managed transition" has been fatally undermined. The Americans were frantically manoeuvring with the tops of the army to replace Mubarak by Omar Suleiman. But now Suleiman has had to go, together with his master.

The people did not trust Suleiman any more than Mubarak. Let us remember that Suleiman told the American television station ABC that Egyptians were "not ready" for democracy. He also warned that if protesters did not enter into dialogue with the Mubarak government, the army could have been forced into carrying out a coup. How could such a man be trusted with introducing democracy in Egypt? One protester said that if Omar Suleiman takes over from Mubarak: "all that will happen is that everyone in Tahrir will rewrite their signs, and then carry on demonstrating".

The regime finally cracked under the hammer blows of the Revolution. On Wednesday, Gaber Asfour, the recently appointed culture minister, resigned from Mubarak's cabinet "for health reasons". Today Hossam Badrawi, the General Secretary of the NDP, the ruling party, has just resigned from it. Others will follow. The rats are already hurrying to desert the sinking ship.

In the absence of any alternative, the army high command has taken over. But despite appearances, they too are powerless. The Army Council has taken over on the crest of a revolutionary wave. Tanks and guns are all very well, but they cannot provide jobs for the unemployed, nor feed the hungry, nor house the homeless, nor reduce the high cost of food. The army taking power under these circumstances, therefore, will want to hand power to a civilian government as soon as possible. It may well call elections in September or even sooner. There is no lack of candidates for the job of president and prime minister. ElBaradei is waiting impatiently in the wings.

But none of the burning problems of Egyptian society can be solved by a "market economy". Egyptian society suffers from rising prices and unemployment. Ten per cent of the workforce is unemployed. Seventy six per cent of young people have no job. Wages are low. Most government workers (about five million people) make about US$70 a month. In the private sector, wages are about $110 a month. There is a severe housing problem and some poor people are living in cemeteries. Four million people are without any rights to healthcare. They are not even recognized as part of the workforce in any contractual way.

There is a burning anger against inequality and corruption. Independent journalists are highlighting the all-pervading corruption that is the chief characteristic of the old regime. Billions of dollars are missing. *The Guardian* estimated the Mubarak family alone to be worth US$70 billion. This has provoked fury and disgust, in a country where 40 per cent live under the poverty level. Now the Egyptian worker will say: "I want my rights, where are our rights?" No bourgeois government can give the workers their rights or solve any of the fundamental problems of the Egyptian people.

The working class is now the real motor force of the Revolution. Until recently the demands of the Revolution had been political, centring on the fight for democratic rights. But the workers are giving the programme a social-revolutionary character. Yesterday we published the programme of the iron and steel workers of Helwan, an industrial city on the banks of the Nile.

This is a very advanced programme that expresses the desire of the workers to carry the Revolution through to the end. Yesterday in Helwan, five military factories were on strike. Today the workers of Helwan Military Factory number 63 were in Tahrir Square carrying a banner that said simply "thawra hatta'l nasr" (Revolution until Victory), and they meant it.

The Egyptian Revolution has begun but it has not finished. In order to solve the problems of Egyptian society, it is necessary to break with capitalism, expropriate the capitalists and imperialists and carry out the socialist transformation of society. This is both possible and necessary. What we have seen today shows that once the workers are mobilized to change society, no force on earth can stop them. It is a lesson that sooner or later will be learnt by the workers and youth of all lands.

The people of Egypt are rejoicing and we rejoice with them. Anything is possible now. Let our slogan be: Revolution until Victory!

• Long Live the Egyptian Revolution!
• Long Live Socialism!
• Workers of the world, unite!

Friday, 11 February 2011

Titles by Wellred Books

Wellred Books is a publishing house specialising in works of Marxist theory. Among the titles we publish are:

Anti-Dühring, Friedrich Engels
Bolshevism: The Road to Revolution, Alan Woods
Chartist Revolution, Rob Sewell
China: From Permanent Revolution to Counter-Revolution, John Roberts
The Civil War in France, Karl Marx
Class Struggle in the Roman Republic, Alan Woods
The Class Struggles in France, 1848-1850, Karl Marx
The Classics of Marxism: Volumes One & Two, Various authors
Dialectics of Nature, Friedrich Engels
The Eighteenth Brumaire of Louis Bonaparte, Karl Marx
The First Five Years of the Communist International, Leon Trotsky
The First World War: A Marxist Analysis of the Great Slaughter, Alan Woods
Germany: From Revolution to Counter-Revolution, Rob Sewell
Germany 1918-1933: Socialism or Barbarism, Rob Sewell
History of British Trotskyism, Ted Grant
The History of Philosophy: A Marxist Perspective, Alan Woods
The History of the Russian Revolution: All Volumes, Leon Trotsky
The History of the Russian Revolution to Brest-Litovsk, Leon Trotsky
The Ideas of Karl Marx, Alan Woods

Imperialism: The Highest Stage of Capitalism, VI Lenin

In Defence of Lenin, Rob Sewell & Alan Woods

In Defence of Marxism, Leon Trotsky

In the Cause of Labour, Rob Sewell

Ireland: Republicanism and Revolution, Alan Woods

Lenin and Trotsky: What They Really Stood For, Alan Woods & Ted Grant

Lenin, Trotsky & the Theory of the Permanent Revolution, John Roberts

Marxism and Anarchism, Various authors

Marxism and the USA, Alan Woods

Materialism and Empirio-criticism, VI Lenin

My Life, Leon Trotsky

Not Guilty, Dewey Commission Report

The Origin of the Family, Private Property & the State, Friedrich Engels

The Permanent Revolution and Results & Prospects, Leon Trotsky

Permanent Revolution in Latin America, John Roberts & Jorge Martin

Reason in Revolt, Alan Woods & Ted Grant

Reformism or Revolution, Alan Woods

Revolution and Counter-Revolution in Spain, Felix Morrow

The Revolution Betrayed, Leon Trotsky

The Revolutionary Legacy of Rosa Luxemburg, Marie Frederiksen

The Revolutionary Philosophy of Marxism, John Peterson (Ed.)

Russia: From Revolution to Counter-Revolution, Ted Grant

Spain's Revolution Against Franco, Alan Woods

Stalin, Leon Trotsky

The State and Revolution, VI Lenin

Ted Grant: The Permanent Revolutionary, Alan Woods

Ted Grant Writings: Volumes One and Two, Ted Grant

Thawra hatta'l nasr! - Revolution until Victory!, Alan Woods & others

What Is Marxism?, Rob Sewell & Alan Woods

What Is to Be Done?, VI Lenin

Women, Family and the Russian Revolution, John Roberts & Fred Weston

Writings on Britain, Leon Trotsky

To make an order or for more information, visit wellred-books.com, email books@wellred-books.com or write to Wellred Books, 152-160 Kemp House, City Road, London, EC1V 2NX, United Kingdom.

|||||| |||| || ||| ||||| ||||| |||| ||
9 781900 007405

Milton Keynes UK
Ingram Content Group UK Ltd.
UKHW042148150324
439550UK00004B/167

9 781900 007405